I0121479

Joseph A. Gwyer

Poems and Prose

Joseph A. Gwyer

Poems and Prose

ISBN/EAN: 9783337098551

Printed in Europe, USA, Canada, Australia, Japan

Cover: Foto ©Thomas Meinert / pixelio.de

More available books at **www.hansebooks.com**

POEMS AND PROSE

BY

JOSEPH GWYER,

WITH

A SHORT AUTOBIOGRAPHY

ALSO

ANECDOTES OF AND PERSONAL INTERVIEWS WITH THE LATE REV. C. H. SPURGEON

AND OTHERS.

LONDON:
Published by F. PERRATON & Co., 28, Kirby Street, Hatton Gardens, E.C.,
FOR JOSEPH GWYER.

MDCCCXCV.

This Book is respectfully dedicated to Mrs. C. H. Spurgeon, as a slight token of the Author's deep appreciation of his acquaintance with her and her dearly beloved late husband Charles Haddon Spurgeon.

Printed at "Caxton House," St. Mary's Road, Southampton.

PREFACE.

"Do not trifle: earth is groaning
Under wrongs and burdens sore:
Be in earnest: put thy shoulder
To the work that lies before.

Every hour is more than golden,
Every moment is a gem:
Treasure up these hours and moments,
There are princely pearls in them."

H. Bonar, D.D.

When a man reaches sixty years of age he has seen enough to estimate most of the things of earth at their real value. If he has any powers of observation at all he has found that much that seems solid is mere shallow, and much that is subdued and seemingly humble and in the background, is after all the true basis of all the solidity that may belong to human affairs. The frown that would once have daunted him has lost its terror, for he has learned its impotence: and the smile that once would have spurred him on to vanity has lost its power, for he has found its emptiness, nay, even perhaps its falsity. So in presenting this volume to our readers in the autumn of life we do so, not longing for the praise of men, or craving for the blame of others, but just expecting it to be received at its true value, whatever that may be. If but one soul is convinced, that even in this doubting end of the century the real things are the things of faith, hope, and love, and God, our object is attained and our labour is not in vain.

A book may be a better one for a simple man to read because a simple man has written it, and it is possible that the records of a man mixing with all classes, doing business in many towns, and sowing beside all waters, in his own blundering untrained way, may wake more sympathy and fellow feeling than would the cold superiority of a giant intellect and a university training.

We send this book out as the record of the thoughts and doings of a man whose heart beats for his fellowmen, and who sees in the prince or the peasant the fellow sinner who needs the cleansing blood, and the saving grace of Christ. What it may accomplish we leave to the Holy Spirit; only anxious that fame and glory be the result to the Almighty power that we believe is ruling in the midst of all the anarchy, despotism, priestcraft, and faithlessness that is apparently around us. Though the waves beat strong about the Rock, the Cross still towers above and points to Heaven, with its arms outstretched to a fearing world, shines with its glory of promise to any who would despair.

We make no pretension to higher thought or clever versification, but give our thoughts and experiences just as it comes to us, inspired by our surroundings, and the always evident Divine designs in life.

Many of these pieces have been written in aid of the stricken and sorrowful. Some deal with the joyful experiences of life, but many record the dark day, when the forces of nature, or the fearful mischance startle with fear and dismay.

Why these things are so, we know not, we leave it to the providence and wisdom of God, but one lesson we learn from them, and this we leave with you, "Freely ye have received, freely give."

CONTENTS.

CONTENTS (Continued).

CONTENTS (Continued).

Copies of this Book can be obtained of the Author, Joseph Gwyer, Beckenham Road, Penge, Surrey, free by post at advertised price.

The following are a few of the many Royal and other Letters received by the Author.

WINDSOR CASTLE, NOVEMBER 25th, 1894.

SIR HENRY PONSONBY has given the Queen the lines which Mr. Gwyer has been kind enough to send him. He has to return many thanks to Mr. Gwyer for the copy he has been good enough to send to his daughter.

COWES, 13th AUGUST, 1895.

SIR,—I am desired by the Prince and Princess of Wales to thank you for the copy of verses which you have sent to their Royal Highnesses.

I am, Sir, your obedient Servant,

FRANCIS KNOLLYS.

YORK HOUSE, ST. JAMES'S PALACE, S.W.,
AUGUST 22nd, 1895.

Major-General Sir Francis de Winton presents his compliments to Mr. Joseph Gwyer, and is desired by His Royal Highness the Duke of York to thank him for the poems so kindly sent.

HATFIELD HOUSE, HATFIELD, HERTS.

DEAR SIR,—I beg to acknowledge your letter of the 24th inst., which I have placed before the MARQUIS OF SALISBURY.

Yours faithfully,

MR. JOSEPH GWYER. R. T. GUNTON

[FROM LORD ROSEBERY],
10, DOWNING STREET, WHITEHALL, 27/11/94.

SIR,—I beg to acknowledge with thanks the receipt of your letter and enclosures of November 24th.

I am, Sir, your obedient Servant,

MR. JOSEPH GWYER. JOHN R. DASANT.

BRAYTON, CARLISLE, AUGUST 23rd, 1895.

DEAR SIR,—Best thanks for the verses which you have sent me. I am glad to hear of what you say about the National Lifeboat Institution.

With all good wishes, I am, yours truly,

W. LAWSON,

ROYAL NATIONAL LIFE-BOAT INSTITUTION,
14, JOHN STREET, ADELPHI, LONDON, W.C.
11th DECEMBER, 1894.

DEAR SIR,—I have much pleasure to acknowledge the receipt of your letter of yesterday's date, and the remittance, as a result of the poem you have written on the Life-Boat Work at Margate. I assure you that the Committee are much obliged for your help, the more so as at the present time the Institution is greatly in need of aid. You will be glad to hear that we have granted rewards for the saving of 613 lives this year.

I am, dear Sir, faithfully yours,

MR. JOSEPH GWYER. CHARLES DIBDIN, *Secretary.*

THE AUTHOR'S BIRTHPLACE AND EARLY HOME.

POEMS AND PROSE

BY

JOSEPH GWYER.

:-O-:

TWENTY years ago I published an auto-biography. The book was favorably reviewed by many papers at home and abroad, and quickly went through four editions.

Some six thousand copies were soon disposed of, and spread broadcast over the world, but just in the zenith of its sale a serious disaster occured, which for a time banished all hopes of even retrieving the serious loss caused by it. A fire took place at the publishers, in which was burnt all the plates of the book, and as they were uninsured, a loss of a most serious character resulted, which for many years banished all hope of ever again issuing my production, at any rate in a book form ; but as my writings, called by one paper of a " prolific character," have been since then of a most varied kind, and have commanded the favorable criticism of the public men and, I have reason to believe, the commendations of many readers, I have been induced to bring before the public some of my latest rhymes, poems, and prose writings.

The persistent and varied enquiries of my appreciative readers who have been continually asking me when I am going to commence a book, so that they may preserve my writings in one volume, especially those which they have most highly prized as landmarks of the nation's history, in which have been depicted events and scenes which will ever be read with interest, and which commemorate red letter days in the people's memories, have led me to carry out their wishes and send another simple and yet truthful annal of work before the intelligent public.

I have taken upon myself the expensive, responsible, and arduous undertaking of compiling the present work, feeling deeply its great imperfections, but with all its faults I hope it will be read with some pleasure and interest. I have already had sufficient reason to know that these simple verses are read by thousands with interest and profit, at least if I may judge by the many who are continually expressing these views by word and pen; and to make it more plain I have had of late a tangible proof of the fact, as no sooner did I announce my intention of bringing out a shilling volume of my rhymes and prose writings than I had eight hundred orders for the book in about three months, some accompanied with the money for their copies; a proof of the faith my friends have in me, as at least three or four months must elapse before the completion of the book. I anticipate no difficulty in disposing of the first edition of twoi thousand, as I expect to receive orders for at least a thousand copies before publication.

It may not be generally known that before publishing my volume twenty years ago, I had become somewhat popular by writing verses on the "Illness and recovery of the Prince of Wales." These verses unknown to me were sent to Her Most Gracious Majesty the Queen, and other members of the Royal household. I received through the gentlemen who sent them, five letters of appreciation and thanks.

These verses afterwards appeared in many papers at home and abroad, so they spread abroad my name and fame the world over.

I will now give a short resume of my life, which was fully given in my former book which I may be disposed to republish, should circumstances warrant the outlay; for I do not intend either to tax my exchequer or my resources, as I only intend to move on just as the Pillar of Cloud and Fire which led the Israelites through their winding desert journey in the wilderness may lead me, for we know that a "Pillar of Cloud led them by day and a Pillar of Fire by night." In a similar way I only want to know the guidings of Divine Providence to follow where He leads, believing that if we "acknowledge Him in all our ways God will direct our path." So in this as in other things I will leave all the issues to Him.

It would take quite another book to truthfully chronicle the events that have taken place, and do continually occur, showing good results arising from the perusal of my first "Life and Poems with sketches, &c."

Suffice to say that our most gracious Queen took a copy to a patient at Clewer Hospital that he might read it. I heard the tale from the patient's own mouth, as he in tears told me of her great kindness to him, and said that in conversation with her he seemed to forget her dignity as she talked and sympathised with him just like his own mother. Perhaps I may as well tell how this came about, or a doubt may linger in the minds of some, though I know not why, as all who know the Queen and her beloved family, have found them to be most generous and kind and unasuming to all. We see this in every distressing calamity that occurs, and why should it not be so. Are we not all made of one blood, with a fellow feeling of human sympathy, no matter what distinctions of position, wealth, honour, or influence may be amongst us.

This man had the misfortune to break his thigh, and was taken to Clewer Hospital, and as he also suffered from heart disease he could not go under chloroform. Her Majesty's doctor told the Queen the operation would be dangerous, so she went to see him herself, and after talking most kindly to him for a time she gave him the present that she had brought wrapped up in paper for him to read. It was my work, so the man told me himself. I have already had about thirty letters from Sir H. Ponsonby of acknowledgement and thanks from the Queen for my writings.

Another case I will tell here. My book was read in the jungles of Africa by a sailor, who knew my name, and wrote home a most kind letter to his mother expressing the pleasure he gained from it, with many others to whom he showed it. No doubt the great day will reveal many trophies won for the Saviour by the instrumentality of this book, through reading its touching incidents, especially as God's own word is secure, and He has promised that His word "should not return void, but it shall accomplish the purpose whereto He sent it." One otber and the last instance I must here record in which good resulted from the reading of my work. A servant at Anerly once told me she had just come from witnessing her father's death in the Isle of Wight, and with tears she told me that the last words her father spoke on earth, were thanks for her ever reading my work to him.

It had been the instrument in the hand of God of his conversion, and he had, his daughter said, gone safe home now to heaven. I asked her "had she still a mother," she said, "Yes, she is bedridden, I am going home to nurse her now and my brother and sisters." I think she said four of them, and she had to keep them. With trophies of this kind for earnest God fearing work it gives pleasure in the midst of my many sorrows to know that God does and will honour any humble work done for His glory and the good of men, "Not unto us, but unto His name be all the glory."

If this should come before any of the members of this Isle of Wight family, as perhaps it may, how pleased I should be to hear from them, and I now so often travel through the Island I could call on them.

I said this should be the last, yet I must record one other instance as told me by the night attendant on a lady. This lady lived at Anerly, was a Roman Catholic, and was forbidden by the priest to read any of my works as they would upset her mind, He knew that she had my book in her possession. The attendant told me that many times she had to read the simple story of my life to her in the silent hours of the night, and that her mistress she believed, received good from it, although told by the priest not to read or hear it.

How often does God use, and how often has He used good books to bring conviction to the heart and understanding by the Holy Spirit blessing the reading of them.

Should this short account of my book excite in any, or many, a desire to see it, and sufficient orders come to me to recoup me for the expense of republishing the same with an enlarged aim, and health and life permit, we think it not impossible we may do so. Such an event could even now be accomplished, but that will altogether depend on the sale and the encouragement I receive from the present editions. If any receive any special pleasure, profit, or encouragement please do not be so unwise as many people who receive good from ministerial friends, either in their preaching or otherwise, and keep all to themselves and scarce ever tell their pastor a word about the good they are the instruments of to them. If so, abandon such ideas, and occasionally at least let them and us know that we are helping you in your upward and heavenward road, or if by God's grace you have been arrested in your downward career by all means let us know something about it, as all workers in the Master's Vineyards have discouraging times, and often like the prophet of old, lament and say, "Who hath believed our report, and to whom hath the arm of the Lord been revealed." My intention was to give in this introduction a short resume of my life, but as I have already in my writings given an inkling of it I shall now take a few pages only just to give a desire for more should there be a further publication.

I was born at Redlynch, near Downton, Wilts, so Downton annals and our family Bible tells me, on the 17th of November, 1835 : I do not like some ladies over 30 wish to conceal my age. I am, therefore, getting to be an old man in my sixties, and have lived long enough to know a little, although I feel it is but very little. At Redlynch, on the borders of the New Forest, my father cultivated many acres of our freehold land, as well as a small farm he rented from Squire Goffe, at Hale, so that our lives were not those of drudgery and poverty.

My dear Mother died when I was eight years old. I was the third child of nine who formed the family ; one brother and a sister being older than myself. I can well recollect the last illness of my dear mother, and seeing her in it. She caught a chill after her confinement and never recovered. I knew but little of a mother's ministering loving care, although so young I recollect her loving smile and tender love. Her death was a great trial to my dear father and to all of us, although we were mostly too young rightly to know our loss.

I went to live with my uncles and grandmother at Lodge Farm near Downton, about a mile and a half from my home. Of the nine children, one, a younger brother had died. There were thus eight little ones left, but the Lord fits the burden to the back, He has been to our dear father and to all of us, a very present help in time of trouble.

I went to Downton British School, and on Sundays to Downton Wesleyan Sunday School. Thus I was surrounded by influences for good, both at home and abroad ; my uncle was a class leader of the Wesleyan Church. My boyhood days could be graphically depicted, spent amid all the rustic scenery of a lonely farm house, nearly a mile from any other house.

At about the age of seventeen I left, to spend a short visit to London, and was so enamoured of my surroundings there, that I determined to brave any difficulties and remain in London. I soon obtained a situation at Bevington Neckinger Mills, Bermondsey, and remained in it about nine months and saw a great deal of sin as witnessed in the characters of those who were my fellow employes. Naturally I was no better than these, but my previous teaching surrounded me by God's providence with something which made me resist many of their sins and temptations. Leaving there I obtained a situation at Messrs. Broad and Sons, Wool Staplers, of Bermondsey. Here I spent some nine or ten years of my life mostly in the happiest way. The masters were connected with the Wesleyan Church, and here soon, through attending the ministry at Hill Street Methodist Free Church, Peckham, I had come under deep conviction of sin for many weeks, but through divine grace I was brought to experience that change of heart, called in the gospel of John, the New Birth; "Except a man be born again, he cannot see the Kingdom of God." It was at breakfast time in our counting house at Bermondsey Street I experienced that change, wrought by God's spirit in my heart, and then and there I was able to rest by faith alone on the merits of Christ, and pleading His precious blood was enabled to say "Abba Father, My Lord and My God," and the Spirit testified with my spirit "that I was born of God." "Old thing had passed away, and behold all things had become new," as the new life I then lived was a life of faith on the Son of God, "who loved me and gave Himself for me."

For some months after my conversion I had a peace which passed all understanding. I felt I must "tell to all around what a dear Saviour I had found," but soon I found trials came fast and thick, but they only grounded me more firmly on the Rock Christ Jesus, and I experienced that whom He loveth He loveth unto the end, for "He giveth unto His Sheep eternal life, and they shall never perish, neither shall any man pluck them out of His hand."

I then joined Rye Lane Baptist Church, as being in more accord with my views. This was a great trial, as I had become so closely connected with the Methodist Free Church, yet I have never regretted the step I took, and believe it was the true leading of Providence with my soul.

Joining the Sunday School I soon became closely connected with all its divine associations. My first Sunday School address I gave in Rye Lane Baptist Churuh before Mr. Congreve, now of Brighton, who has built at his own expense the splendid Baptist Chapel at Hove, now presided over by the Rev. David Davies, formerly of Regent's Park Chapel, London.

In later years on going into business I became connected for a short time with the Metropolitan Tabernacle, under the Rev. C. H. Spurgeon. My after associations with Mr. Spurgeon became of the most friendly nature.

It would be too long a task to follow all the leading of Providence through its winding turnings. Suffice it to say I left the Metropolitan Tabernacle and came over to reside at Penge, from whence I married my wife on June 4th, 1864, at Old Croydon Church, since burnt down. Here we soon became connected with the Penge Tabernacle cause in its very earlist infancy.

Although I had grown very cold in divine things for upwards of a twelvemonth before this, here I was aroused and sought and found a fresh grip of divine things. The Lord gave unto me the joy of His salvation, then I taught transgressors His way, and sinners were converted unto Him. I did a goodly share of Evangelistic work in the open air and elsewhere, and tried in my humble way to preach Christ and Him crucified to the people. He says, "I, if I be lifted up will draw all men unto Me."

I soon joined the Temperance work, so that my engagements for Evangelistic Services and Temperance platform work became most arduous, while an increasing business and other calls upon my energies soon strained those energies to the utmost limit, but still I felt like the Master that "I must work the works of Him that sent me while it is day, for the night cometh when no man can work."

I was laid aside for nearly twelvemonths with diseased bone in the leg, the pain causing a large abcess; it was most unbearable, and to make matters worse I had to go into St. Thomas' Hospital, which was then carried on in the Surrey Gardens where Mr. Spurgeon preached while the Tabernacle was being built. It was thought that I should probably be compelled to have my leg amputated, but the Lord restored me without this trouble, and thanks to His kindness I am able now to walk about better than I ever was able.

After being there for two or three months I came out with all my resources drained and had to begin life afresh. Now it would be too long to enter into the details of all the harrowing trouble that came to our lot, but the Lord fulfilled His promises, "thy bread shall be given thee, and thy water shall be sure." I am here tempted to tell how the Lord removed my gloom and sorrow respecting the bread that perisheth; I became somewhat desponding as to the future of earthly things, but being led to buy a large mass of burnt clay ballast, which lay behind the Penge Pharmacy, giving but thirty shillings for it I was able to make upwards of £30 of it, and the work of sifting it really restored me to health, Just then my wife sickened with fever for weeks, and laid between life and death for several days, but the Lord restored her and we commenced business in a small way and soon made a really thriving business until again my health broke down. Surely mine has been an up and down hilly life, and yet by God's grace we continue to the present day.

The Penge Tabernacle has grown from a little one to a thousand. We are led to exclaim, "what hath God wrought, and who are these that fly as a cloud and as the doves to the window." I commenced about this time publishing an almanack, and prefaced it with local and popular events of the year, and for nearly twenty years I continued it, getting from £30 to £40 per year for advertisements in its pages, without paying a single canvasser.

I put in from year to year my own Poems, which were written on a variety of subjects, and many pounds collected for various charitable and philanthropic objects through the sale.

About this time my popularity rose to its zenith, in consequence of my writing verses on the recovery of the Prince of Wales, which verses drew from Her Majesty the Queen, and other members of the Royal Family, many letters of appreciation; about this time also I was made somewhat popular in London and elsewhere, by the publicity resulting from my catching a swindler at London Bridge, who afterwards got five years transportation. The whole affair is described in my book, in many pages of verses.

Through my last illness four years ago, extending over a twelvemonth, I was obliged to give up my business, and have for nearly three years been travelling for Bentley and Co., and find this has given me an opportunity for an increased information of all parts of the country, which I hope my readers will find interesting upon perusal, and hope also they will find my life's work has not been in vain.

Here I should like to describe how I first became a traveller for the respected proprietors of this firm, and I would say I have worked for upwards of three years with them in the greatest unanimity and content. Never once to my knowledge has any unpleasantness cropped up the whole time. The partners are kindness itself to me, and seem thoroughly to appreciate my humble endeavours to serve them, which appreciation compensates for any unpleasantness, such as occurs in any sphere of life, especially that of the road through having to meet with so many different temperaments. On the whole the tradesmen are exceedingly kind, and I have not much fault to find with any, as after all life is to a great extent what we make it ourselves.

I began to fear my life's work was drawing to a close, and that no other sphere would open for my future. How unfounded my fears. Well the poet puts it—

Begone unbelief,
My Saviour is near;
And for my relief,
Will surely appear.

As I was musing and sheltering from a storm on the top of West Hill, Crystal Palace Road, Upper Norwood, thinking of my hopeless condition, and fearing in sinful unbelief that all my earthly hopes were dark, a gentleman, one of the proprietors of Bentley's, with his wife and family, went by in his wagonette and accosted me thus "Mr. Gwyer, jump up, and go home with us. My partner and myself have been talking about you; we have got a job for you, we want you as our traveller and collector." He then told me what business it was. I told him I should be no good for it, but still they said I should. They wished me to ask my friend, Mr. William Bertram, of the Crystal Palace, what he thought of their goods, as I had done business with him and Mr. Roberts for many years.

Mr. Bertram kindly said to me, "By all means take it on, these goods will sell well, they only require introduction, and you are just the man for that. You will have the pleasure of riding about the country selling their goods, viewing Old England's scenery, and you will be able to write sketches of scenery in prose and rhyme till further orders, and mark my words your straight blunt way may not at first be understood by all, but you will get a connexion you never dreamed of, and will be able to sell anything worth selling that you may introduce to the tradesmen's notice.

Those who are acquainted with Mr. Bertram know well he has no fulsome eulogy for any one, but I thought his kindly feeling toward me might be exaggerated, yet, though I have nought to boast of, his remarks in a measure have already come true. I may further say that I had been known and on intimate terms with the proprietors for over twenty years.

Closing my life story with this I will now relate a circumstance connected with my book. A lady used to be amused and interested by my rhymes. I asked her if she would like to read my book as I thought, probably she might be amused if not interested in its pages. She perhaps had an idea that she was going to have a pleasant amusing reverie upon its perusal, but calling upon her afterwards and asking if she had been amused she said, "No, but I have been greatly interested in reading the book, and if you are right sir, I am wrong, I have never experienced that change of heart you speak of." In tears she told me of the impression it had produced in her heart of searching for better things, and I trust that some day this lady will be found amongst "the bloodbought throng," who have "washed their robes and made them white in the blood of the Lamb."

I heard C. H. Spurgeon once say that such books as the "Dairyman's daughter," "The Little Cottager," and the "Shepherd of Salisbury Plain," and others of their kind would bye and bye be shown to have done, by divine instrumentality, more good than all the splitting of straws so general to theologians. So by God's blessing I hope some good may be accomplished through the reading of my humble efforts.

Another instance I will recite of how a bright jewel was won to the Temperance cause, who has accomplished by his extraordinary genius and talent a great deal of good in that cause, and in the proclamation of the Gospel of Jesus Christ. The Primitive Methodists had taken possession of the room used by we Baptists in Hawthorne Grove, Penge, upon our removal to Penge Tabernacle. I told them whenever they liked to send over their preacher to dine with us they could do so. They sent us a Mr. Elford, a preacher of no mean order, who for nearly twenty years was like an angel in our house, and whom I had the pleasure of connecting, through a curious coincidence with the Temperance Work, the story of which coincidence may be interesting to our readers. The temperance star was then in the ascendant. As he was in my house on Sunday dining, and spending the afternoon, I told him I should have to leave as I was going to the funeral of a dear fellow worker, who had died suddenly, and was to be buried in Forest Hill Cemetery. It was Mr. Scott, of Peckham, a worker in the sewers beneath the ground, yet who for years had done good work in the Temperance and Gospel work. He was a genius of no mean order, and an original talented speaker for a working man. Mr. Elford accompanied me to this funeral, having read the account of him in the Temperance Star, and was so struck by the sight of the thousands who followed and packed the way leading from the Melon Grounds, Commercial Road, Peckham, right up to the Forest Hill Cemetery, that, he said to me, "Mr. Gwyer, if this is the outcome of Temperance work, this deep respect that all pay to his memory; even publicans and others, never again will I touch a drop of intoxicating drink;" and he never did, and Mr. Elford for nearly twenty years worked hard and gloried in the Temperance work, as in the preaching of the glorious gospel of the blessed God. He always had an open door at my house, and no one was ever more welcome whenever he came on Sundays or week-days. He was a bootmaker and I could tell how this good man of God was often tried in temporal things. The miles he used to walk and the arduous work he did for the Primitive Methodist Cause is well-known by some of their older ministers and members, as he preached the Gospel for nearly fifty years. I think he has told me he preached when only seventeen years of age to large congregations. Certainly you would like to hear how this good man went home to Heaven. I had been saying to my wife "How is it Mr. Elford does not come," when lo after dinner a minister one Sunday called at my house, and told me "Mr. Elford is seized with illness, and would not die without seeing you; will you kindly go and see him at once." I did so. He lived at Sutton in Surrey. I shall never forget going into his bedroom. His thin wan face lit up with a heavenly smile. "My dear friend Gwyer," he said, "my desire is granted, I feel now like Simeon, when he said "Lord now lettest Thou Thy servant depart in peace according to Thy word." "Come, said I, whats the matter." "I am going now" he said "to be with Jesus which is far better." "Oh, come" I said "you may be getting better." "Never, never," he said with emphasis "I am going home, I am dying now; do not think by my talk that my mind is gone, never was intellect brighter or my memory more acute. I do not know where Heaven is, but this I know I am going to be with Him whom I have long served, and whose Gospel I have for nearly fifty years tried to preach, and trusted him amid all my creature imperfections."

The tears of joy ran down his furrowed face as he told me this, and I felt the place was hallowed. "Now, friend Gwyer, I must hear your voice once more in prayer. You and your dear wife have been kindness itself to me for so many years. I have enjoyed the hospitality of your humble home, surrounded by your dear children, and now I am going home, and by and bye "We shall meet beyond the River where the billows cease to roll." And, as I poured out my soul to God in prayer for our dear brother, and prayed that God would support his dear wife and beloved children, and give him in his own good time a happy entrance into the everlasting Kingdom of His dear Son, then I prayed for my own family, and asked God to give each of our children His saving grace, whatever else betided them; alas! this prayer is not answered yet, but it is on the golden file, for how blessed to know that for Christ's sake no faith is vain, for is it not said "Instead of the father shall rise up the children, which shall be princes in all the earth," and "the fervent effectual prayer of a righteous man availeth much." I rose bedimmed in tears, and then our friend, as Joshua in departing told the leaders of Israel, told me "My friend, God will answer your prayers, your house will be saved. I have faith to believe. Shall I tell you how the Lord answered my prayer for my dear children. I had been preaching anniversary sermons at Winchester, and coming home along a dark lane one Sunday night, I poured my heart to God in prayer for my dear children that God would save them all, and this prayer is answered. One of my sons is in Jersey preaching the Gospel with much acceptance to the people. And all my children are in the good way. Cheer up, now, good-bye, we shall soon meet in Heaven." He further told me that for nine weeks he had only beef tea, yet although he had experienced fifty years of the love of God in Jesus Christ, he had felt more of that love in that little room, and on that bed, than ever he had been able to preach about in fifty years. We thought as we left him for the last time on earth of one of old who said "Let me die the death of the righteous, and let my last end be like his." I hink he passed away some three or four days from this interview.

I am tempted to tell of other good done by the death of Mr. Scott. He was to have given a temperance address in the open-air the same week in which he died. I was to take the chair, being tasked by the Temperance Society to do so, but when his death was heard of we could obtain no suitable supply. I had to fill up the gap and give an address, and I asked if there were not some young men who would fill this vacant place in our ranks and identify themselves with this grand Temperance Crusade, and especially we wanted, I said, intelligent Christian men to advocate the claims of the Temperance cause, and denounce the drink which was blasting, blighting, and mildewing happy homes, and ruining the bodies and souls of many thousand people every year. There were three brothers standing, by name Hutchings, who were members with us in the Penge Tabernacle, and strange to say such was the effect, that Stephen Hutching said at a meeting when leaving for Australia, " It may not be generally known how it was that myself and my brothers joined the Temperance ranks, and then he recited to a large crowded meeting at the Penge Hall the incident that I have related, and how he and his two brothers at this out of door meeting, under these untoward circumstances, each one of the three on the spot pledged themselves, unknown to each other individually, to become abstainers, and have been so ever since, and he said " You all know the work we have accomplished, and we are now determined to go on in the same in a foreign clime if God spares us, amongst strangers. So be encouraged friend Gwyer and other workers in the good cause, " In the morning sow thy seed, and in the eve withhold not thy hand."

This man was Stephen Hutchings, gardener, of Penge, the man who first wrote asking Mr. Spurgeon to send a student to Penge. Mr. Cox came, who was the instrument used in commencing the cause, and building the fine Penge Tabernacle. His two brothers are dead, John and Charles, but kept to their pledge till death, and were good workers in the cause. Mr. Hutchings possesses with his family a good quantity of freehold land in Australia, and still carries on the Temperance and Christian work. He is in a good position, and has done a grand work in Australia. At one time, in Penge, he was in such dire distress that I asked a gentleman for a small gift for him and family. This gentleman gave half a sovereign for him, and afterwards found him a lot of work. This gentleman's name may be told here. It was Mr. Croaker, an honoured and beloved deacon for many years of the Penge Tabernacle. So we see our influence is not lost even at death, for Mr. Scott being dead yet speaketh. Sow seeds at random wherever you be. Surely such a life like Samuel's, devoted from early life to the Master's service, is more honourable than wielding an empire or wearing an earthly crown, unless wearing it in the fear of the Lord, and doing everything for his glory and the good of men. To be honoured of God in being brought to Him in early life, and being instruments of good in leading men through God's grace from darkness to light, for "he that converteth a sinner from the error of his ways, hideth a multitude of sins."

My experiences of the late beloved C. H. Spurgeon, commenced a few weeks after he came to New Park Street Chapel. I went to hear him preach on Thursday evenings, and continued to hear him for nine years, being employed then at Messrs. Broad and Sons. I well remember Mr. W. Olney telling Mr. Broad "We have got a young man at New Park Street, who is destined under God to do a remarkable work in the Master's vineyard." "See, said he, if my words do not come true." This induced me to go and hear him preach, and those who remember the old times will bear me out in saying that earnestness was not only marked upon the preacher's utterances, but solemnity pervaded the whole services. We all felt that "it was none other than the house of God, and the very gate of Heaven." Soon, a bitter persecution commenced, and Mr: Spurgeon became the song of the drunkard, and was caricatured in the comic papers. By these means his notoriety extended, and crowds came to hear the young Baptist preacher. Soon after the building of the Metropolitan Tabernacle I joined their communion, as I had a business in Walworth, but soon after left it for Penge, where I stayed till I became nearly the oldest member of the Penge Tabernacle.

We first worshipped in the room in Hawthorne Grove, since which two large chapels have been built. Last year the new one at a cost of six thousand pounds, where a large congregation meets, and a good work is being carried on under the ministry of the Rev. J. Wesley Bond. There is now a membership of six hundred. Surely in this we may well say "what has God wrought." "The little" has literally "become a thousand." When Mr. Spurgeon came to reside at Westwood, Beulah Hill, Norwood, I became on very friendly terms with him, and often had business to do with him or his that brought me into close contact with him.

Mr. Spurgeon was one of the wittiest and most friendly gentleman that one could meet. One could not be in his company a minute without feeling quite at home, and he always courted conversation from one. He was a master of puns, but never of those which could injure and annoy. I remember once, his taking me by the arm and leading me to the bottom of his garden at Westwood, and telling me how he came into possession of that house and grounds in a most curious way, indeed, most remarkable, which I am not at liberty to relate here. Suffice to say, it was a most wonderful providence, and I know Mr. Spurgeon viewed it in that light. "The privacy of the place won my affections," and now he said, "what do you think; the builders are again making inroads upon our home as you see. They have begun to build at the bottom of our garden. I have purchased these plots so that they cannot build at the back of my garden, what do you think is best to be done to make it more private that people may not be looking over?" "Well," I said, "they all like you, so they all want to look at you, but I should advise you to plant some poplar trees in front of your plots, and they would grow up almost in a night like Jonah's gourd. They would be bare of leaves whilst you are enjoying your second summer at Mentone, and the trees would be richly covered with leaves to shield you and your beloved wife from the gaze of the public when you are at home, moreover, Mr. Spurgeon, you had better have some apple trees planted so that then you can walk among the apple trees of the wood." "You are a funny fellow Mr. Gwyer," said he, "As if you were not of the same type," I replied. He received this joke with a hearty laugh, which all who knew him will realise. We walked arm in arm together in his meadow. I remember the spot well, and I should like to commemorate the place in the same way in which Wilberforce's oak was commemorated, when he brought about the abolition of the Slave trade. "Comrade," he said to me, "when I think of all the goodness, mercy, and loving kindness of our God "I am lost in wonder, love, and praise," and all that He has wrought instrumentally through me in this great city and throughout the land amazes me. I am amazed at his taking a countryman from that little village and town of Colchester;" and as he said it the tears ran down his face and dropped on his boots, and we wept together for very joy. Oh! the deep humility of that man; he was ever ready to confess he was most unworthy. Surely I felt like Moses who had to take off his shoes when he saw the bush burning and the place whereon he stood was holy ground, he could scarcely have felt more than I that this was holy ground. No one was ever more ready than C. H. Spurgeon to give all the glory to God for all the good accomplished.

On another occasion we were at Westwood carting some hay. Mr. and Mrs. Spurgeon were about us off and on all the day, and as we were shaking up the hay together for a short time before carting, as I did not consider it quite ready, he said to me, whatever you and your men may require to drink there is ginger beer, lemonade, cocoa, tea, coffee, and milk here. If any stronger drink is required you must go to my neighbour over the way, for we do not give it house-room at Westwood." I said, "But how came this about? this has not always been your experience respecting the drink." "No," he said, "but it has of late years. I saw some declensions of church members through the drink; alas, some in the church of which I am pastor, and I made a solemn pledge that I would never touch another drop," a pledge which I believe he kept inviolable to the last. He had no misgiving about their conversion, but their fall was great all through the drink. Would that all seeing it in the same light would resolve on the same Christian, manly, and heroic way of action! But still we must not be too harsh. To their own Master they stand or fall as Christ's servants, not under law, but under grace. In the afternoon we were busy carting the hay, and I was pitching the hay from the van to the stack. Mr. Spurgeon said to some one standing by the stack, "Why, how true is the old adage, 'it never rains but it pours.' Why, here we are blessed with two poets on one day: there is friend Gwyer on the load of hay, and here comes Charlesworth (the Master of Stockwell Orphan Home) down the garden." When I had finished, the perspiration was streaming down my face, as it was a very hot day in June. I said, "Mr. Spurgeon, what did you say just now?" Mr. Charlesworth was standing by his side. When he repeated his words, I replied, "Why, Mr. S. I call this hard prose not poetry, what say you Mr. Charlesworth? and it strikes me you have something besides poetry-writing to do with all those young boys of Mr. Spurgeon's at the Orphanage." Mr. C. replied, "I know I have." Mr. Spurgeon joined heartily in the laugh. He then dilated to me on what happened some time ago to him and Mr. C. in London. They had just got into a hansom cab, when after a little pleasant conversation, Mr. Charlesworth took out some paper, which Mr. Spurgeon was in hopes had been a legacy left to the Orphanage, when to his dismay he heard it was a poem on himself. Quick as thought he whipped the paper out of Mr. C.'s hands, and tore it up in front of his lordship, and was in hopes that that would have been the end of it. Not so, however; for one night at a large meeting at the Tabernacle, after Mr. Charlesworth had ended his address, this said poem, to Mr. Spurgeon's dismay, came on as a tail-piece. "Why," I said to Mr. S., "did you take the chair on this occasion?" He replied, "Yes." "Well, then, I should have called him to order at once as being too personal, and stopped him." But Mr. C. H. S. said, "You see what a pompous gentleman he is. The papers next day would have had displayed in

SEE PAGE 11.

large type, "An unseemly quarrel at the Tabernacle last night, between Mr. C. H. Spurgeon and the Headmaster of the Stockwell Orphanage. This would have been most unseemly would it not, so I was obliged to let him finish it."

Two months ago at West Cowes Regatta I met Mr. Charlesworth, with a Baptist minister, and taking a short walk with them, spoke of this occurence and of pleasant times we had together with the dear departed, and Mr. Charlesworth made the remark, "Just like him Mr. Gwyer, we shall never behold his like again, shall we, we both knew more of him than some folks."

I do not know how I have been led into this strain of writing on Mr. Spurgeon, but I think it may be more interesting to some of my readers than my own history.

Let that be as it may it rests agreed that I put what I like into my own book, so I will continue a little more with these, my most delightful recollections of the friend whom I so greatly loved, and who through grace I look some day to greet in the New Jerusalem. I had collected a goodly sum for many years for the Stockwell Orphanage, nearly all in pence, through the medium of my rhymes, and when taking, I think £2 to Mr. C. H. S. one afternoon, Miss Thorne told me he wanted to see me round in the library. This happened to be a Thursday afternoon, and I saw his notes in front of him and was reminded that it was his preaching night. He told me to take a seat close by him and shook my hand heartily. His two secretaries were sitting at the large table. He said to me, "Why, you must be known as well as I am, to collect all the money in pence that you do for our Orphanage." "Oh no," I said "it is your Institution that draws it." "Not a bit of it," he said, "unless they knew you they would not give it," so you see he would not take the praise. "Be that as it may, so we work and you receive, to the Lord be the praise." "Do you ever have any unpleasant remarks made respecting these collections." "Well, very rarely, as the roughest men I think believe that it all goes in the channel collected for, and many of this class give me a penny." "Well," Mr. Spurgeon said, "if there is a word said, shall I tell where I think it comes from, is it not from your own tradesmen." "Yes," the other day I called upon a draper, he said he would give me something, BUT! "Well," I said, "what is the But to do with?" "Well," he said, "you must have a motive for all this collecting that is made each year." I said he was quite right, I had; "But how," said he, am I to know that it goes for that object." "Who do you doubt, Mr. Spurgeon, the Institution or myself?" "No, not exactly in that way," he said, "but you must do it to get trade or notoriety." But I had that without it, and if so that had not to do with him, as motives which are unseen are unknown, but the work is seen and known. "Well," I said, "I do not want YOUR penny," and a happy thought came into my mind. "Do you know how you can get a good advertisement?" "No," he said. "I'll tell you then: whenever a lady comes to buy a silk dress marked in your window at five or six pounds, and a hat at twenty or thirty shillings and has paid for them, kindly pull her sleeve as she passes the door and say, 'Excuse me madam, I know how liberal your heart is towards the poor, I have a collecting paper, and should like to see your name with the others on it,' and then she would go and tell others what a liberal hearted man you are, and you would have your shop crowded with customers buying your silk dress material, and hats and other things, all through your kindness and liberality, as the public would think much of you and are always so fond of giving." Mr. Spurgeon after a hearty laugh at my recital said, "that served him well right."

"Well now" Mr. S. said, "allow me to congratulate you on your last poem." I looked around and saw a pleasant twinkle in his eye, and thought to myself what's on the board now, as a short time before he had told Mr. Samuel, pastor of the Penge Tabernacle, "that if I could write poems as I sell potatoes, I should make a mark in the world, and my rhymes are not exactly like the Irishman who could only play two tunes on his fiddle; when he had done one he said, do you want to hear t'other?" I said, "what poem Mr. Spurgeon?" He said, "On the Bulwarks of Old England," calling up Tennyson. "How is it you wrote that, I consider it very good, the best I have seen of yours, by all means send it to Alfred (meaning the then *Poet Laureate*).

I stood up and asked Mr. S to rub that little praise well in between my shoulder blades, as his praise like oil was running down my back delightfully. I turned round and saw that his face shook with laughter, in which his two secretaries joined heartily, then he said "you know Mr. Gwyer, I only say what I think, and by all means send it to Alfred." He knew I should get a letter back from him, which would do me good in business; for asking me if I had sent afterwards, on my replying "No," he said, "You have done wrong." He had an eye for our temporal, as well as our

Yours truly

C. H. Spurgeon

spiritual good. Afterwards I sent the verses I had written on Mr. Spurgeon's decease, and received from Lord Tennyson a very nice letter in reply.

One day Mrs. Spurgeon sent to ask me to try to get her a large sugar vat to put some grains in for the cows, and the next day being out with my waggonette I bought a vat at Croydon and put it with some boards behind on my waggonette and took it up to Westwood. On the way I met a farmer, Mr. Murphy, with whom I had done a deal of business for many years. "Why," he said, "what have you got a sugar vat for?" "Don't you see I am going with this up to Mr. Spurgeon's?" "What," said he, "the great Metropolitan preacher, C. H. Spurgeon?" I said "yes" "Can I go with you, shall I be likely to see him." "Very likely," I said, and as we entered his stable and carriage yard there was Mr. Spurgeon ready to receive us. "Why Mr. Gwyer, whatever have you got?" "A vat for Mrs. Spurgeon," I said. "Why, you are kindness itself, it was only last night she sent to you for it, we must be a terrible bore to you, for you to be at our beck and call for so many things that we are constantly requiring." "No" I said, "not so Mr. Spurgeon, I feel it an honour to be privileged to do anything for you.

I introduced my friend to him, and he had a chat with him, and after calling his gardener to help us down with the vat, he said to me, "What is the charge?" "Four and six." I said. He winked across to Mr. Murphy and said pleasantly, "Why Mr. Gwyer cannot get five shillings out of this deal." Mr. Murphy, an Irishman and a Catholic, said afterwards, "I am not surprised such a man as he is, is liked; you cannot help liking him. Such is the testimony of all who came in touch with him.

I will insert here an extract from my Almanack for 1885, which I think will be an interesting conclusion to this record of my dear friend.

"We have to congratulate our respected neighbour and beloved friend, the Rev. C. H. Spurgeon, on the completion of his fiftieth year, which was made the occasion of presenting to him a valuable purse of gold. He, in his usual magnanimity, gave it nearly all away to various objects that lay near his heart. We say, "Well done John Ploughman, this is the way to grow fat and flourishing." If good John Bunyan's rhyme is correct, in which we are disposed to think there is more gospel than some niggardly souls suppose, it runs, as most all know—

> "There was a man—
> Some thought him mad—
> The more he gave away the more he had!"

Nevertheless, if this is not always correct, we feel assured that in John Ploughman's case it will prove true, for there are thousands of loving liberal hearts who would feel it a great privilege to contribute towards such an honoured Ploughman were he ever in need. But in showing their love and respect for John they have an excellent opportunity of expressing it to him by supporting the many claims that must press upon him in these hard times, when farming is such a bad business and scarcely pays for the ploughing and sowing. As the corn is so cheap, John must be a wonderful ploughman, as we know he is, if he does not sometimes get into Doubting-street, but faith is better than doubt, and more honoring to God. Therefore, we feel assured that what God has done for our beloved Ploughman in the past he will do for him in the future; for is He not an unchanging God, "The same yesterday, to-day, and for ever." Will many of our readers send a small gift, and some a large one, to John Ploughman, to help him feed, clothe, house and educate 500 bright-eyed intelligent boys and girls, at "Stockwell Orphanage," which are daily provided for by a grateful benevolent public purse, which has never yet run dry. This will greatly cheer the venerated Ploughman, as he has got now the seedy side of fifty, and needs fresh and increased sympathy and help from all on the farm. Bill Smith, our Shepherd, says his eyes will soon be getting dim, so that he will not be able, through infirmity, to see so clear ahead, or be able to hold such a straight furrow, or be able to walk with such elasticity over the hard ground that he meets with while turning up the fallow land as in the past, when youth and vivacity made him whistle while driving his team from hedge to hedge in turning up his long furrows.

Their son, Tom, from New Zealand, has been paying his dear father and mother a visit for the last few months, and was received with open hands from all quarters of the farm. He must have gone back to his "Brighter Britain" well laden with a harvest of grateful recollections for the mercy and kindness of his father's and mother's God, as well as his own, and thankful for the generosity of his many friends. He is a thorough "chip of the old block;" he must have learnt his ploughing through driving his father's team. He will be sure to carry off many a prize in future ploughing matches. We hope that in "Brighter Britain" the soil is not so sterile as it is in Old Britain; nevertheless, if it is the same good seed sown broadcast there, it will grow in the hardest soil, if our gracious husbandman sends down the fertilising and refreshing showers, to cause the seed to germinate and grow. We pray that he may long be spared to follow in his father's footsteps, and scatter the good seed over all sorts of soil in that genial clime, and that by-and-bye the ploughers and sowers, the reapers and mowers, may meet in the Father's garnery above.

The other day we heard a plough-tail rhyme very wrongly quoted. We were giving a little advice to Ted Giles, our young groom, to abstain from intoxicating drinks, when he replied in the following couplet, very out of place for him, but was, we think, very nice, as it relates to John Ploughman's son. It reads:

"My father's father held the plough,
Content my father holds it now;
And I, with every rising sun,
Will spend my days as he has done."

Sam Stiles, our thatcher, told us that John Ploughman's wife was continually sending about large parcels of books to poor shepherds on all sorts of farms, in all out of the way places, and strange to say, we were spending a few days with Farmer Hodge, near Salisbury Plain, some time ago, and Dick Jones a Shepherd from the New Forest, came over on the Sunday to preach at the little chapel in the village, and he told, in Farmer Hodge's house, such a tale, how one day Mrs. John Ploughman had sent him such a lot of books to read that made someitt run from his eyes like rain drops, and he wondered however she found him out, on his out of the way farm, right in the New Forest, amongst the young wild colts. We all said, God bless dear Mrs. John Ploughman. We know all the shepherds like her, and suppose some of their flocks could send her some wool, for Dan Sharp, our cowman says, "tis all fish that comes to her net,' for she turns everything into books for the shepherds to read while 'their flocks are lying down beside the still waters, or feeding in the green pastures." We always thought that John Ploughman had got a good kind-hearted wife, and this undoubtedly has wonderfully helped John in his ploughing, and made him so often whistle behind his team, and helped him to carry off such a lot of prizes in the ploughing matches.

Mr. Thomas Spurgeon, during his visit here, preached several times for his father, and elsewhere, and gave an interesting lecture in various parts of this country on his experiences in New Zealand."

Writing as I am now, at a Temperance Hotel in Canterbury, November, 1894, I think it may interest some of my readers to know that searching in my bedroom for a Bible I could find none. Oh, how I wish each bedroom in every hotel and lodging house was supplied with a copy of God's holy word. Looking round the room a text hung upon the wall I found was the same as that which was the means in God's hands of bringing divine light to dear Mr. Spurgeon. When labouring under a deep conviction of sin he entered a little Primitive Methodist Chapel near Colchester, and this text was given; It was, "Look unto Me, and be ye saved all the ends of the earth." He looked by faith that Sunday morning, and received the adoption of sonship. "Being justified by faith, he had peace with God, through our Lord Jesus Christ."

I am continuing notes, but am now writing in a bedroom in the John B. Gough Temperance Hotel, Sandgate, which was built to commemorate the great orator and reclaimed drunkard, who laid one of the stones in the wall on the 50th anniversary of his first leaving Sandgate.

What hope for any desponding one there is in this. If such a man could be saved, not only from the drink but from sin by God's grace, and snatched "as a brand from the burning," surely all can be saved who are brought to see their own sinfulness.

What thousands were reclaimed from both drink and other sin by his instrumentality. I myself became an abstainer through hearing his graphic and thrilling lecture at Exeter Hall thirty-eight years ago, and continued so for three years, but having signed no pledge and not attending other temperence meetings, when an attack of illness came upon me I again took moderate stimulants, but never to excess. The unfaithfulness of an abstaining friend, who, on my expressing a desire for stout instead of dissuading me, actually sent out for it, largely contributed to this regrettable declension. Ten years after I became an abstainer fully pledged; signing with a man that often gave way to excessive drinking that I might stand by him. He was an intelligent Scotchman, and I know for years, as long as he was in my knowledge he kept the pledge.

I have never regretted this step, it having turned out to be a great safeguard in many temptations, and a more powerful example to others than I could have otherwise shown.

There is a little house near here, opposite to the spot where Gough was born, and in the wall is a stone bearing this inscription—

JOHN B. GOUGH,
TEMPERANCE ORATOR,
Born 22nd August, 1817, in a cottage near this spot;
Died in America, 18th February, 1886.

In the "J. B. Gough" Temperance Hotel, above one hundred people slept on the occasion of the Sandgate Landslip, by the kindness of the manager. Verses on this event may be seen in this book, which realized seventeen shillings and sixpence for the Sandgate Fund, and a like amount for the Liberator Fund, in pence as collected by their circulation.

This affair, sad as it was, took place without loss of a single life, a fact which seemed to us at the time little short of the miraculous, and to many others too who witnessed the sad havoc made at the time.

I happened to be at Sandgate at the time of the Guy Fawkes Carnival, 1894, which on account of rain had to be postponed a day. Coming home from the Carnival, on entering the Hotel and coming into converse with a Balaclava hero, bearing the name of the missionary "Martyr of Erramango," John Williams, I found he was seventy-eight years of age, and had enlisted in the Sappers' and Miners', on January 16th, 1840; afterwards incorporated with the Royal Engineers; the Duke of Cambridge, after the Crimean War, bringing this about with the remark that these men knew as much as the Royal Engineers. He was before enlisting by trade, a stonemason, and had also learnt the art of diving. A vessel was sunk outside Balaclava harbour during a gale in 1854, blocking the entering of our vessels. He was ordered to go down and cut the mast which he did. He has been a pensioner for thirty-one years, and has also been a prominent member of the "United Service" Good Templar Lodge, No. 2,253, founded in 1871, ever since it was formed, going through all its offices. He with his wife also suffered by the landslip. His wife being an invalid was kindly cared for by the station-master of Sandgate. She has since died in the Infirmary at Folkestone.

I was sorry to hear that this old and valued servant of our nation is only in the receipt of five shillings weekly, a fact I was told, not by himself, but by a gentleman. Not enough to keep body and soul together. I hope this publicity may make things easier for the aged saint for the few years, perhaps months, that he may remain in this world. I heard he is in connection with a Christian church. After a few years, coming from the Crimea he received his pension and was put on at Shorncliffe camp as the manager and inspector of the drains, and superintended the whole of the drainage of the camp.

About four years ago General Nicholson was inspecting the Company and the works of Shorncliffe, as he was Inspector General of Fortifications, Head of the Engineers. The General was afterwards promoted to be Governor of Gibraltar, but has since died. Meeting Williams he said, "Oh!" and took hold of his hand and shaking it said, "What are you about now? looking after drainage still." Williams said, "Yes Sir," and the General remarked, "It seems to me it does not do you any harm." "No, Sir, I have not had a day's sickness since you put me on, nineteen years ago." "Well well," he said. Williams then asked how the General was, his ladyship and all his family. He said, "Quite well, thank you, ten of them;" he then shook up his shoulder and laughed heartily.

Before going to the Crimea, Williams had to try experiments at Woolwich Arsenal in this fashion. He made twenty-three charges he said, and put them down in different places in the river, one under an old boat, and blew them all up at one time: the old boat went flying up in the air, and the officers and gentry laughed heartily to see it. It was done with a galvanic battery, with a small copper wire covered with India rubber attached to a big copper galvanised wire attached to the battery, the batterys all working in acid, when at a given signal by touching with a wire the whole exploded. They know when it is in working order, by a clockwork arrangement called a galvanometer.

He was with Admiral Sir Charles Napier in the Baltic, taking the Bomersounds, and gained a medal for it. When going up the Baltic in shallow water, his ship ran aground, and they threw some of the guns overboard. He with others had to go and dive for them. One of the divers going down into the bottom fell into a deep hole and would not go down again. They then sent for Williams, got the apparatus on deck, and asked if he thoroughly understood the diving apparatus and air pump. "Yes sir," he answered, "I know everything about it." If there is anything broken can you repair it?" "No, Sir, I am not a smith but I can take it to pieces, clean it, and put it together again." "That's something," they said. Sir Charles Napier was then looking on with the officers. "If you take charge of them, what do you expect," they asked? "I leave it to the generosity of you officers entirely," he said: Then I tell you, said the Commander, "We give our divers one shilling an hour, and will give the same amount to you." So he got all the guns up.

After taking Bomersounds he came back to England, and quickly went back to the Crimean War, after four days. In this time the experiment before related took place. The Admiralty had made arrangements with the principal Whitstable diver, Mr. Dean, to go out and blow up the Russian ships that were in the way of our ships getting to Seba-tapool Harbour. The engineers would not give over the diving apparatus to the Admiralty until Williams came home to try these experiments.

Mr. Dean saw the experiment at Woolwich and said to him, "Where did you learn this." He said, "it must be a very poor Sapper that does not understand that," and the officers turned their backs and burst out laughing and said, "This is how we blow up all our fortifications," and Dean said, "I could not do better myself." "Then tell me where you learnt the diving?" "Over the wreck of the Royal George at Spithead." "What," said Dean, "under General Paisley;" "Yes, Sir, he was my commanding officer at the time." "And did you know me there?" "Yes, Sir, a blowing up a ship, the Southsea Castle, and you nearly blew us out of the water." And Dean said, "Yes! yes! yes! I know it well, and we used to hoist the flag."

Williams also told me an incident which occured in the trenches at Sebastapool. A bomb shell falling near him, he laid flat down on the ground; the bomb bursting actually tore up the earth and covered him over. His comrades thought he was killed, but when he was uncovered they found him unhurt, and he continued his fighting in the trenches.

One day when instructing some men in the art of diving with his apparatus, going down first in the Sebastapool Docks to show them how, to his surprise on feeling about, he found a cannon on wheels with the horses harness attached. They drew it up with ropes he put round the wheels. This gun had belonged to the Russians, who in their haste must have unharnessed the horses and escaped, running the cannon into the waters of the dock, to keep it from the clutches of our army. Williams said that this incident served him well, twenty-five years after, at Shorncliffe camp. The major's servant came to him one day as he was at work, and asked him if he knew anything about diving. "Why do you ask that," he said. "Is your name Williams?" "Yes." "Then you are the man these officers have been reading about in the Journal of the Crimea, how you found a cannon." Ever after this they seemed to regard him in a different light.

I should like to describe a Sunday I spent at Bournemouth, December 3rd, 1894. I penned some verses on "The Sabbath Dawn" in the early morning, and then I wended my way to the Richmond Hill Congregational Church, where the eloquent Rev. Ossian Davies ministers to a most aristocratic congregation.

The church is one of the finest and prettiest that I have ever seen. It is lighted by electric light. I attended the morning prayer meeting before the service, at which the pastor presided. There earnest supplications were made on behalf of all church workers and churches.

We listened to a thrilling discourse on the text "The fool hath said in his heart there is no God." The preacher said he must be rightly designated in the face of all that we see in nature, providence and grace. He told of an Infidel dining with a Christian; the sceptic remarked, "how nice this pudding is." "Well," said the Christian, "it has had no cook, according to your principles." "You say this beautiful earth came by chance, without a creator." He said, you might as well say St. Paul's Cathedral and Westminster Abbey and such places, have been built without architects or builders." Altogether it was a most profitable time.

We then went through the Golf ground that had been opened on the Wednesday of my arrival. This ground occupies about seventy acres of heathy common land, which with another eighty acres had been made over to the Corporation of Bournemouth, by Sir George Meyrick, the Lord of the Manor, after paying out the various men who exercised common rights on the land. The Corporation had spent about twelve thousand pounds in making roads, laying out the ground, planting shrubs and building.

The Corporation being allowed to sell nine thousand pounds worth of the land, for the purpose of meeting the expenses, surely the £13,000 has been well expended and will bring into Bournemouth athletics of every description, for they are now making cricket and football grounds on part of the other eighty acres. This will take the point from the remark I heard made at Margate recently, viz :—that Bournemouth was greatly composed of sick folk in Bath chairs; but we ought to remember that they were there from other places, to enjoy the healing balm of Bournemouth and recruit their health. Wending my way through the golf ground, I came on the right to Bournemouth Cemetery, where the silent dust remains in quiet and ease from strife. We could not but admire this cemetery, a prettier one we never saw. Here lies much that was beautiful in life, and now in death is surrounded by beauty. Here everyone should pay a visit; it may remind them of their last earthly home, and may show them life is so brief in which to do all the kindly acts that they can do for their fellows.

"So let us live that we may dread,
The grave as little as our bed."

Entering the Cemetery, one sees on each side of the roadway, about fifty of the most beautiful monkey trees I have ever seen. There is a beautiful shrubbery and firs and pines growing in all their profusion. The cemetery Church is one of the finest and largest; as forsooth everything in Bournemouth is fine. I am like the Americans, fond of large things, but in monetary matters, I am more like Southampton in the doggrell rhyme following, which I heard a short time ago :—

"Romsey on the mud,
Southampton on the stones.
Romsey eats the meat,
Southampton picks the bones."

Not very complimentary for Southampton. If this verse had been quoted in verses on the "Beauties of Southampton," we perhaps should have had the "kick out," so we had better let it be here, but not because they do not eat meat at Bournemouth. The butchers' shops were laid out on Friday as though the bones would take a lot of picking before they were seen.

I then, wending my way to Boscombe, began to find dinner had been forgotten, and searching my pockets, found a slice of bread and butter and three apples, and really had a sumptuous dinner in this humble repast which I enjoyed, having the best of sauce, even better than Bentley's, in a keen appetite which made a remarkable relish. Finding myself at Boscombe Salvation Army Barracks, and seeing the color-sergeant with the flag I asked if I might accompany him, and found him a most agreeable companion. He took me to an out of door service which they had in the public road at Boscombe, having a ring of large dimension with an excellent band. The collection box was the flag, which they put on the public road. Some may object to this, but what is the wrong; they must have money to carry on the work, and in all sea side services, and in every place of worship, they have collections. Why not in the open air, which is their sanctuary?

They obtained ten shillings and twopence, twopence more than the amount required the Captain said on that occasion. At least they are good beggars, and therefore ought to be supported, for they are doing a good work in reclaiming drunkards, and bringing salvation to many a home. May God bless them all in all their enterprises in His service.

The Captain asked me to read a portion of Scripture, and give a short address in the Barracks, which was packed, it holding some three or four hundred people. Reading and commenting on the xxiii. Psalm, I told them how meeting a navvy last year in the Boscombe Chine, I tried to capture him for King Jesu's army, and found he was one of their soldiers, having been converted through their instrumentality. He told me that seven years ago, he with others went to disturb the meeting held by two young female captains, but the Lord met him, convinced him of sin, and saved his soul. We meet many such cases when going through the country. May the Lord bless them as He has done in all their work and labor of love. It was pleasing to know this soldier was standing true to his colours, though gone to seek employment elsewhere.

After taking tea with a respected friend, late of Upton Park, London, I came back to Bournemouth and heard a talented and fluent Baptist minister, reminding me of the old days at Park Street, when C. H. Spurgeon first began his ministry. He was the Rev. W. Minifie, late of the Pastors' College. We did hear that an aristocratic London Church had been trying to decoy this young pastor to more luxurious pasturage. Sheep stealing seems to me bad enough, but when officers of churches flagrantly try and steal by sinful pelf the shepherd of the flock, when he is doing a grand work in the sphere in which he is working, the sin ought to be well punished, if they are not hung for it, as men used to be for stealing our four-legged sheep. This somewhat unsettled the people, but we hear to the pastor's credit he has withstood the temptation, and is still to remain, till God pleases, the pastor of Lansdowne Baptist Church, Bournemouth. They are contemplating building a larger church, and friends will do well to assist them in their struggles, as they are crowded out, being packed like bloaters in a case.

Mr. Minifie preached a sermon from the ten lepers, only one returning to give thanks, and he a Samaritan. He said the most unlikely got saved, and those who were the greatest sinners generally showed the most gratitude to the dear Saviour for their cure, hence to night there might be the poor drunkard, or the great sinner who had gone deep into sin, who would return like the Samaritan, to give thanks for the Divine healings, while the most moral and self righteous Pharisee would be amongst the nine. The whole sermon was fraught with useful lessons of gospel truth.

The Lord's Supper was celebrated after the service, and all through, the day was full to overflowing of spiritual blessing.

Some eight years ago I had the removing of a family from Penge to Lyme Regis in Dorsetshire. We had some four miles to go from Axminster Station. It was in the month of May, and the country looked in its prime. Three out of the four miles was up hill, and as we looked back over Devonshire, with its hills and vales, its rivers and woods, and green fields of corn, and meadows with grazing cattle, Devonshire lay as a panorama of beauty before us, and we realized God's work in nature as excellent. The birds were singing their songs of grateful praise, and gratitude seemed stamped on all around.

When at the top of this hill, looking down into the placid waters of Lyme Regis, with a background of hills, we saw Devonshire in all its pristine spring beauty, whilst in front were miles of expansive blue sea, forming a sight most beautiful to behold on that spring evening. After we had finished our removal the next day, we were intent to see all we could of the place.

Picking out an elderly man from about a dozen fishermen, I said, "Here my friend, take a walk with a stranger to this neighbourhool this evening," not offering him anything, and he accompanied me at once. I thought of the Master, as He called His disciples from the craft, and said to Peter, "Follow Me, and I will make you fishers of men." My old fisherman was about 65 years of age, He told me how the waters had made inroads into the land since he was a boy, he having been born there.

He took me to a point, and showed me where acres of land one morning tumbled into the sea, and a road that was not allowed to be used by any heavy traffic for some years past, for fear it would do as the land in Sandgate did. He showed me the corner of a churchyard that had already one morning deposited several coffins into the sea beneath. So at some parts of our coast the land recedes, while at other places the sea gives way to the growing land. As we travelled along together, I asked him if he had by grace found the road to Heaven yet, and was he on it; "No," he said, "but he had a great desire to get on." I told him the royal road to Heaven was repentance towards God and faith in our Lord Jesus Christ.

I found he attended the Baptist church, and his brother, he said, was a Christian and a chapel keeper of the same church. We then came upon some stalwart fine looking fellows. Never imagining they were lifeboat men, I picked out the oldest and said, "My friend, the stream of life is getting narrow for you, have you yet found the heavenward road?" "Thank God I have, for many years," was his frank reply, "ask my men if I have not." He had been the Captain of the lifeboat for many years, and had with his crew been the means of saving many a shipwrecked mariner, and I found they were nearly all total abstainers. To hear some people talk you might suppose that no one could face the storm but those who drank spirituous liquours, but this is a fallacy, as in the lifeboat crew at Eastbourne there are many abstainers as here; we conclude all could be so if they chose, and all would be far better without the fire water than with it.

Then I commenced a Gospel Temperance address, and got a good many listeners of the well to do sort as there were many there. A barrister who heard, said he was so much interested in our address, that he must give a friendly word, which he did. It was quite a treat to hear his oratory and pungent speech. A collection was then made for the Lifeboat Institution, and about £1 5s. subscribed, a soverign of which was given by the barrister, so we were enabled to do a little in the good work even though on business. The next morning we went off by the coach for the station, and left Lyme Regis and sweet Devonshire behind for the dingy London smoke.

The father of the Duchess of Edinburgh, the then Czar of Russia, paid a visit to this country in the year 1874. Coming up the river Thames, his vessel got aground near Gravesend, which mishap impeded his landing on British soil for several hours. As we were waiting at Windsor for the royal train to arrive, I improved the time by giving a Gospel Temperance address in Windsor Park to a goodly and attentive audience, mostly aristocrats and well to do people. A gentleman present, who was a New York banker, gave me his card, and invited me to visit him, if ever I went across the "herring pond" to America. I told him the only thing that would prevent my doing so was the lack of the dust that I saw by his card he dealt in.

This temperance address did me good service some years after. A lady stopped me when I was out with my van, and said to me, "Will you tell Mr. Gwyer to call upon me, my address is in the Crystal Palace Road," at the same time giving me her address. "Tell him, he will remember giving a Temperance address some years ago, in Windsor Park, prior to the arrival of the Czar of Russia. I was amongst his appreciative hearers, and told my husband how I had been interested in his address, and how, if ever we went to live near the Crystal Palace we would be customers to him." I said, "Yes madam, I remember it well." "but," said she, "surely you are not the gentleman I heard.' "Well," I said, "My name is Gwyer, and I remember giving the address you speak of." She then became a customer, and continued as long as she lived in that neighbourhood.

My friend, Mr. Baker, now of Southend, and I, conducted a Gospel Temperance Open Air Meeting one Sunday afternoon, in Prince Arthur Road, Beckenham, many years ago, to an audience mostly composed of brickmakers, navvies, and men of that sort. Amongst the crowd were several lads, who listened very attentively as I described a christian teetotal home, with all its joy and comforts. I told them God was able to change the hearts of any of their fathers or mothers, who by sin were depriving their children of these things, if only the lads would ask Him in faith to do so. One lad unknown to me, took me at my word, and asked God to save his father, who was a drunkard, and we must not say surprising to relate, his father a short time after was brought to attend a Primitive Methodist Chapel, and got savingly converted and became an abstainer, and the children experienced that my description was a true one, they having a delightful home from that time.

This only came under my notice a few week ago, when a gentleman of good appearance spoke to me in the street of Upton Park, Essex, and telling me he was this lad, thanked me for the words which had led him to his prayer, which was so gloriously answered. He told me he was now an wholesale jeweller's traveller, going all over the country. This event should give great encouragement to all engaged in Gospel or Band of Hope, or Juvenile Templars work amongst the young.

Leaving now these humble sketches with all their imperfection; I ask the kind forbearance of all my critics, hoping only and always that they will be read with interest and profit to the cause of temperance, benevolence and religion, even when my course on earth is over, and my pen no longer moves its accustomed journey, in the prose and rhyme narrations of a somewhat eventful life.

My one hope is that I shall meet in the Better Land many of my readers, who like myself, shall have learned to look above the trials of life, and see in them the kindly discipline of a loving Father's hand.

DECEMBER 28th, 1894.

FOLKESTONE.

We were on Folkstone beach at five,
For we this morn did early rise,
And as we sat the muses came,
Alas! 'twill spread abroad our fame.
The rising orb proclaimed its power,
In beauty from the east that hour;
We never shall forget the sight—
Which gave to us such grand delight;
Behind the sandy cliffs; we gazed,
And forth her warming rays she blazed;
The sea in grandeur fore us spread,
Our upward thoughts to God thus led.
With merchandise its ships did see;
Those mighty towns upon the sea,
And from their funnel left in line
Their long and smoky vapours fine;
To Watt's mind while yet a boy,
Which gave him then the greatest joy,
This latest power of steam not known,
The kettle lid revealed alone.
George Stephenson the railway king,
We ever must his praises sing;
Now what without this mighty force
Could guide these great Leviathan's course;
But still a providence most kind
Revealed it to the youngster's mind.
One vessel bound for London Town,
Now others gliding channel down.
P'rhaps one for China or Japan,
Or to Egypt for the Soudan.
The fishing smacks they spread about,
And singing boatmen too were out.
The mansions large they towered high,
And hazy clouds sped long the sky.
The marine gardens promenade,
A pleasant sight it truly made;
Some lodging houses fine and tall,
Were built just neath the sandy wall,
These homelike residences seen,

Are sheltered from the cold winds keen.
Before we quit this lovely spot,
Which now two hours has been our lot,
At lifeboat house just built we stay
A pleasant visit to it pay.
It has seven hundred pounds just cost,
We know this money won't be lost.
The Lifeboat is a ladies' gift,
To save poor mariners adrift,
While Folkstone promises to pay
All future debts incurred this way.
Lifeboats round our sea girt isle,
Shows loving deeds in best of style;
Our noble lifeboat crews so brave,
Save many from a watery grave.
Let's send our contribution then,
To cheer these brave and valiant men;
One other thing on beach we saw,
Which seemed to us without a flaw.
A tram does climb the sandy wall,
Another coming down the tall.
With electricity comprest,
This mighty silent worker's drest;
We climbed the steps of sandy bank,
And nature's beauties full we drank.
A pleasant seat in half moon style,
And then a little time did wile:
Here sixty steps and six we climbed,
And now these flag stones we have rhymed;
Then ninety-nine we travelled o'er,
And sixty-six put down before.
In climbing up a steepened hill,
We use our energy and skill,
Now here's a seat and down we sit
For rest we want, a little bit.
Our Sandgate rhyme we give to one,
And now will tell what it has done:
A gentleman was passing by—
As on the Leas we stepped up high,
Our rhyme of Sandgate gave to him,
It did from him a shilling win.
We're tempted now to tell his name,

And us we hope he will not blame;
He lives by death, suffice to say,
By burying those who pass away.
For his kind act and deed we'll praise,
And when are stopped our humble lays,
This our wish when passed from here,
He'll bury our remains with care.
We asked his name, he Handbrook gave,
And kindly to us did behave,
His mansion on the Leas can see,
In front of the wide rolling sea,
If you the beach to Sandgate walk,
And with companion you should talk,
The sight you'll find a pretty one,
At least we found it beat by none.
There cabbages so large did grow,
Near sea, with ebbing tides that flow,
They did potatoes dig in May,
We saw them as we passed that day.
We must not touch on Sandgate here,
We've shed before the falling tear;
But still we hope there's brighter store,
Reserved for it than heretofore;
God works by means that's sometimes strange,
Disasters oft he doth arrange,
To teach us lasting good each day,
That we may trust the Lord alway;
And when our troubles blind our eyes,
Our faith shall know His purpose wise.
Now since we wrote the rhyme above,
We know full well that God is Love;
We heard from some, two months ago,
The darkened cloud did rainbow show.
An ornament the pier doth stand,
Victoria's name much loved, so grand;
One Penny is the only charge,
To visit it and walk at large.
We could write many verses more;
For we have lots of rhyme in store,
Of Folkstone and its healthy clime,
And mansions large could put in rhyme.
The truth of all, you sure will find,
And Folkstone people very kind.

THOUGHTS SUGGESTED BY SEEING THE DISASTROUS SLIP AT SANDGATE.

We oft are awed with trembling fear
When gazing on some trouble near,
But unbelief hides light from view,
Of mercies that are ever new.

A prettier view could scarce be found
Than Sandgate's scenery miles around;
The hills protect from Northern wind,
The bracing sea-breeze suits mankind.

Alas! the 5th of March, at eight,
The people were in greatest strait;
The earth began to move and quake,
And many hearts seemed like to break.

With anxious fear—what does it mean?—
As out their houses many came,
The walls they cracked, and ceilings fell,
And many now the story tell.

If it had been a midnight scene
Far greater had the horror been;
For if they all had gone to bed
Most likely some would now be dead!

A little girl did lose her sight
(So we were told) on that dread night,
No other accident occured,
A miracle, indeed, we heard.

The John B. Gough's Hotel, they said,
Found many folk a nice, warm bed;
And all the friends most kindly sought
To shelter neighbours, as they ought.

In God's kind providence there's room
To praise His Name amid the gloom!
For, while exposed to dangers many,
No sudden death occurred to any.

To Sandgate send a brighter day,
Though this disaster shades their way;
May cheerful givers aid their loss,
To help them bear their heavy cross.

If John B. Gough had been alive
He would have helped the funds to thrive;
For good he did—his birthplace there—
In gratitude his place we'll share.

Our Queen subscription, too, has sent,
Her heart is always kindly bent,
With tender sympathy and care—
God spare her long to us down here!

The rich will send a generous gift,
To give the sufferers a kind lift;
The poor will give their humble mite,
To light the shadow of the night.

WRITTEN ON THE BEACH AT HERNE BAY.

I sat upon the pebbly beach,
To hearken what the sea would teach,
It taught me lessons rich and rare,
Of God's kind providence and care.

The rolling waves and ebbing tide,
And calm and spray, and storm beside,
Reveal God's wisdom, grace and love,
Which shine resplendent from above.

And as I gazed across the sea,—
I'll tell the lessons it taught me;
The changing scenes of life, at best,
Are like the tide—they have no rest.

Close there the children build with sand,
A garden planned, like one on land,
But soon the tide will sweep away
The efforts of their childish play.

So like the children playing there,
We build our castles in the air,
Till down they come with such a dash,
And all our castles gone to smash.

Is there another lesson taught
Of house that's built upon a rock.
How storms and tempests rage in vain,
Yet safely doth the house remain.

"So I by Faith in Christ shall stand,
All other ground is sinking sand;
His righteousness my only plea,
And that He lives and died for me."

IN MEMORIAM

OF THE LATE

PRINCE ALBERT VICTOR

DUKE OF CLARENCE,

Born January 8th, 1864. Fell asleep January 14th, **1892.**

The fourteenth of this month we mark,
A cloud fell grim, and black, and dark,
And like a pall it hung that day,
When Albert Victor passed away.

The paper decked in mourning spoke,
To those whose hearts were nearly broke,
Of him who late we did esteem,
Whose sad departure seemed a dream.

O Lord in pity hear the cry—
We know that Thou art ever nigh,
Thine ear is listening to the prayer
Of all who cast on Thee their care.

To those whose loving hearts are riven,
May Thy supporting grace be given,
Heal their bereaved hearts, we pray,
Be, Lord, the parents help and stay.

And while in pitying thought to-day,
We pray for those bereaved who stay,
A darkened Palace home to mourn,
The loss of him who's from them torn.

Those bitter pangs and trials given,
Be ladder steps to lead to Heaven,
May they be sanctified by grace,
And lead us all to seek Thy face.

The sisters and the brothers too,
Their sweet affection ever true,
This sad bereavement such a grief,
Lord only Thou canst give relief.

For his beloved, betrothed bride,
Who looked to be his joy and pride;
We pray she may supported be
In all her bitter agony.

Our Queen beloved, her trials great,
May she in prayer with patience wait;
Cheer thou her heart, O Lord we pray
Her faith be strong on this dark day.

The Nation mourns with loyal heart,
In tender sympathetic part,
Condoling Royal hearts bereaved,
And prays that soon they'll be relieved.

Albert Victor loved his mother,
Father, sisters, and his brother;
Affection great marked here his stay,
Was kind disposed in every way.

His resolution formed was high,
To do the right, he said he'd try;
And at the Blacking School did say.
Clean boots the best, my boys each day.

Although the Nation reckoned here,
Upon his head the crown he'd wear,
We hope that bright upon his brow,
The Saviour's crown is shining now.

Blest Jesus wipe the scalding tear,
Which on their cheeks will sure appear,
When visiting the silent tomb,
And with Thy light remove the gloom.

Thou who did'st weep at Lazarus' grave,
Jesus so mighty still to save,
Speak to each soul and gently say
I am Thy life, Thy truth, Thy way.

And while the Nation mourn with those
Whose promised joys are turned to woes,
For every worn and tear-stained face,
We asked the Father's love and grace.

17th January 1892.

THE ROYAL MARRIAGE,

Of His Royal Highness the Duke of York, to Her Serene Highness Princess May of Teck, on Thursday, July 6th, 1893.

The Duke of York, in nuptial ties,
  Is bound to Princess May,
The joyful news resounding flies,
  The empire's various way.

A happy life we wish them both,
  And may they long be spared
To prove the virtue of their troth,
  Their confidence is shared.

With health of body and of mind,
  Give pleasant times we pray;
Lord grant them this, for Thou art kind,
  And guide them in Thy way.

The good man's portion may they share—
  Sweet children round their board,
May they be free from pain or care,
  With blessings from the Lord.

His parents we respect alway;
  Both Prince and Princess too;
The parents of our Princess May,
  Give Lord a blessing true.

Our gracious Queen's great heart of love
  Is deeply touched we know,
And for her children's children strove
  Her loving care to show.

Her sympathy doth not there end,
  She loves her subjects so,
That when calamities attend
  Her purse strings quickly go.

The fireworks, fine, in grand array,
  Show forth the joy we feel;
May cheerful tidings greet their way,
  'Mid future woe or weal.

The nation joins in jubilant song
  To wish them cheerful glee,
And hopes in distant future long
  The Duke our King to see.

Along the route are mottoes grand,
  God bless the happy pair,
Long may they live in this our land,
  Thou God of Bethel hear.

The Prince and Princess, bless, O Lord!
  The Duke and Duchess both,
Give to them all a cheery word,
  And to the pair betrothed.

God bless our gracious Queen, we pray,
  Spare long her life to reign,
Impart great joy to her alway,
  If this Thy will contain.

John Bull's old England, join in one,
  Kind greeting give we all;
From mansions to the cot there's none
  But blessings on them fall.

Most costly presents, too, were sent
With gifts and jewels rare,
For rich and poor, they both were bent
To show the love they bare.

No Royal Wedding ever had
More links of loving chord,
With loud acclaim we're sure 'tis clad
With blessings from the Lord.

Upon the Royal heads, we pray,
Heaven's benediction rest,
To Bridegroom and to Princess May,
God give that which is best.

May they so live 'mid honours here,
To seek for heaven above;
Come joy to them or sorrow's care,
Be cheered with Jesu's love.

Then when earth's race by them is run;
(Life's schooling days soon glide),
May they each hear Christ say: "Well done,
In heaven with me abide."

THE BIRTH OF THE FUTURE HEIR TO THE THRONE OF GREAT BRITAIN.

The bells rang out most merrily
All o'er the country cheerily,
To tell an infant Prince was born,
Who may some day the crown adorn.

From Richmond Park the news was spread,
Throughout the world it soon was read,
The cannon loud did shake the earth,
To greet the Royal infant's birth.

God bless, we pray, the mother dear,
Guard Thou the babe with Thy great care,
Each may Thy providence preserve,
And may both live Thy cause to serve.

The telegrams were sent with speed,
The telephone was much in need,
The papers sent the news abroad
To rich and poor, countess and lord.

For wheresoever you may call,
You find the Duchess loved by all;
Here kindly feeling won her fame
When Princess May was still her name.

The Duke as father now we know,
In him a parent's love doth show,
His wife and son, so very dear,
He always now will love and cheer.

The mother's Ducal mother bless,
Blest Jesus, with Thy righteousness;
She knows that faith's a greater gem
Than any earthly diadem.

The Prince and Princess bless we pray,
Now their grandson is born to-day;
May gratitude their hearts inspire
To live with aims both true and higher.

Our gracious Queen both true and good,
We long her love have understood;
God bless we pray our noble Queen,
Long be her line in safety seen.

For all their honours incomplete,
Unless they prize Thy mercy-seat,
And though temptation them assail,
Thy grace for them will never fail.

June 25th, 1894.

IN MEMORIAL OF MARY ANN TIPPLE,

AGED 43 YEARS,

Who passed away December 5th. 1893, and was buried in Grays New Cemetery, December 11th, who left nine children to mourn her loss.

Their mother's landed now in heaven,
Her bark to harbour safe is driven;
While here encountered many a storm,
But now is safe from any harm.

She ne'er could think so short her stay,
Behind the loved ones passed away;
But Jesus took her home in love,
To dwell with Him and them above.

The children nine now left behind,
Who mourn bereaved both parents kind,
The Lord will give His helping hand,
This promise good for ever stand.

Bind up their hearts by Gilead's balm,
Their griefs assuage, their sorrows calm,
Give them, O Lord, Thy grace we pray,
Provide and guide them all their way.

And though they mourn kind mother gone,
And Father loved whose race is done,
A brother late so true and brave
Was drowned beneath the ocean's wave.

Raise up for these bereaved, O Lord,
Helpers, according to Thy word,
The widow and the fatherless,
And orphans Thou wilt ever bless.

WRITTEN IN BOURNEMOUTH GARDENS.

While travelling for T. H. Bentley & Co.

The feathered songster's notes rang sweet,
The blackbird's song our ears did greet,
It dipt it's wings in flowing brook,
It's plumage beautiful did look.

The Rhododendrons all in bloom,
In Bournemouth gardens there is room
And scope for sweet poetic muse,
Grand thoughts of nature to infuse.

The trees, and varied shrubs looked green,
Sweet coloured May and flowers were seen;
To those in search of vigorous health,
The pines are full of odourous wealth.

That June's Lord's day will ever be,
Loved for its song-bird melody;
The river Bourne's bright waters clear,
Will long remain to us so dear.

The river pictured life to us,
Amid its worry and its fuss,
Our life stream glideth swiftly by,
Into the sea of eternity.

So teach us Lord while here we stay,
Like this bright stream do good each day,
That when our voyage here is past,
We may find peace in heaven at last.

10th June, 1894.

IN MEMORIAM.

Verses penned through paying a visit to the graveof **a brother Forester**, beloved—the late Mr. THOMAS DEADMAN, **who died on** Easter Sunday, and was buried In Beckenham Old Church-**yard** on Friday, April 22nd, 1892, and who had also been **a respected** neighbour for upwards of twenty years, and **was much** respected by all who knew him. His late beloved **wife** was buried in the same grave 15 years ago.

A brother Forester lies here ;
A friend so true and neighbour dear,
We've known for twenty years or more—
Till now his life's short journey's o'er.

His wife some fifteen years ago
Much loved, he lost, a crushing blow,
But as in life they both were one,
They're joined in death beneath this stone.

So life's short journey soon is done ;
It's fleeting moments quickly run :
God give us grace to live aright,
And shed abroad His Spirit's light.

By his grave side we shed a tear
His voice seems sounding in our ear;
Our lives are short it seems to say,—
And all are passing swift away.

Affection's tribute on this mound;
Encircling wreaths which fade around
Yet show the love that's followed thee,
Will bless thy loving memory.

To rhyme the wishes here we'll try,
Though sad at heart we heave a sigh;
Here's one "our loving tribute pay,
To our dear Father this dark day."

Little Willie has shown his love
He had for Grandpa now above;
And in his simple loving word
His tender sympathy we've heard.

A wreath of wild flowers now we see
To bless Grandpa's sweet memory;
From Sissie dear, and brother Fred,
Whose young hearts must have nearly bled.

And yet a grander wreath we view;
From dearest friends "styled old and true;"
In loving memory to him,
Who did while here their friendship win.

Then many loving wreaths we read;
Spoke tender words to him who's dead,
Consoling those who mourn his loss,
Who feel it such a heavy cross.

To all the dear ones left we pray;
Be Lord to each their help and stay,
And bring them all to meet above,
With him to share Thy home of love.

WATCHING THE FIRST RAIN AFTER A LONG DROUGHT AT BOURNEMOUTH.

The rain comes pattering down at last,
We hope that long it will rain fast!
The earth's wide gaping mouth shows wide,
As asking it on every side.

The pasture's dry, and parched and bare,
The farmers need it everywhere;
O may these showers of heavenly rain
Resucitate the earth again.

The cattle grazing on the mead,
So much they do the rain drops need;
The feathered tribes they sing with glee,
'Tis real happiness to see.

We saw from window at Bournemouth,
The showers came sweeping from the south,
This early morn at five we rose
To hear the grateful cawing crows.

O may our grateful prayer arise,
To praise the Lord for He is wise,
And though the drought has been so long,
We'll praise Him with a cheerful song.

May all our thoughts of His great love
And His compassions from above,
With earnest zeal our faith inspire,
To live a life for Christ entire.

Like showers refresh the earth below,
So heavenly showers will God bestow;
For sovereign grace our hope and stay
Will guide us through our earthly way.

Our faith will soon be lost in sight,
When we shall leave this earthly night,
Hear Jesus say to us "Well done."
Thy sorrows drought's now past and gone.

23rd June. 1 [illegible]3.

IN MEMORY OF MAY KENNETT.

Born 8th May, 1891, in High St., Beckenham, Kent, fell asleep 25th May, 1892, was Interred in the Crystal Palace District Cemetery, Elmers End, Beckenham, on 31st May, 1892.

Our darling babe is now at rest,
So short her journey to the blest,
Her feeble bark to harbour driven,
So soon she's landed safe in Heaven.

She was so frail and weak while here,
And down her face oft ran a tear,
But Jesus wiped them all that day,
And took our babe to Him away.

Though only turned the twelvemonths old
With joy her prattling tongue oft told
The love that dwelt within her heart,
And now in ours is left a smart.

These tender tendrils how they twine,
In sweet affection to combine,
Parental love's drawn close together,
Death alone can ever sever.

We named her May, and strange to say,
'Twas in that month she passed away;
Our sweet May bud in Heaven will bloom,
Unprisoned by the silent tomb.

So teach her parents here, O Lord,
To walk according to Thy word.
Give grace to equal all their need,
For thou are still a Friend indeed.

And when we meet on Canaan's shore,
We'll see our babe, a babe no more
But praising God with angels bright—
A worker crowned in heavenly light.

So when our earthly course is run
We hear the Master's word "Well done"
Resounding from the heavenly shore,
By Jesus when our journey's o'er.

3rd July, 1892.

PRESENTED TO A YOUNG WOMAN.

On her 21st Birthday, October 21st, 1892.

On a bed of sickness, lonely, languishing in pain.
In London Hospital Nellie laid, but never did complain.
The days seemed long, and weeks and months passed by
She bore affliction patiently, she felt that God was nigh.
In all her agony of pain she said, I know He loves me
now, [bow.
For Jesus helps me by His grace, and to His will I
No complaining word, ungrateful, would she say,
Although the bitter pains, kept by her night and day,
The cancer wrought its deadly work, for eight long
years or more. [scanty store,
She's now a sufferer at home, fed by her mother's
The Lord by this affliction, brought her to feel her need
The Saviour sought His wandering sheep, her to His
fold did lead. [full and free
She found His pardoning grace and love so rich so
And will throughout her life, however long or short it
be. [from heaven so great,
Five years she has enjoyed this blessing, a boon
It has kept her in the wintry night and cold, and
sultry's summer heat, [with many a thorn,
So come what may, though rough her road, and strewn
A diadem will by-and-by through grace her head adorn.

SONG OF THE CUCKOO,

As heard at Northfleet, 14th May, 1892.

As I lay musing on my bed,
Some grateful thoughts pass through my head;
I heard the Cuckoo's first glad lay
On this the fourteenth day of May.

Remembering winter now is past,
Although so long it seemed to last;
Its biting winds, its frost and snow,
Are gone for weeks just now we know.

The Cuckoos licked all up the mud,
And flowers appear from bursting bud;
He brings with him sweet melody
And gladsome is his plaintive glee.

Our lives with all their varied change,
God's providence doth wise arrange;
His counsels are a channel deep,
His loving kindness doth us keep.

But p'raps there may be some who see
These lines and say, they're not for me;
I'm still a wanderer from the fold,
And find the world is bleak and cold.

Now Christ saith "sinner enter in,
My grace can conquer all your sin;
Come unto Me, ye weary one,
Of all who come, I'll cast out none."

Come then in penitence and faith,
Believe the word that Jesus saith,
And all your sins He will forgive
Because He died that we may live.

Then yours will be a happy life,
Amid its conflicts and its strife,
And you with us will join the song
Some day in heaven's eternal throng.

THE MYSTERIES OF LIFE.

The keys of life He holds in hand,
  Though rough the path He leads aright;
Through flowery meads or desert land,
  His loving kindness shines so bright.

The road we take is sometimes straight,
  Then long it crooked turnings be;
The night seems very long and dark,
  The keys of life He holds for me.

Each trembling saint He'll safely guide,
And makes him too in grace to grow;
His promise firm is on our side,
The keys of life He holds we know.

In darkest doubt we long had been,
The night seemed black with storm ahead;
Our faith beclouded scarcely seen,
He holds the keys of life we read.

We tempted sorely were, and sad
Which on our spirits long did stay,
But faith triumphant made us glad,
He holds the keys of life alway.

In our perplexity we sought
Sweet pardon at the throne of grace;
And faith applied Christ's blood that bought,
He holds the keys of life could trace.

IN MEMORIAM OF ELEANOR JANE RELF,

Who fell asleep in Jesus August 11th, 1893, Aged 18 Years; buried in Old Northfleet Churchyard August 16th.

"I love them that love Me, and those that seek Me early shall find Me."

Some verses now we would indite,
Lord guide our pen while thus we write
The parents, hearts bereaved to cheer,
For loss of her they loved so dear.

Thou who did'st weep at Lazarus' grave,
Dear Jesus merciful to save,
Now though their hearts are crushed and sore,
Thy love remaineth evermore.

In pity look on them, dear Lord,
Sweet comfort send from Thy blest word;
For Jesus once said, we have read,
"The Damsel sleeps, she is not dead."

"She's safe in Heaven at home with Me,
Like all who follow Me shall be;
Life's journey here so quick doth fly,
For feeble man is born to die."

When Jesus said "seek ye My face,"
She sought and found His pardoning grace.
She was by all much loved alway,
Yet destined short on earth her stay.

The Shepherd took her to His fold
From storms and tempests, bleak and cold,
This lamb for whom the Saviour bled,
Has now a crown upon her head.

Three weeks she bore the greatest pain;
To her God's will it did contain;
And then her soul went safely home
To hear her Master's words "well done."

Lord, Thou alone can'st give relief;
Her parents' hearts now wrung with grief,
Bind up their open wounds we pray
By Gilead's healing balm to-day.

Her brothers and her sisters mourn
Now their loved sister's from them borne
May grace in early life be given,
And so may each meet her in heaven.

Her dust in Northfleet now doth lie,
Within the Parish Churchyard high;
An ancient church of many a year,
And thousand forms once loved dwell here.

Now weary, worn, bereaved and sad,
Tell Jesus all, He'll make thee glad;
He'll turn to joy thy great sorrow,
Thee heavenly blessings give to-morrow.

While thou art treading life's rough road,
To Father's heavenly blest abode;
Jesus will soon say thus to thee;
Come home, my child, and dwell with Me.

28th September, 1893.

WRITTEN AT BOURNEMOUTH

Through seeing the first verse hung up in my bedroom.

"My Jesus as Thou wilt,
All shall be well for me;
Each changing future scene,
I gladly leave to Thee."

Then come to me what may,
I leave it to Thy care;
I know that as my days,
Thy promises I share.

These riches will sustain
My soul in every strife,
'Twill ease me in all pain
And will preserve my life.

Then when my race is run,
As soon it sure will be,
I'll hear the Master's word "well done,"
Come home my child with Me.

"I WILL NEVER LEAVE THEE NOR FORSAKE THEE."—Heb. iii., 5.

Written at the Red Star Temperance Hotel, Poole, Sunday, September 3rd, 1893.

When our hearts are faint and sad,
His promises do make us glad;
"I will not leave in time of need."
Should quicken all our heavenward speed.

If doubts or fears perplex our way,
"I'll not forsake," shall be our stay;
Our trials here are sent in love.
Prepare us for our heaven above.

If friends far of removed be,
He's said, "I'll ever be to thee
A refuge and a stronghold too,
And guide thy path thy journey through."

For God will aid us by His grace,
If long our stay, or short our race;
"I'll never leave thee" cheers our hearts
And heals them of their inward smarts.

When tempted sore, and sorrows press,
We'll plead the Saviour's righteousness;
Our advocate's gone up on high,
And hears the groanings, or the sigh.

In sickness or at lonely death,
"I'll never leave," the Master saith;
"My grace is strong in love and power,"
"My staff supports the dying hour."

And when on Canaan's shore we meet,
The ransomed spirits us will greet:
And we shall hear in Christ's own word,
Enter the joy of Thy blest God.

IN LOVING MEMORY OF HARRIETT MITCHELL,

Died November 17th, 1892.

Our tender Mother's race is run,
Her constant work on earth now done,
She's heard the Master's welcome voice,
Enter my glory and rejoice.

Full threescore years and ten had she
Past on this frail mortality:
Still wisely ordered are God's ways,
For these are man's appointed days.

A sufferer she for many years,
Her face oft wet with sorrows tears;
But Jesus wiped them all away:
She smiles in Heaven's Eternal day.

Though grace she bore it patiently—
Trial, we know, God's saints all see:
But still He gave her here to say,
His grace is equal to my day.

Her husband there had gone before,
About six years or little more;
He greeted her upon the shore,
In bliss to dwell for evermore.

Her death came sudden too, at last,
Which on her children all did cast
A solemn gloom.—now Mother's dead,
And all their hearts with sorrow bled.

Her children ten, with falling tear,
All followed close behind the bier;
And relatives some forty strong,
Made the funeral very long.

In Kingston Churchyard is her grave,
Near where the Oceans waters lave,
The sands of time she's left for aye,
For sea of God's Eternal day.

So teach the dear ones left, O Lord,
To walk according to Thy word;
Give each Thy grace, O Lord we pray,
That all may meet in Heaven some day.

FLOWERS SHED FRAGRANCE SWEET.

Written at Eastbourne after a long drought, May 17th, 1893.

Sweet flowers they stud the land,
  And shed their fragrance sweet;
The roses choice on every hand,
  Our eyes with pleasure greet.

The Artist's handiwork we know,
  His paintings rich and rare;
The landscape grand doth show
  A Father's loving care.

He's dressed the earth in green,
To cheer and do us good;
The trees their foliage seen,
The fields provide us food.

The drought as well, He's sent
It long with us did last;
His hand with blessings pent,
The rains now pouring fast.

So we obey His will,
So we would throw away
Our own pretended skill,
And live by faith alway.

What stupid folly this
To doubt our Father's love;
We many blessing's miss,
He's promised from above.

In wintor time may we
By faith rest on His care,
Or summer's calm it be,
We know the answered prayer.

WRITTEN AT PORTSFIELD ELMSWORTH SHEPHERD HILL, NORTHCLOSE (Near the Sea, Isle of Wight).

The Isle of Wight so sweet its scene,
With hills, and vales, and sea;
And studded here and there are seen
Sweet homes that would suit me.

Speak not to me of city life,
With all its chafing care;
But let me live with my dear wife
On this sweet Island here.

The larks high up with cheerful notes,
These songsters up on high ;
Praise God so loud with bursting throat,
To copy them would I.

The insects humming round I hear,
And birds of chirping glee ;
And cackling hen just caught my ear,
With prancing foal I see.

The trees their varied foliage round,
And nestling near the wood ;
The cattle grazing all around,
All speak that God is good.

The welcome baa of sheep ahead ;
Their young were calling out,
And o'er the pastures wide they spread
Till shepherd dog's about.

So may we then in fields be seen,
When Jesus leads the way ;
We know like Ruth the time to glean,
When Boaz comes our way.

And when the Shepherd's dog doth bark,
For Satan oft does roar,
Though like a lion prowling dark,
God's sheep he tempts the more.

The hedgerows circling fields of corn,
With honey suckle grow ;
And wheat and other grain adorn,
This Island home below.

The pastures pant, the drought is bare,
With gaping cracks the earth,
Is longing for the showers down here ;
Send Lord the treasured worth.

With heat and drought, we see the cows
All scampering up the mead ;
Their tails high up did us arouse,
And filled our heart with dread.

So pants our soul for living stream,
Like earth's dry parched land,
Till from God's fountain forth it teem,
By grace alone we stand.

O may the streams of heavenly grace
Now saturate our soul ;
No drought of earth we there can trace,
Thy touch can make us whole.

Then when our life's short journey's past,
Though rough the storms of life ;
Our soul will safe be anchored fast
Beyond the reach of strife.

30TH JUNE, 1893.

STANZAS ON "THE GRAND OLD MAN,"—W. EWART GLADSTONE AND HIS BELOVED WIFE.

As life is drawing to its close,
Give to our gallant friend repose ;
Good Lord be Thou to them most near,
At eventide their hearts to cheer.

Let them Thy grace and glory see,
And humble trust alone in Thee.
Be Thou to them a refuge strong,
As Thou hast been to them so long

The measures fraught for good we pray,
With victory crowned be some day,
And though they meet with many a blow,
Like others passed which well we know.

For good laws on our statute book,
The "Grand Old Man" hath ne'er forsook,
O'ercame the obstacles so great,
And honors many for him wait.

But still there yet is work to do,
Which he our gallant leader true;
Until they're passed will not forsake,
On statute book these laws to make.

May our loved Gladstone with his wife,
Have God's protection all through life;
And His rich grace be each their stay,
Until in heaven they meet some day.

August, 1893.

AN APT REPLY AT A TEMPERANCE HOTEL.

Entering the house at Basingstoke,
I thus the conversation broke;
Please tell me now what is the charge,
For bedroom airy, clean and large.
Where I can lay my weary head,
Upon a soft and downy bed,
And rise refreshed at morning light,
Resuming work with brisk delight.

The host replied, "I cannot say,
Refreshment comes perhaps not that way;
But still I think you'll like my bed
To rest to night your busy head.
Refreshment does depend we find,
Upon the state of health and mind,
But as my charge is very small,
It suits Commercials one and all."

ON THE SABBATH.

The Sabbath dawns, O blessed day,
In Zion's courts we meet to pray
Amongst the saints to bless the Lord,
In harmony, with sweet accord.

Though here at Bournemouth far from home,
We do not feel we are alone;
The Lord is still our hope and stay,
To cheer us on our earthly way.

Show, Lord, Thy servants how to preach,
Apply the message unto each;
May they the Spirit's lesson learn,
That all our hearts with love may burn.

Disperse we pray the gloom of earth;
Fill up with joy our barren dearth,
Into our hearts let spring be given,
To end in summer up in Heaven.

The humblest work for Jesus take,
And do it for His own dear sake;
You will not lose the great reward,
But get good interest from the Lord.

Like those who met their risen Lord,
Who helped and cheered them by His word;
We shall by faith the Manna eat,
And gain our strength from Heavenly wheat.

DECEMBER 3RD, 1894.

A STORM AT MARGATE.

With their two Lifeboats, the "Quiver" and the "Moss."

When north wind blow in dreadful form,
And ships are drifting in the storm,
Those dauntless men so brave and true
Launch out the Quiver lifeboat true.
Their other lifeboat, too, we tell,
The noble Moss has done right well,
And many precious lives it saves
From sinking in their watery graves.
These men a record here deserve,
Who never from their duty swerve.
They have our thanks, the best we pray,
Both in the calm and stormy day,
To risk their lives they do engage
When hurricanes and storms do rage.
It was to us a pleasant sight
To see these valiant men last night,
They watch amid the storm and wind
To see if stranded ones they find.
Ahead the gale was blowing then,
We thought how dreadful for these men.
And then we asked them, "Would you go?"
"Yes sir, we would our courage show."
Now here we must relate to you,
What here we heard so very true;
They cannot launch in stormy night,
When spray and wind and waves do fight,
Because the north wind drives them back
Upon the dangerous rocky track.
But from a gentleman we heard
A hundred pounds, or less, his word,
If anchored cable they could place
To run beyond the beach surf's race.
They could with wheel or turnstile guide
The lifeboat to the ocean wide.
Then surely money should not stay
This Godlike work a single day.
If we had money we would spare
No longer they should want it there.
We heard it said at Margate too,

A simple statement and quite true,
The lead a licensed Victualler takes
As Lifeboat Secretary, makes
Our hair to stand quite up on end,
Although we know one may offend.
With such a noble work in view
To risk the lives of men so true,
We want not men with such a trade
That many moral wrecks have made.
The Quiver's donors can't, we know,
Conceive these things are really so.
What can our Temp'rance friends be doing
To let these men be lured to ruin.
No wrecks so numerous on the sea
As strong drink makes around to be.
One other thing we heard one day,
And now at Margate this we say,
While launching boat one day in storm
And mariners were suffering harm,
Some five or six were coxwains many,
And so the work's undone by any.
In future, though a novice, we
Would recommend that one there be,
Then Æsop's fable will come true,
One give command to launch, not two.
No venom poison in our line,
That's never in our flowing rhyme;
Unless the cap should fit the head
Don't take offence at what we've said.
One word more ere to Town we haste,
Your precious time no longer waste:
The noble lifeboats manned in style
Around Great Britain's sea girt isle
Commands from all the best we give
For precious life to longer live.
Send large subscriptions or a mite,
If a poor widow latter's right.
The Quiver's readers all must thank,
They highly in our verse shall rank.
And when we find another place
They'll give a similar one with grace;
For he that hath to him is given,
If saved through grace 'twill take to heaven.

:S OF MARGATE, RAMSGATE, WESTGATE-BROADSTAIRS, BIRCHINGTON AND THE ISLE OF THANET.

At early morn we rose betime,
Commenced again our work of ryhme;
A young man met and thus did say
Seeing no other on the way:
"My friend, life has commenced for you,
Our years are here but very few;
Now, shall we meet in yonder home
When life's short work on earth is done."
He said, "I hope we shall my friend."
We said, "Our friendship here will end,
But are you on that happy road,
Which reaches that most blessed abode,
Then stop at once, and let us pray
For those who seek can find to-day
God's pardon free: His grace is free,
Confess thy sins, He'll pardon thee."
With handkerchief we wipe the seat,
With joy were sheltered from the heat,
And into conversation we
Did quickly join most easily.
With one more man that passed close by,
And in his face we could espy,
A man of sterling worth we saw,
And we did him in converse draw.
"In what of life's great task share you,
Will you, dear sir, please tell me true."
"My work, my friend, is selling corn;"
"What brings you out this early morn?"
"I further diamonds black do sell;
Pantechnicon van to move as well."
We answered, "Few days do we stay;
Soon round the coast we are away,
We're Bentley's traveller you know,
Selling some tons where'er we go:
Many pounds we've taken here,
Selling our goods with greatest care;
And early morn's the only time

We can write down our flowing rhyme.
How strange, said we, our previous work,
For twenty years we did not shirk ;
But illness came, restored then we
Some other work were brought to see,
God's Providence is a safe chain
When one link snaps, He mends again,
Our tangled threads of life He takes,
And beauteous patterns of them makes ;
So then our friend, we say to you,
Whatever life you may pursue,
Keep this great fact before you well
Where'er we go this truth we tell.
The seeds in life we sow to-day,
Shall future harvest all display."
He futher said, "How strange it seem
Down here, with fog the air doth teem ;
While up on yonder cliff close by
The air is clear ; no cloudy sky"
We said, "Just like the vapoury cloud
Of earth, which hangs like darkest shroud.
But up in yonder Heavenly seat,
Our Captain's guidance is complete ;
He knows our fog, our storm, our rock,
He guides our ship to His great dock :
Now is he, Sir, your Captain too,
On Christ the solid rock are you."
We left the message then with him,
How by God's grace Jesus can win.
If others on life's sea are out,
With fogs of fears that hang about,
Let pinion wings of faith arise,
To clearer visions in the skies.
Should there be one or more that read
These lines, we pray that they may lead
To God, who hears the humblest cry,
And deep contrition's feeblest sigh ;
Then sinner, come to Him and pray,
And find sweet pardon on thy way.
Our conversation ended then,
And who should pass, but two dark men :

"Our friends," said we, "why early out.
What brings you thus so soon about?"
"We've walked from Wales," was their reply,
One said with tremulous sad sigh;
"Our work was with a travelling show;
Two years I've been with it you know."
We said, "why, how comes this about
That from that service you've run out?"
"Well sir, a fortnight back or more,
No bed had we, us to restore;
I overslept just for one hour;
The master's wrath on me did pour,
He sacked me there, without a warning,
And we to Margate came this morning?"
We asked them for their history,
"Once sold like cattle Sir, were we,
I was born a slave sir," one said,
"By grand emancipation freed:
But only three years old was I,
When we obtained sweet liberty.
Just then my father died, I've heard,
From my own mother's blessed word."
"Where did you live," we then replied,
"Before your own dear father died?"
"In Southern Carolina State,
Cotton Plantation too first rate."
"Please tell me now, how you became
Possessed of your full free man's name."
"Our master's name was always given,
Until our shackles all were riven.
McAlister I'm named you see,
In father's master's memory."
We for this information thanked,
In Margate's verses it shall rank.
At Wenham's Coffee Stall by sea,
Give in this note and breakfast see.
We must resume our notes again,
Our verse on Margate must contain
A word of the Jetty's renown;
Crowded when Londoner's come down.
Where Sally, Molly, Jane, and Kit,

Oft on its seats long hours do sit,
And watch the ebb and flowing tide
And calm and storm o'er ocean wide;
And both the poor man and the peer,
In close proximity sit here:
Nor is that such a mighty stoop,
For both alike will have to droop;
What matters it, when all on earth
Dissolve to dust of little worth;
May this lead us in very deed
To cheer and aid the poor in need.
The "Margarrett," a vessel grand,
Lands thousands on the Margate sands;
If shillings five, you here can show,
A "Soveriegn" ride you sure can go.
Save up your money we would say,
And give the wife a holiday—
Give them a sea trip they will prize,
We well this trip would advertise.
On the parade near harbour meet
Hundreds of loving couples sweet:
In fashions gay and finest dress,
With cheerful smile and love caress.
While on the sands they sit about,
As happy as a cricket out.
One day in evidence did we,
Such manifest affection see:
The lovers heads in sweet maids laps
Beguiled within their silken traps.
We gave a speech of deep import,
Impromptus though of friendly sort:
We told how Justice Clarke would take,
Bentley's fine Relish case to make
When long drawn cases did appear:
From tickling found his throat 'twould clear.
Some loving couples looked our way,
We fear they will be old some day.
Now this excited many a smile,
From fairest ladies for a while:
While we depicted Bentley's Relish,
The very thing they all should cherish;

And if our Lemon Squash they use,
The men will not their wives abuse.
So on the sands some thousands heard,
Our Temperance speech, so plain in word ;
We pray the seed sown, then may prove
The root to grow strong drink to move.
And while we thus did spin on rhyme,
We by this speech used well our time.
Some readers, perhaps, are glad to know,
The way we thus the seed did sow ;
The Minstrels Black had placed around'
Some chairs upon the sandy ground :
And for some time they were absent,
For lunch we heard, they just then went ;
We stepped right in and thus begun,
The rhyming verse that here doth run ;
The precious seed of truth we sowed ;
Our priceless time, too quickly flowed.
In Perkin's machines you read
Of Bentley's goods what we have said,
When bathing, there you ought to go,
Our Testimonials read you know.
On Sunday's you must never come,
No Lord's Day work by Perkin's done ;
Now we must never fail to sketch
How Punch does all the children fetch ;
And many, too, of older growth,
To see his pranks were nothing loth ;
Punch well his Judy doth caress,
He gives her kisses and doth bless,
But soon his sticks in use we tell,
To reprimand and thrash her well.
Once we did hear a parson say
Old Punch had charms for him alway,
If round the corner he could spy,
His own delight was very high.
The acrobats with drolling too,
Some laughter gave to not a few ;
While clown and fool with funny mien,
So clever on the sands are seen,
While thousands sit about and loll,

The children playing with their doll:
We saw the pails and wooden spades,
Fine castles in the sands are made,
So we like children, thought we there
Build careful castles in the air;
The tides of time sweep them away,
And we are left in blank dismay,
Unless in Christ by faith we stand,
"All other ground is sinking sand;"
The banks of earth oft break we know,
But faith in Christ will stronger go,
Till when the tide of death is run,
We shall in harbour hear "well done."
The Town Band we'd not leave outside,
Their music echoed far and wide;
These men deserve the highest praise,
Give them a copper then always.
The photographers' busy art
Takes portraits on the sands so smart;
While Bentley's Lemon Squash so nice,
Is sold there at a moderate price;
Your fruit and cakes and sweets can find,
Of many sorts to suit your mind,
And crippled children there we saw,
So brightly drilled without a flaw.
Then friends, when fine, held meetings there,
And found kind givers everywhere,
They said their quarters were at Bow;
Send them some cash, and kindness show.
We once for months were crippled too,
So kindly please this for them do.
A children's service on the sand.
In weather fine does always stand,
While singing through the children's hymn,
We thought how Christ their love did win.
On Sunday also, one can hear
Salvation Army band so clear;
Their testimonies very bright,
God's pardoning grace gives them delight:
The Baptists too, a meeting hold,
To speak out truth, are very bold,

The pastor, Mr. Briggs we heard,
Most earnestly speaks out God's word;
And they collect for objects good,
Full many pounds we understood.
For Doctor Barnardo's homes that day,
Collections were we're pleased to say,
Five guineas haste to him to send
The last half crown was from a friend.
The Wesleyan's have a mission band,
Who pray and preach upon the sand,
And thousands there the gospel hear
Who never to a church go near;
We wish these friends to take a leaf
From out the Baptists' gospel brief.
Throw overboard what people say;
Collect for objects good alway.
Let Satan's cavillers only, find
Excuses varied as their mind:
Doctor Stephenson's home you've got,
Collect for it, forget it not,
No matter what the cavillers say,
Collect for orphans any day.
The Regatta on its day took place,
The Jetty full of wealth and grace;
And pleasant men and modish way,
Of those who took this holiday;
The smiling ladies we could see,
Were just as happy as could be;
The sweethearts too, of ladies fair,
Were watching o'er them everywhere;
The day was fine, the sight was grand,
With sunshine on both sea and land,
And more than that we're pleased to say,
Our Margate Coastguards won the day.
The cliffs were lighted up at night,
With brilliant fireworks glorious light.
We further could relate you know,
Of sturdy rowers in the show.
The Margate Fort Arcade we see
High up above the rolling sea;
A sight in store of grandeur great,

Which you will think, we say, first rate;
As vessels pass of every sort,
A-sailing up to London port
With merchandise, a precious freight
Of many hundred tons of weight,
Whilst others going out to sea,
To foreign ports pass frequently:
In summer days large boats and grand,
With freights of human souls are crammed,
And when on briny sea you quaff
The vigorous breeze, 'twill make you laugh,
Restore to you your health again
And drive from you all weary pain,
And thus while you enchanted are,
You find your sorrows driven far;
So to the Fort a visit pay
When spending Margate holiday.
Jubilee Clock Tower may be seen,
A tribute to our gracious Queen:
And Albert Terrace, Margate too,
To honour good Prince Consort true;
Large Marine Palace Baths we say
Are held in high esteem to-day:
It joins the Fort and Jetty pier,
The swimming bathers watched with care.
For sixpence only sum so small,
Which suits the pocket of them all,
With private baths both hot and cold,
One Shilling only charged we're told.
The Grotto and the Cavern too,
A Druidical Temple true,
A million studded shells are there,
Grouped in wreaths and flowers with care.
This shellbank bedded in cement
Reveals the Druid's genius bent:
Then to this shrine a visit pay,
When you to Margate go one day.
Lord Sanger's wild beast show to see
Whene'er at Margate you may be:
We nursed a cub some years ago,
Two baby lions in the show.

Should you be pleased some time to give it,
The gardens too will pay a visit ;
Please also aid with kindly care
The Cottage Hospital when there.
Pay it a visit if you can,
To cheer the sick and dying man.
These institutions, nobly grand,
To aid and help in this our land,
And Convalescent Homes also,
Which will be glad of help you know ;
Of Scrofula, Oh ! pity such,
Your sympathy they merit much ;
The deaf and dumb large schools down here
You'll aid and help, we have no fear ;
The Cripples Nursery very good,
Has need of help we've understood,
We once for months were crippled too,
So fellow feeling have that's true.
We many others here could name,
But search them out and find the same,
As many mickles make a muckle,
Pay up like men and do not truckle.
This will we know your pleasure aid,
If for these things your money's paid,
Found in December forty-nine,
In Margate was an eagle fine,
On the house steps it there was caught,
To naturalists' a blessed thought ;
In ninety-three last year did we,
A swallow's nest with young there see
Within three yards of our front door,
It had built there for three years o'er ;
Margate's aspect here we name
Has spread abroad its healthy fame,
While Institutions rich and rare
Have convalescent homes down there ;
We fear our sermon best had done,
You'll think it an unending one
If we go praising up each place,
In every one great good we trace.
And now a ride to other place,

You must in this our sketch book trace;
To Westgate then by coach we go,
A pretty ride for threepence know;
But if you walk along the shore,
You then enjoy the sea breeze more,
Can gambol then upon the grass,
Or rest awhile with your sweet lass.
The field of corn you there can see,
And ships a-sailing on the sea.
To Fife was royal honour paid,
When Duke and Duchess both here stayed.
At Westgate then we happed to be,
When Royal Duchess came you see,
The Duchess nursed her infant there,
And tended it with watchful care;
He cried like other infants do,
As if his heart would break; its true,
The Duchess nursed her child first-rate,
Awhile the carriage did her wait.
When a Sunday, we at Margate stay,
At a friend's house we spend the day;
At eve to Westgate Chapel go,
The Wesleyan cause, you should know;
Our host is Chapel Steward there,
And of its business takes great care;
With pleasant walk along the beach,
Our converse did rich lessons teach.
The sea in grandeur for us spread,
Our thoughts to God are upwards led;
The earth full burdened with its food
Which God supplies so sweet and good.
The yellow corn in shocks we see,
Glad autumn August memory;
We talked of life, its shades and lights,
Its sunny days and darkened nights
Both health and sickness too are sent,
Our children too are only lent
To draw our thoughts to One above,
For God does all his children love;
Their death is precious in His sight,
In life or death all things are light;

Our friend was called of late to part,
His dear son's death ne'er broke his heart,
The broken heart God's balm doth heal,
All that He does is right we feel.
We much enjoyed this pleasant walk
And also profitable talk,
And at the chapel soon arrived
To come no parson had contrived,
This Sunday eve no preacher there
Turned up at all from anywhere ;
They asked us, would we kindly take
The service, and them happy make,
The Lord gave us a word to say,
We hope the right one on the way ;
Our hearts did burn with love we know
While talking o'er His grace below ;
He touched our lips with live coal flame,
And thus we praise His holy name.
In weakness did we sow the seed
The spirit helped us in our need.
When shaking hands the grasp we felt,
A truest meaning language spelt ;
While, said our friend in kindly word,
To-night we've had with us the Lord.
With this in mind, while homeward bound,
What strange and wondrous feelings found.
Old Birchington we must not skip,
While we through Isle of Thanet trip ;
These sea side homes of modern date,
Just suit the folk of style and state.
Lately a village quiet and old,
But now its called a town we're told :
Its country lanes and walks are grand,
And high in our esteem do stand.
We mention now within our page
Birchington Church is of great age,
It will repay a careful visit,
Search it through and do not miss it.
For mariners its shingled spire,
Guides vessels from the rocks and mire ;
While in the church, we know its true,

The gospel also guides men through.
With six grand bells, whose merry peal
Oft makes the saddened joyful feel;
The rich and poor both there have wed,
Some thousands to the altar led;
Here too, the sinner and the saint,
Have poured to God their soul's complaint;
Here too the careworn and the sad
Have found rich grace to make them glad,
And sought God's pardoning grace and love,
And triumph now with Him above,
Within its hoary ancient store,
Lies honored dust of days of yore.
The painter and the poet too,
Lie there: Rossetti good and true.
With space for ten centuries found,
For worthy ones from miles around.
Some years ago we moved from here,
A lady home to Anerly there;
On Sunday morn to Margate walked,
And with cheerful companions talked;
And thus beguiled the lengthened way,
And pleasant memories last to-day.
Some four miles there it is about,
A pleasant walk when you are out;
Along the road we heard the bells,
Their merry peals sweet music tells,
Reminding us of Sabbath rest,
One day in seven God says is best.
We to His house did then repair
And found His blessed presence there;
But back to Birchington we go,
Our sketch just now is there you know;
But when we're out, like bees on wing,
We gather honey home to bring;
For this digression pardon give,
And buy our books that we may live.
To pretty Quex Park pay a visit.
You will be pleased if you will quiz it;
And Waterloo's grand Tower we see,
And yet not pay a single fee.

We must soon halt upon our way,
Or we shall have too much to say;
Near Birchington, St. Nicholas see,
This too an ancient memory;
The Church near thousand years is old,
And built of sea worn flint we're told;
While Sarre is from there a mile,
You can with profit stay awhile.
The Wansterne channel so we read,
Was then a mile in width 'tis said,
But narrow now its stream is found,
What once was channels, now dry ground;
The coaching half way home is Sarre,
Where they a little while do tarry,
The visitors, refreshments get,
The horses, too, they "get a wet."
From Ramsgate and from Margate jetty
They daily run to Canterbury;
We Monkton, too, with pleasure trace
Some mile and half from Sarre place:
This pretty village you will say
Will give you pleasure on your way.
If you should from Old Minster go,
To Sarre you pass it you know:
From pious monks it took its name,
We wish not here to spread their fame.
St. Mary's Church will well repay,
A visit or a longer stay:
A lady there does highly boast,
For three good husbands did her toast;
Frances Blecheden her name,
Three husbands win her honoured fame:
Sixteen hundred and eleven she died,
Her friends they grieved from far and wide.
Old village stocks near church we see,
Of old notorious memory:
We quickly now our verse must end
To other business must attend.
Our verse we hope's not penned in vain,
Our Thanet sketch will long remain
A trophy of the modern style,

In which we spend our time awhile.
If you should think our style is quaint,
Of our book all your friends acquaint;
As once was done, please do and act,
The following is an actual fact.
Some twenty years ago we trace,
This suprised ladies' pretty face,
She stopped us then on life's rough way,
And thus she spake "I'm pleased to say."
Why, Mr. Gwyer, we've read your book,
Great pleasure 'twas in it to look."
"Why madam," thus we then replied,
"Our life is read on every side,
But when dear lady did you buy
Our honored book, you value high?"
"My neighbour kind, lent it to me,
I could not purchase it you see."
"Why madam," thus to her we said,
"Of strangest ladies we have read;
How could you dare to hinder us,
With such a lot of useless fuss,
You've hindered us a lot of time,
With all your gushing talk of rhyme,
And yet you say you can't afford
To buy, we don't believe a word,
Why houses many you possess;
If true the book you would possess."
Perhaps readers may think us most rude,
To lose two hundred pounds we stood,
Two shillings was the published price,
Six thousand sold out in a trice:
Then fire in Cowcross Street did rage,
Destroyed the plates of every page;
So get your friends to purchase on,
And then our arduous work is done.
We cannot publish without cost,
Bring out the money, 'twont be lost.
To Broadstairs you by rail can go,
Or its a pretty walk you know:
Or you can ride for little charge,
In waggonettes both fine and large.

Find houses there of great renown,
Which in your diary should go down.
Bleak House, forsooth, where Dicken's first
For writing novels had a thirst,
Where weeks and months he spent each year
Making his varied books appear.
And it some time you wish to wile
See houses here of ancient style,
Things, too, of ancient date and style,
Attract our fancies thoughts awhile.
At Broadstairs, too, are relics found
As you may see for miles around ;
York Gate, five hundred years has stood
In Harbour Street ; if speak it could,
What scenes it would depict of yore
Of our forefathers gone before.
In Household Words, Charles Dickens drew
Of Broadstairs pier a picture true,
While on the balcony he then
Penned down his thrilling tales of men.
When jaded by life's toil and spent
Oft to quiet Broadstairs he was bent ;
And thus his strength renewed with zest,
Its briny waters health posses't.
With an old tar we converse had,
His graphic talk made us so glad.
We asked him, "Had he ever seen
At Broadstairs Dickens when he'd been
"Why, Sir, I was his boatman here
And daily rowed him out with care,
A kinder man not breathed than he,
And also paid me well you see."
"Dear friend, life's drawing to a close,
Its ebbing tide with quickness flows,
Now, are you on the heavenly road
To our good Father's blest abode,
If not, dear friend, come now you may,
Our Saviour blest turns none away,
Who knocks in faith at mercy's door
Will find unlocked its treasure store.
God give you grace we humbly pray,
Repentance unto life to-day."

With parting shake of hand and cheer
We turned away with starting tear.
Our Lady Bradistowe gave name
To ancient Roman relic fame.
A flint Chapel upon the way
At Broadstairs see while there you stay.
Old mariners saluted it
By lowering topsails just a bit,
And thus implored the Virgin's aid
In answer to the honour paid.
Those superstitious days are o'er
We fain would wish for evermore.
The ladies like Broadstairs we hear,
It suits their children loved and dear:
The country round looks quite as grand
As any places in our land.
Here relics, too, of olden time
We fain would mention in our rhyme.
For we were here Regatta Day
And much admired it in our way,
Thousands here of every station
And lady swells in proud elation.
We saw a handsome lady fair
In smart bicycle suit dressed there.
Her pretty dress and pleasant mien,
Is why within our sketch she's seen;
We called her "Miss," but soon we heard
"My wife, Sir, please," in kindly word,
We entered into converse sweet,
Well pleased this happy pair to meet.
We gave the "Royal Infants" verse
And still kept on to hold converse;
"We are upon our holiday,
Pleasant has been our happy way."
We thought they'd figure in our sketch
And our fair readers' fancy fetch,
"A Tricycle sketch, we'er on," we said,
"That in the future you may read
A fortnight's tour we had last year
Through Isle of Wight, soon will appear."
A few things now we note with care,

At Broadstairs saw Regatta there,
The little boats so swiftly rowed,
And calmly too the water showed.
The swimming matches good to see,
While swiftest men swam playfully.
The first a tie, which made the sight
Doubled in interest's delight.
The sweep and miller in combat
With soot and flour, well stocked at that,
While they rowed well each little boat
And seemed just like Jack Tar afloat.
To all a merry time the cause
Amid a thunder of applause.
Then climbing of the greasy pole
For a large leg of mutton whole.
This pleased the people very well
And all went like a wedding bell.
We many other things might name
Did not our space forbid the same,
We were at Cowes Regatta week
Yet can for Broadstairs praises speak ;
This day like Margate's it was fine
And near all day the sun did shine,
Upon the cliffs we saw the sight
Which gave so many great delight.
To Broadstairs is St, Peter's near,
A pretty village, bright and clear,
With country sights that are as sweet
As any on the Isle we meet.
But now we haste upon our way
By coach to Ramsgate for a stay :
The corn they're cutting with all speed
Supplying all our creature need.
We turn to God in thankful lays
For all the mercies of our days.
Our readers, perhaps, would care to learn
The midnight oil we used to burn,
But now we turn our pillow round
To where the first faint light is found,
And wait with curious look we ween
To where the first pale streak is seen.

The blind we pull up to the top
And sometimes let the curtain drop,
For by this course we get the light,
The morning's most delightful sight.
Neath Dover's chalky cliff we write
This morn of Ramsgate clear and bright,
The sight at first enchanted me
Some twenty years or more you see.
While we at Ramsgate then did stay
With our dear wife for holiday;
For weeks before her fevered breath
Was panting at the gates of death,
But God's kind providence did give
Her back to health and now she live.
Those days restored to health again,
Our wife from all her aches and pain.
Those days at Ramsgate will not be
Erased from our fond memory;
Those hours of talk, the walk, the drive,
So long as on the earth we strive.
Yet Ramsgate now hath charms you know
Which here do follow on below;
We well remember on the sand
We near the pier did mount a stand,
And sounded forth the gospel clear
Upon a Sunday night while here.
Our hearts were full of grateful praise
For all God's goodness through our days,
And sickly faces many here
Were brightened by the Gospel cheer.
We really further must not stay,
We must resume without delay;
We pointed out God's hand in it
And hope its lessons well did fit.
Who'er you ask, on whom you call,
The Ramsgate sands are liked by all,
And when the tide is ebbing low
You can to Broadstairs walk you know.
The well-built Pier and Promenade
Is by the visitors well made;
A pleasant place of glad resort

To watch the great waves dashing sport.
The pier light-house gives light so clear
Points out the course the ships should steer;
This honour long to them be given
To save the toss'd and tempest driven.
And lifeboats round our "sea girt isle,"
Old England loves in best of style;
Then let us give to them our aid
By large or small subscription paid;
The Sailor's Home has often seen
Harrassing scenes of woe we ween.
At Goodwin's treacherous sands close by
Thousands have met their fate to die;
In length these sands ten miles are found,
And dreaded by all sailors round;
In width two miles. in peril great
Many brave men have met their fate.
From Royal Harbour Ramsgate, they
Are five miles out o'er ocean's way;
The Ramsgate pier and promenade.
Five hundred feet in length was made.
In eighty-one 'twas built with care,
Ten thousand pounds it cost them there,
But mariners are warned, we know,
By glaring lighthouse just below:
Yet stormy tempest sometimes drive.
And ships with gallant crews arrive
On Goodwin Sands, their death to meet,
Unless the lifeboat men they greet.
These gallant oarsmen oft do save
So many from a watery grave,
Those Bradford townsmen praise, we will,
Who pay this boat for Ramsgate still;
And thus have sheltered from the storm
Those filled with fear and dread alarm.
New roads now made gave us delight,
They have improved the sea front site.
From Royal Hotel, by the sea,
A noble widened road we see,
A great improvement, very smart
This feat of engineering art,

So when you go to Ramsgate, find
And ask to see the Granville, mind ;
It is right up o'er Dover rail
A sight of grandeur you will hail ;
And as you climb and stand and gaze
The scene around will you amaze :
The God that made the mighty sea,
Beautiful flowers that we see,
And hills and valleys decked with corn,
And fruit that doth the earth adorn,
Shall have all praise from day to day
For gracious mercies every way.
On the left the Granville there
A spacious block of building rare,
Where rich folk spend their summer stay
In really sumptuous holiday.
Sir Moses Montefiore's good name
Did win for him the highest fame,
This Jewish baronet its shown
For hospitality was known.
His home so fine we here can see
Is East Cliff Lodge close by the sea,
In Mausoleum, Jewish style,
He with his wife is laid awhile.
Of Ramsgate sands we could say more
Of sights that often are in store,
It is the same of Margate, too,
But we must haste for hours are few.
The fishery, too, of Ramsgate's good,
And tons are caught we've understood,
And sent to Billingsgate each day
To thus provide good food alway.
Get up at early morn, at four
And see a feast of fish in store,
The pleasure boats we can't leave out,
And fishing smacks do lie about ;
It you a shilling pay, you know,
You can out there a-fishing go
With a large smack that draws a net
With gallant men a hardy set.

Go out with them, you'll find this true
They will the fish divide with you,
Which you can to your lodgings take
And will your wife most pleasant make.
Do not neglect when coming here
To enter in the house of prayer,
In varied sanctuary meet
"And thus surround the mercy seat."
Your purse should ever open be
That all your sympathy may see,
In winter season bear in mind
They cannot then the money find.
On East Cliff Albion House is seen
Where lived in early life our Queen,
Duchess of Kent, her mother dear,
Did with her daughter live just here.
If climbing Jacob's ladder mind
From Pier to West Cliff you will find
A flight of stone steps, leading high,
A grander sight you could not spy.
To Minster old a visit pay
And to the churchyard make your way,
Augustine's memorial cross
If you don't see, you suffer loss;
It was built by Lord Granville good,
Since eighteen-eighty-four has stood:
They say it marks the very site
Where Saint Augustine did alight.
King Ethelbert's statue, we met
The memories grand we don't forget;
The early date does history fix
As five hundred and ninety-six.
Here was Saint Augustine's well,
Where did this saint his thirst dispel,
We here enshrine within our page
Augustine's well of hoary age.
Nor must we from our sketch leave out,
Sweet Pegwell Bay we'll write about,
Its here we penned a poem long
In younger years when we were strong;
Some quarter of a century past

And now our autumn tints are cast.
We sat upon that cliff that morn
With health in us again new born.
While walking through St. Lawrence, we
To a baker read our poetry.
" From these sweet verses you have read,
"Where can I get them, Sir," he said.
He thought we culled them from a book,
From nature's book those thoughts we took,
Those lines we here would like to print
They came so fresh then from the the mint,
Alas ; we mourn them gone and lost
Like much we've written at such cost.
While passing through St. Lawrence, you
Its churchyard, green, must visit too,
While passing through we seem to think
Some epitaphs we'd like to print.
But time and space forbid it now
Or down we'd place them here we vow ;
And many a gallant sailor brave,
By storm, met here a restless grave ;
Their bodies washed upon the shore
Lost to their friends for evermore.
Here, too, is precious dust of old
Of our forefathers, we are told ;
Who fought out life's allotted strife
And long have entered into life.
We often think in old churchyards
Of times of Earls, of Dukes, and Lords,
Who fought their battles through the land
Where now these crumbling ruins stand.
Mementoes of their warlike mien
No more those darkened days are seen ;
When cruel anarchy and strife
Compelled all men to fight for life.
The rich and peasant both here lie
Their mortal dust dissolves close by ;
Oh, would that kindly measures here
In life were fraught with godly care,
In times of need, some kindly deed
Would deck the grave with wreaths indeed,

How frail and short our life at best,
Ere comes the final judgment test.
Oft epitaphs misleading are,
For praises high they spread afar,
But that the truth they do not tell,
Many who read them know full well;
May we all learn in life's short stay
That acts of kindness cheer the way,
By sovereign grace meet those above
Whom we have won by acts of love.
So read us now, nor wait instead,
Until some day you hear we're dead;
And now the bait entices much
To give an historical touch,
The third King William oft stayed here,
At Manor House, a mansion near.
In sixteen hundred fifty seven
One Henry Crispe was seized and driven,
Three thousand pounds he had to pay,
Being found Puritan that day;
Now noted too for shrimps alway,
The finest caught is Pegwell Bay,
And largest lobsters there abound
As any on the coast around.
The fishing there is quite a trade,
The lobster pots are strongly made.
Here, too, the place, so we are told,
Where landed Augustine of old.
Here Roman armies too did land,
And terror spread with every band.
The epitaphs of those now dead,
Are in St. Lawrence churchyard read,
They're strangely funny, you will say,
Though we can't spare a longer stay,
Old Minster Church will well repay
A visit from you on your way.
There's some old things we revel in,
Such as this Minster walk within,
Churches, Castles, and Gospel old
Have all a charm for us we're told.
While 'neath their hoary roof we stand

Awed by their age and memory grand,
The gnawing tooth of time is shown,
To us in crumbling granite stone,
A deep solemnity creeps o'er,
While thinking of the days of yore,
And while our thoughts the future view,
It matters much what here to do.
While thoughts like these do us impel,
If we are Christ's, all things are well.
By Him again have we been born,
Now by His love we're not forlorn;
And we can Abba Father say,
Our darkest night is turned to day,
There in the future shall we be,
In Heaven with Christ most happily.
But you who live in sin think not,
That this will ever be your lot,
Unless your heart is changed by grace,
You'll never see the Saviour's face;
No matter what your honours here,
They're fleeting, frail, and full of fear;
Your health and treasured wealth may go,
But if we're Christ's alls well we know.
If by the Spirit's work within,
We're cleansed and purified from sin,
And live by faith in Christ alway
And love the throne of grace each day,
Then bye and bye when life is past,
We'll reign with Christ in Heaven at last.
Our sketch we soon will have to close,
But news of Sandwich must disclose,
We think it is the quaintest town
That in old England is set down.
The Isle of Thanet shared its fate,
Away from very earliest date;
Anno Domini Six hundred too,
As a port t'was known all England through,
Then merchants with their shipping trade,
An honored name with wealth had made,
But war, that savage monster, strife,
Soon sucked the blood from out their life,

In eight hundred and fifty one,
The King of Kent a sea fight won,
Took vessels nine, so records say,
And left the Danes to dread dismay,
This was enacted near the town,
Since then the seas receded down.
Two hundred years from this again
Poor Sandwich was in greatest pain.
Because the Danes with sword and fire,
Fell havoc made of it entire.
But then in great Queen Bess's reign
Sandwich did flourish once again;
More factories were built with speed,
When men of Flanders took the lead,
In sign of which you still can trace,
The Dutch House in the Market Place,
These stirring tales remind us still,
Of men of grit and strongest will.
Three parishes with churches old,
Historical mementoes hold,
To all the churches then repair
See the records and offer prayer.
What good men our forefathers were
To build these churches everywhere,
Our verse prolonged, we know, has been
Of things in Thanet we have seen,
We hope not prosy much or tame,
Though oft we fear its been the same.
To an old man of sixty mind,
We feel our readers will be kind,
And make allowance for our age,
By friendly reading of our page.
There's many a rare and tempting sight,
To give our fancied pen delight,
But our long Thanet yarn must drop,
Our reader's patience soon will stop.

:-o-:

Personal reminiscences of a Ride on the Tantivy Coach of Messrs. Ames Brothers, from Bournemouth, around the New Forest, September 7th, 1893. 48 miles.

This morning Mr. Ames did say
Now, welcome on my coach to-day;
You will enjoy a pleasant ride
To view the country far and wide.

So now we try to tell the tale
Of things we saw through hill and vale;
And starting off this morn at ten
With ladies fair and gallant men.

Mounted Tantivy's coach so grand
Of Ames' Brothers,' four in hand,
A ride so sweet through country rare,
Seven shillings only for the fare.

We had relays of horses fast,
Which made the miles glide quickly past,
With brisk converse and cheerful glee
The hours rolled by most merrily.

The ladies' company so nice
Gave all a relish just like spice:
Their happy joyous converse sweet
Gave just the zest we love to meet.

The Bourne's most famous mouth we leave,
The "Happy journey" we receive,
And drive by Boscombe past the Chine,
In rugged beauty very fine.

The guide tells out in language clear
The deeds of old of many a year:
Old English history repeats
And all our question quickly meets.

We cross the Stour and thus arrive,
As o'er the bridge we slowly drive,
And enter Christchurch, ancient town,
And salient points we now jot down.

Up on the hill the re, on the right,
The ruins show a pretty sight,
A Norman Castle once so bold,
Upon whose walls old Time has told.

The Priory church, where many a saint
Has poured to God his sad complaint.
In worship humble, bowed in prayer,
How many God has answered there.

There, too, have many a pair been wed,
And sacred vows from lips long dead
Have bound affection sure and fast,
Those old love stories of the past.

Please, reader, pardon for this break,
This sketch needs light and shade to make;
This licence often we require
For pictures given by J. Gwyer.

An old thatched Inn of ancient time,
The "Cat and Fiddle," next we rhyme,
Six hundred years its course has ran,
So we are told, since trade began.

We stopped for food and water here,
Of horses we must take great care,
These precious gifts are helps indeed,
Our strong and faithful friends in need.

With lemonade and ginger beer,
And varied drinks our throats we clear;
And then refreshed and full of glee,
The New Forest we go to see.

As on our route again we start,
The horses trotting with good heart,
Sweet nature new refreshed with rain,
Autumn's rich tints are cast again.

The golden grain just housed with care
Leaves fields all ready to prepare;
Our grateful thanks to God we'll raise,
For food supplied in all our days.

The partridges by sportsmen sought
Are often up to London brought,
A week ago as tame as cats
But now as wild as any bats.

Now of a glorious scene we tell,
By Sir George Meyrick's land, known well;
The Forest Gate we enter in
And here the Forest glades begin.

Six miles brought Lyndhurst to our view,
The noble trees around us grew,
The air was filled with rapturous song
Of birds, who praised the whole day long.

Rough ponies with their colts so young,
And pigs who roamed the trees among,
And sheep who to our minds did show
A scene of fifty years ago.

When we, not far from here did keep
And tended then our uncle's sheep,
When sad a thunderstorm arose
And filled our childish heart with woes.

We rushed for shelter to a house,
With heart as timid as a mouse,
While loud and long the thunder roared
And sorrow on our young head poured.

Such rattling claps, so loud, the sheep
We quite forgot to tend or keep;
The sheep so frightened went astray
And homeward found their straggling way.

We through the Forest sobbed and cried,
As in the shades of night we plied
Our homeward path, its course to take,
And sobbed as if our hearts would break.

When, lo! we found them at the fold,
Let not "like silly sheep" be told!
We found our sheep secure that day,
Two miles or more they found their way.

All men are not so wise, we ween,
These sheep teach us a lesson keen,
For though like them we go astray,
We cannot find our homeward way.

We need a Shepherd in the storm
Who will our straggling ranks reform ;
Who will not leave us in alarm,
But safely fold us from all harm.

Now to resume our tale again,
And points of interest retain :
Miss Braddon's house upon the right,
The novelist whose works are bright.

In Lyndhurst at the Crown Hotel,
We relish luncheon laid out well.
With "Bentley's Sauce," which takes the cake,
And keen our appetite does make.

The jovial hostess' cheerful word
Told us of things that had occurred,
She seemed for sure quite up to date ;
We hungry ones her viands ate.

Next at a fine old church we look,
With pillared aisle and shady nook,
Some epitaphs we penned with care ;
Sir Frederick Leighton's picture's there.

The Queen's house then we go into,
The old Court Room in this we view,
Where many curious things are shewn,
Some interesting ones we own.

A relic hangs up there of old,
King Rufus' stirrup, we are told,
Of Norman days, those days of force,
It tells its tale of knight and horse.

Relays of horses here do wait,
And tired horses go to bait.
While we again get on our way,
To further share our happy day.

We Lyndhurst leave with happy mind
From Stony Cross more beauties find,
Southampton's Waters grand we view,
And miles of country landscape too.

We by the Forest Kennel run,
And muse on sport that they have done,
And Minstead Park just on the right,
Shines gaily through the trees so bright.

Sir William Harcourt's house we view,
We hope the nation's heart beats true,
To show his worth and honoured fame,
We speak in praise his noble name.

Amid our joy we give a thought,
To those who are to suffering brought,
From Netley's ward our warriors brave,
Have often gone, to fill the grave.

But oft renewed in health and strength,
They face the foe again at length,
Our thoughts of Crimean time prevail,
And of the blessed Nightingale.

The horses halt upon the hill,
And for some minutes they are still,
While we walk down into the plain,
Where Royal Rufus once was slain.

The guide, in voice both loud and clear,
Said "spend only ten minutes here,"
There's twenty-five miles yet to go,
And you will want to dine you know."

We view the iron Rufus stone,
For kings must meet death quite alone,
No arrow, from the bow that's shot,
Will miss its aim, if such our lot.

We view with pleasure and surprise,
A few yards on before our eyes,
Two trees are joined, quite twined together,
Oak and chestnut quaintly tether.

We climb right up the hill again,
And find our coach does now contain
A cargo, valuable and rare,
Of ladies beautiful and fair.

Our gallant Jehu drives with speed,
With careful ribbons keeps the lead,
And through the forest, beauteous sight,
The varied landscape gives delight.

Right in the road there stood a calf
Which made the people loudly laugh,
It then moved off so very slow,
We feared the horses it would throw.

Just like this calf we see some men,
Who play the whole day long, and then
They only stick in others way,
And vain expect a harvest day.

We soon at Ringwood stop for tea,
A beverage that refresheth thee,
And stimulated now we start
With prancing horses fresh and smart.

We now have fourteen miles to go,
Its scarcely seems it can be so:
The steeds from Lyndhurst will rest here
And fresh ones take us on with care.

We passed a smithy: shod was there,
Sir Walter Tyrrel's horse with care;
That horse's shoes placed the wrong way
To guard him from his track that day.

The Avon near, he then did cross,
With danger great and risk of loss,
But soon his journey here did close,
He quickly out of England goes.

The trees with apples gaily hung,
Their fruit to cool our parched tongue;
And pears and plums our eyes did greet,
And blackberries were ripe and sweet.

At six, we reach sweet Bournemouth Town,
So glad that we are here put down,
The ride we can well recommend
To strangers, or to any friend.

Personal reminiscences of a Ride in the Tantivy Coach of Messrs. Ames Brothers, from Bournemouth to Wimborne and back, September 8th, 1893. 10 miles each way.

On Friday Mr. Ames did say
"I have a shorter ride to-day,
Could you to Wimborne now contrive,
To take a lovely country drive."

"My Tantivy coach starts at three,
You can at Wimborne get your tea;
You'll say the drive is very rare,
I think the weather will be fair."

In just a word we now would say,
How rhyming verse came in our way,
Suffice to say the Prince of Wales
Could since his illness tell the tales.

In London then, we wrote in verse,
Some simple stanzas, very terse,
Upon his illness which we know,
The nation felt a serious blow.

A gentleman these verses found,
And scattered them for miles around;
They brought the tear drop to his eye
And spread our name both far and nigh.

To our most gracious Queen he sent,
These simple verses which were bent
To bring the tears to Royal eyes,
And thus our fame to advertise.

The Queen sent to us her best thanks,
Her letter now the highest ranks;
Three other Royal letters then,
And from the Prince some nine or ten.

While twenty others from the Queen
Convey her thanks for poems seen,
These humble verses that we write
Once more in journals see the light.

Since then we write on merrily,
As in our books the public see ;
We leave this egotistic style,
For precious time we must not wile.

Our notes of Wimborne we resume,
Though not in best of rhyming tune,
In beating thus about the bush
Our writing some may think profuse.

The Ames Brothers we should say
Do now four coaches run each day ;
They are well known both near and far
For enterprise quite up to par.

We start now as the coach is full,
We hear this is the usual rule,
And yesterday we realised
The fact, and so were not surprised.

Our driver has a pleasant grace,
And witty humour lights his face ;
We presently may perhaps afford
To give our coachman just a word.

The guide is bland, courteously free,
And that we wish in him we see,
And as he figures in our sketch,
We perhaps from him some thought may fetch.

On leaving Bournemouth soon we view
A Cemetery, its wall looks new,
But fifteen years it has been there,
Most precious dust to keep with care,

Though Bournemouth is a pretty place,
Still here grim death we have to face;
We must not moralize too much,
Or we shall give too dark a touch.

On left and right is Talbot Wood,
Guide said, "A lover's walk" so good:
"At Winton "Gladstone" chops the hair
From Whigs and Tories, dark or fair."

On counties two, the people perch,
On left of Winton, Moordown Church,
In Moordown village we were told.
The little school is very old.

At Christchurch Priory we do peep,
Which on our memory will keep;
Pass "Horse and Jockey," sporting name
To this four miles, we find we came.

Then Redhill drying ground so trim,
Our kind respects the Laundress's win;
"Here donkey died," said guide, "one day
Because he could not have his way."

Ansley Vicarage now we pass,
Where lives the friend of every class,
The Gospel lived and preached can win
Our Saviour's wandering sheep to Him.

Pretty "How" village we pass by,
Asked how they named it, wonderingly:
Names are sometimes strangely given,
Only one will lead to Heaven.

West Kinson Village in our road,
And Colonel Russell's sweet abode;
Crimean hero, who lived here,
His memory cherished far and near.

At Dolphin Inn, a minute stay
To water horses on the way,
That brought along the coach so fast,
And scenery delightful passed.

Soon on the road with fresh delight,
The view to all, a pleasing sight;
A relic too, of olden time
We now put in our simple rhyme.

Upon the right, old Kinson Church,
Where many people for it search.
Nine centuries their debt have paid
Since first so firm its stones were laid.

On left, a large dimensioned dam
Proclaims the Waterworks Long Ham,
Supplying Bournemouth from the Stour
Quarter million gallons an hour.

The water filtered pure and sweet,
Doth up to date true science greet;
We hope all towns will lessons take
From our poor Worthing's great mistake.

The Councilmen of Bournemouth bear
A noble character we hear;
The Mayor and his honored clan
Will still do all the good they can.

We ride to Wimborne, bear in mind,
To this digression please be kind,
For here we do confess our fault
And not so long again will halt.

Then close at hand, four cross roads meet,
Poole, Ringwood, Bournemouth, Wimborne,
Now on the road to Wimborne haste, [greet,
Our four in hand no time to waste.

When lo! the finest sight that's seen
Makes our company feel serene,
There on the right Lord Wimborne's seat
Where Albert Edward friends did meet.

On this we must not paraphrase
The bait is tempting to our gaze,
For Bournemouth Recreation Ground
He opened then midst cheers profound.

"Flags and festoons," the guide did say,
"Were closely hung for miles that day
Along the route were thousands seen
To cheer the son of our loved Queen."

With game, the place, seemed swarming too.
And pheasant, partridge, hare, all grew,
And there the Prince of Wales has shot,
Some scores of game came to his lot.

The guide to us did point a place
Where royal sunshine did him grace,
"And where he sat, the mushrooms grow,
Such humour, witty people know."

Our yarn we fear is much too long,
And on our road, we know its wrong,
Yet when upon our pastime rhyme,
So quickly goes the hoary time.

At Model Houses now we glance,
The best in England, or in France;
His Lordship's rent is One Shilling,
Weekly it is paid so willing.

A Model Laundry, too. is there,
Where women wash with cheerful care;
The guide said, "there's a Model School,"
Where model children are the rule."

And in this village has been passed
A Veto Bill, long may it last:
No public house has been allowed
To cast around its darkened cloud.

We reach Wimborne in quickest time,
Ten miles the journey most sublime,
Just half an hour we stay for tea,
Start back for Bournemouth merrily.

Now Wimborne is an olden town,
In Norman days, we think, laid down;
We found that it was market day
When healthy farmers came that way.

The "Minster" deserves a visit,
It lost its spire, oh, pity is it,
Of other places, too, so bright,
Had we the space we soon would write.

We came back miles another way
Towards the closing of the day,
We then were stopped most pleasantly,
A noble church in front to see.

The coachman said, with funny wit,
"What other place could better fit,
Now at this church collection take
For me, and guide our fast to break."

The ladies laughed with might and main,
We shook our sides, yes, and again,
Right well they earned our willing gift,
And we with pleasure gave a lift.

At six in Bournemouth we arrive
And ended thus our pretty drive;
Three happy hours we did beguile,
Then to the Square came home in style.

IN MEMORIAM.

LORD TENNYSON.

Born at Somersby Rectory, Lincolnshire, August 5th, 1809; Died at Haslemere, Surrey, 6th October, 1892: Buried in Westminster Abbey, October 12th, 1892.

In Westminster there lieth one,
A poet great, whose work is done;
Yes, while the tears bedim our eyes,
Silent in death the patriot lies.

His wisdom great, wondrous his skill,
His work inspiring, strong his will,
His genius shone through every line,
Will give a light in every clime.

Lain in that sacred, hallowed ground,
With scores of honoured forms around,
Like them his name has perfume spread,
As theirs his virtues shall be read.

His epitaph world-wide is known,
In loving hearts his memorys sown;
And while with grief our hearts are sad
We know his spirit's bright and glad.

To one sad heart, now left alone,
We pray God's comforts may be shown,
The Lord says, "Widow trust in Me,
I will thy Husband ever be."

Weeks and years may pass along—
Then, joined in one eternal song,
Husband and wife shall meet again,
And never more feel parting's pain.

The son who lost his father dear
Will find that still the Lord is near;
And, though his heart is wrung with grief,
The Lord will give him sweet relief.

Though sorrow-stricken every heart,
In heaven they'll meet, no more to part,
Strengthen each heart, O Lord, we pray—
Be "sovereign grace," their hope and stay.

To our beloved Queen, we know,
His sudden death is a great blow;
We pray that God may cheer her heart
In this and every other smart.

:-o-:

BOURNEMOUTH, BOSCOMBE, AND SURROUNDING TOWNS.

Bournemouth and Boscombe have charms alway,
In summer heat or wintry day ;
Its rugged rural country round
Is sweet as any can be found.

The merchant who is jaded out,
Or housewife worried much about,
Or peasant weary from the soil,
Or children from scholastic toil.

Or others seeking needful change
Try Bournemouth if you can arrange,
And if a visit there is sought
Your healthful glow will back be brought.

And should you wish while there to roam
The coach can take you far from home :
Through the New Forest's lovely drive,
If you the money can contrive.

To Rufus' Stone they daily go,
Some fifty miles, or nearly so.
To view the stone that yet doth show,
Where the Red Prince in death laid low.

Last autumn we were treated rare
With ride the cheapest, best of fare,
On Ames' Tantivy coach and four,
The ride extol we to the door.

Sweet Boscombe as you ride there through
Its Chine doth nature's freaks outdo.
With garden shrubs and pretty flowers,
Where you may spend some happy hours.

A Cottage Hospital is there
And if some money you can spare,
Please send J. Gwyer a stamp or two
To aid this Institution true.

We could not end our yarn to-day,
Before we Christchurch do display,
Where battle scenes did once engage;
Historic Normans fought with rage.

There river Stour with sluggish stream
With salmon constantly does teem
Which often caught with heavy weight,
Make nets be broken with the freight.

Near Parkstone, too, a pretty sight
Will give the tourist great delight:
When driving through to ancient Poole
Where smuggling once was quite the rule.

Near Poole is Titchbourne of renown,
The claimant thought he'd pitch him down,
A claim in England must be given
Before estates are robbed and riven.

We cannot leave neat Winton out
While riding through Tantivy's route,
Near Wimborne Lawson's Bill has brought,
The peace and happiness it sought.

Permissive Bill is passed and done
As through his vast estate we run
No public house on it is seen;
Abstainers say: "This is serene."

The people there they rent a house
As snug as any little mouse,
One Shilling is per week the rent,
We wish that we could there be sent.

When you at Wimborne please attend,
Some minutes at the "Minster" spend
And all the thoughtful ones will say
They useful lessons take away.

The Bible there with chains so fast
You then will see them tightly cast,
We hope this blessed book you'll read,
Taught by the Spirit, without creed.

And there if you in summer, please
You take sea voyage at your ease;
Pretty Isle of Wight you visit,
And spend some days to see and quiz it.

Each sect has churches large and grand,
Which in Bournemouth's environs stand;
And preachers, too, with talents rare,
The Lord's good work are doing there.

So go to Bournemouth for a stay,
May healthful vigour speed your way;
You'll find the change so good and rare,
If time and money you can spare.

For invalids nice walks are there,
'Neath shady trees so rich and fair:
The sick can pain and care forget,
And kindly seats are often met.

There in the garden so we heard,
A place is named, most fitting word,
Its the "Invalids walk" they call,
'Mid oily pines so cool and tall.

These firs dispense their healing balm,
There odorous med'cine rich and calm;
The patients sit about at ease,
Have shady walks just as they please.

The sick ones need the Master much;
Lord Jesus give Thy healing touch;
As once the blind were brought to Thee,
So let these sick ones healed be.

But if Thy wisdom this deny,
And some are there that soon must die,
Give all, O Lord, Thy saving grace,
And help us each to seek Thy face

That when our race is run down here,
We hear the Master's welcome cheer,
"Come home, my child, in heaven to be,
In happy bliss to reign with me."

10TH JUNE, 1894.

A TRICYCLE RIDE FROM A BRIGHTON CENTRE.

Through Littlehampton, Arundel, Lewes, Eastbourne and Hastings.

Our riding tour in Isle of Wight,
Describing which gave us delight;
We little thought would make a book,
Yet many men who in it look,
Say " don't you see enough to write
Of our dear home so sweet and bright,
While you praise others to the sky.
You let ours in oblivion lie;
This sarcasm cannot be said
Of Brighton, which the world has read.
The "Grand Old Man" doth take its part,
He says no air is half so smart,
Its often nerved him for the fight
This Brighton air so clear and bright.
We too, our testimony give,
That Brighton people long do live;
Hove church we found when there also,
Men of greatest age doth know,
The Pyramids are mountains high,
In grandest height they scale the sky;
So you can Brighton's "queendom" trace.
See from the Downs the watering place;
Not here the feeble candle light,
Here with the electric blaze at night
Shines Brighton forth in dazzling flame,
Its lights do credit to its name.
We walk its Sunday promenade,
And wonder how the fashions made
Here ladies fair, with pretty face.
Help on the sunshine of the place;
It seems a pity that grim death,
With fell disease should load his breath,
To take away such beauties fair
With smiling face and riches rare.
Here dandy gents do stalk about,
And quaff their spirits and their stout:

While still most goodly men they are,
Who'd drive the stuff from them afar.
Here mansions are of sumptuous style ;
Hotels where you the time may wile,
To give a view of Brighton's grace,
Would fill a book for this one place ;
And if from London you should start,
Don't criticise and be too smart,
For Brighton only second is
To London in its mightiness,
Its environments too are grand,
As any in our native land.
Go to the Devil's Dyke, and see
The grandest nature mystery ;
The great Aquarium see, now mind,
A thousand sorts of fish you'll find ;
Some tons are daily caught off here,
Sent to London with haste and care.
We must no longer halt or stay,
With our three wheeler we're away ;
And now we ride down Promenade,
Which by most clever men was made.
Our steed is oiled and painted smart,
And off we go with a good heart,
And Hove we soon pass through, and call
On shops, for Bentley's suits them all,
They say we know that man is Gwyer,
For he to try does never tire ;
We orders get which act like oil,
Our friends to push is pleasant toil.
We fear some reader, perhaps may say
This is an advertising lay.
But they must bear in mind this thought,
That we no sketching tour had sought,
But paid by Bentley's firm, and sent
To sell their goods we were intent ;
If here digression you'll permit,
We'll tell a tale that this will fit.
A gentleman in Patsy's land,
Did at a peasant's door once stand.
He asked him then which was the way,
The road that he should take that day.

"Will you dear Sir, come in and dine,
We've just commenced, have me and mine;
You're welcome as the flowers in May,
Come rest with us a time and stay."
When by the door a sow walked through
And in the corner rolled its true,
In kindly tone the gent said there,
"Do you allow a pig in here:"
"Why Sir," the peasant thus replied,
"She has more right than all beside:
Her young ones pay the rent each year,
And thus provide we have no fear."
So this we now of Bentley's say,
They pay our rent and board alway,
And were it not for them you'd not
This book been able to have bought.
If us you would help o'er the stile:
All Bentley's goods please buy on trial;
A wink as good as you have heard,
To those not blind, as singing bird.
Our steed resumed, we're off again,
Our sketch must real news contain:
Yet still a little space is nice,
If not bought at too high a price.
Portslade we ride so slowly through,
Here still a little business do:
Here grocer and draper were combined,
If we the dry goods line entwined.
We here a line of each could have,
And much expense we thus could save,
But Gwyer's friend at Penge would say
Keep from the drapers' trade away.
A Plymouth lad once prenticed there,
Left it quite soon, as you shall hear;
His mother taught him not to tell
A lie, for trnth did suit her well.
Some flannels cheap looked strong and rough,
Marked up, All Wool, the best of stuff;
Some lady came, and she did say,
"My boy, is this all wool to-day?"
"No, there is a cotton in it,"
"Then I won't take a little bit."

The master called him up to him
With rage, then boiling o'er the brim;
"My mother taugh me not to lie,"
"Go home to her then boy and die."
He wended homewards then his way,
But is still living to this day;
Some sixty years have passed since then,
He's now a hearty hale old man;
With honour great, he is renowned,
And much respected all around.
O'er seventy pounds ten years ago
The folk at Penge gave him please know,
And a gold watch to keep good time,
And now we praise him in our rhyme.
The honours of Penge Hamlet won,
For unpaid work which he had done,
He is an heir of heavenly birth,
Though still possessing earthly worth.
So readers all who this peruse,
In doing right you cannot lose
If seeking first God's kingdom here,
Through life He guides you with His care
This moral here we point as truth,
Be true to God from early youth:
We now resume our rambling sketch,
And information we must fetch;
Upon the road we're off again;
Once more the scenes we will explain,
Another order get its true.
In Southwick as we're passing through
We viewed old Shoreham just ahead,
In its grand church have many wed;
Within its churchyard halt awhile,
Our carriage waiting near the stile
Old histories flit through our mind,
Such interesting things we find;
A thousand years and more have sped,
Since first the monks its floor did tread:
We view its crumbling mortared stone,
See what the teeth of time have done;
Look centuries back when darkened days,
And fell oppression blocked men's ways,

And thanking God for light like this,
Are grateful for our present bliss.
On grocers through the town we call,
Get orders quick from nearly all ;
Each minute of the day soon gone,
And lo, another day's work done,
Of rest we must be thinking now,
On downy bed our head must bow.
The Temperance place we found was full,
Which is indeed the general rule ;
We then enquired of one close by,
If we should find an Inn near by.
"Yes Sir," replied the strolling host,
"My house I can with pleasure boast,
A half crown a night's my charge,"
We think you'll say it wasn't large.
"If were we rich it might be small,
But as we're poor and only tall
Could you not take a lower price,
Then we should think it very nice."
"No Sir ; no smaller price we make,
Therefore your offer cannot take,"
But soon we found upon our way
With pleasant folk a place to stay ;
Now Sandgate's slip had lately been,
And all its sad effects had seen
Its tragic scene we put in verse,
And Bentley's firm did them disperse.
The money paid we freely gave
To Sandgate Fund, the poor to save ;
To Liberator Fund some went,
Our sympathy was both ways bent.
The person where we lodged did say,
And told us in an anxious way ;
"There stays with us a lady here,
Who lost her all it doth appear,
In Liberators' dreadful smash,
The culprits I would like to thrash."
When in the morn we out did go,
This lady said, "How do you do,
Can you dear Sir, a moment spare,
While I to you my woes declare.

Seventy-four years is my age,
We here record it in our page.
Her bank showed a goodly sum,
In hosiery trade for years had come;
Her hosiery business she had sold,
The Liberator she was told
Was safe as any bank that's found,
In any place all England round,
We knelt and thus to her did say,
We'll pour our cry to God this day
That He would aid the widow here,
And screen her with His tender care ;
We knew the Lord our prayer ha l heard,
The widow's trust was in His word.
This case is one like many more,
We hear as we go England o'er,
The guilty consciences must know
They caused this misery and woe.
The Shoreham Poor Law gives we're glad
Some shillings weekly this case sad :
She still lives there, and does not know
How she's provided here below ;
God answers prayer, He doth provide
For all His saints the whole world wide.
We must not further linger now,
Or friends with us will have a row,
With watching, waiting, patience pressed
Our pretty course with sunshine dressed.
Across the bridge we go with speed
It was a pleasant ride indeed ;
Our horse is ready for the fray,
We leave Old Shoreham quick that day,
These incidents do thrillings make,
Exciting interest through a brake ;
They'll surely help to spread our book,
If in its pages some will look ;
The ups and downs of life are many,
But few experience learn, if any.
The cap we make will suit most all,
Whoever on these lines may fall ;
O give to us the country fair,
With pleasant homesteads everywhere.

The spring when starting life is born ;
The summer fields of growing corn,
Or autumns golden tinted sheen,
The jewelled fruits that we have seen.
Nor can we leave the winter out,
Though tricycle can't roll about ;
The hoary frosts of winter too
In panoramic glittering view.
The icicles with flashing rare ;
God's handiwork is everywhere.
This incident I think of here,
A scoffer asked a child ; with jeer,
" If you, my dear, will kindly say.
Where you can find your God to-day,
A present then I'll give to you,
Of real worth a treasure true."
" If you dear Sir, will tell me now,
Where God is not, to you I'll bow,
But as He's everywhere you see,
The Holy Spirit here must be ; "
Thus children in simplicity
Make scoffers in the dust to lie,
Oft simple words the blind to lead
From out the mouth of babes proceed ;
God uses often children here,
As instruments, His words to bear ;
We must not further halt to-day,
But Worthing next must be our stay.
A pleasant ride four miles or more,
These simple things a mine in store ;
We soon to Worthing come with speed,
A happy ride it was indeed,
Our usual work again we ply,
All can on Bentley's goods rely.
Some orders quick we get from there,
Treasures we prize with greatest care,
We now reminded are its true ;
We neglected that we ought to do.
Our spanner we had left behind
But here a gentleman so kind :
" Your tricycle to my house take
I'll screw it up, and oil, and make

It right and ready for your route,
Till safe and speedly it will suit;
I've read your verses, Sir, so rare,
My daughter rhymes the same with care,
I'll tell her now you're coming in,
You'll feel at home with her within."
Her talent as a poetess,
The magazines do all confess;
She praised ours, we scanned her verse
With talent rare, and rich, and terse.
Not quite an hour did there beguile;
Her father screwed our steed the while,
These pleasant memories of our way
Are not forgotten since that day.
We do at Worthing like to call,
We're kindly spoken to by all;
This lady's name is known to many,
We won't reveal it here to any.
The kindly father here we thank,
Who highly in our sketch does rank,
A bitter taste with every sweet
In life's great journey here we meet,
With sugar cane oft gall we drink.
Which makes our heart with sorrow shrink;
To day with plenty we abound,
To-morrow poverty all round.
In vigorous health to-day we be,
And shortly bed of sickness see;
To-day surrounded by our friends,
Then only doctor soon attends.
Life's varied changeful fickle skein,
Short days of life does here contain;
The fever here commenced to rage,
No medicine could it assuage;
The cause was tainted water bad,
Recorded in the papers sad.
In a few days it spread so wide,
Hundreds were stricken down and died;
Death's angel spread its sombre wings,
And banished all the joyous things,
Which do belong to June's bright morn,
And laughed them all to bitter scorn.

Of harrowing cases we could tell,
In families whom we knew quite well;
God gave His grace to them to bear,
The chastening rod which fell just there.
Though many a saint He took in love
To dwell with Him in Heaven above;
A man of faith, and loved by all,
The Vicar soon did have to fall.
The sick around him did confess,
Both night and day they did him bless;
He comforted the fevered one,
And read what Christ for them had done.
He prayed and helped them with his purse,
And for the sick did daily search;
Alas, one day the fever germ,
Upon his strong heart took hold firm,
And he like others had to die,
We know full well the reason why,
In bitter grief the people mourn,
For him they loved, now from them torn.
Two other cases we recite,
Wherein the fever dart did smite;
Two tradesmen lived close together,
One lost his wife, his son the other;
"This blackened garb, what does it mean,"
With tremulous tones we said when seen,
"Come in. I'll tell my bitter grief,
The Lord alone doth give relief;
My wife beloved is gone you see,
And much I mourn in memory;
Its well with her, I know its bright,
The Lord He doeth all things right;"
Thank God, we said, this is the way,
He gives us strength from day to day.
The tears that fell were garner store;
In God's own bottle evermore,
This brother is indeed a friend,
We oft in prayer our voices blend.
At Penge we often bowed in prayer
For Baptist brothers. both we were,
Within two doors the grocer lived,
Who also lately was bereaved.

"My friend. that black does give alarm,
That now we see upon your arm;"
"Yes, Mr. Gwyer, my heart is sad,
I've lost our son, that made us glad;
But like a shining pearl we saw
The life of faith without a flaw;
Our Heavenly Father's will be done,
Christ's helped us say of our dear son."
These memories of darkened days,
Will still remain with us always,
We may one other case reveal.
Which shows a nature hardened still;
To them not any sickness came,
We will not here divulge their name,
With wealth of gold and freeholds theirs,
No thanks to God for lives he spares.
For trifling losses they sustained
They murmured long and sad complained.
Thank God, its over long ago,
Now Worthing's healthy well we know:
When next a sea resort you seek,
Go down to Worthing for a week;
Or longer time will you repay,
If you at pretty Worthing stay,
Though sad the news which here we've told,
We've written what we did behold.
On iron steed away we drive,
And thank the Lord we're still alive;
Along the lanes in pleasant mode,
With clear blue sky above we rode.
Now in the village Augmering,
We did some trade which made us sing;
We found a titled man lived there,
With mansion large and park so rare;
He much respected is, we heard
From many people's ready word.
To Littlehampton we did come,
And much enjoyed the ride we'd done;
This quiet watering place is smart,
So trim and nice, laid out with art:
The children and the sick ones there
Enjoy a pleasant seaside rare;

The walks and country lanes are grand,
And high esteemed by most they stand;
Some houses, too, are very fine,
While other, cheaper do combine,
To save the pockets one or all.
At Littlehampton next we call.
Now here we did a roaring trade,
And customers to Bentley's ma le.
We then to Arundel did start;
Four miles along we rode so smart;
We then returned quickly to rest,
Our weary body made it best.
A re sume to give we'd like,
Unless our readers do dislike;
The fine Cathedral on the hill,
The Duke of Norfolk built with skill;
The Catholics here do hold the fort,
We heard that this was their resort.
The castle and the duke's fine park,
Both make in Sussex a land mark;
The Duke we heard is not behind
In kindness unto all mankind.
His purse is ever open found,
To sick and poor for miles around.
Some few small orders we got the e,
We value them, yes, everywhere;
From Brighton, Tuesday morning borne,
Now Saturday is come this morn;
And so the week rolls round apace,
And each day we God's mercy trace.
Our tricycle was out of gear,
We took it to a maker near;
Repaired again we wend our way
To Brighton, fifteen miles that day.
No travellers Saturday expect,
For business wait till Monday next.
But still upon the road we found,
That orders did for us abound,
The recollection of that ride
Will ever in our life abide;
A stiffish hill when going down,
We saw an old man of renown;

We put on brake, and then went back :
" Do you the one thing needful lack ?"
"My life's great race is nearly run ;
Eighty years marked the setting sun ;
Timber felling did in that wood,
My master was so kind and good ;
I from my youngest days lived here,
And now am tended with great care."
" Have you kind aged friend," we said,
" In penitence to Christ been led,
And found His blood to cleanse from sin,
Through faith in Christ made meet within ?
And are you walking in the light,
And does His grace give you delight. :
Can you now Abba Father cry,
Is your rich portion fixed on high ;"
Evasive answers told us this
That these great blessings he did miss,
We pointed him to God's great love,
In sending Christ from Heaven above,
How He had suffered bled and died,
And opened still His wounded side.
We soon again were on the road,
To Brighton, our destined abode,
And prayed that God the word would bless,
Spoken of Jesu's righteousness.
He only can the blessing give,
Who died for us, that we might live.
Some fifteen miles on this hot day
We had to travel Brighton way ;
The country picturesque did look.
Its pleasant scenery in we took,
Poor Worthing Town we saw on right,
The thought of fever was not bright ,
With bread and cheese, and ginger beer,
We soon recouped our strength and cheer.
We supple now our steed with oil,
And vigour fresh makes easy toil ;
And through the country lanes we run.
While on our head shines burning sun ;
Those miles of pleasant scenery long,
Will years remain in verse and song.

Grand nature's volume open lies,
Shows its Creator good and wise;
While song from jubilant birds that soared,
Proclaimed the goodness of the Lord.
Soon evening's freshening breezes came,
Our strength renewed by it again:
We joined the road just the same way.
That we rode down the other day,
We have already told the tale,
Of this grand road, o'er hill and dale,
One thing we quite forgot to say,
The other day whilst on this way;
We saw a lady pass, its true,
Who lives at Penge, and whom we knew;
The lady's smile and coachman's mode,
Made pleasant greetings on the road.
Neath shady trees, on grassy plot,
We rested while the sun was hot:
And little thought on this lone road,
To see one from our Penge abode.
'Twas pleasant thus our friend to greet,
Where Shoreham and where Worthing meet,
So back again we came that night
To lovely Brighton clear and bright;
With sleep refreshed, our slumber sweet,
With light returned the Sabbath greet;
We to the house of God repair,
And found His holy calm to cheer;
His pardoning voice, how sweet the sound,
With faith in Jesu's blood abound.
A clan brother, Davies by name,
As preacher won an honored fame.
The church is grandly large and bright,
His preaching gave us great delight;
'Twas built by Congreve's purse we hear,
Who is renowned both far and near.
We joined near forty years ago;
When he a deacon was you know.
The Peckham Rye Lane Baptist Church,
When we for futher light did search;
At Peckham oft we walked together,
In summer and in winter weather.

We would recount to you awhile,
How he once helped us o'er the stile.
The first address to young we gave,
We sought by grace their souls to save.
This gentleman was present then,
When first we sought the erring men ;
Though then with tremulous voice we stood ;
"Dear friend," he said, "this gospel good
Will not be cast off, you shall hear,
The gospel message you must bear."
Some forty years have quickly flown
Since Mr. Congreve's act was done,
This deed to us was very bright.
The very thought brings heavenly light.
Kind words never die, no, never,
Nor from our memory can they sever ;
Sow then, thy friendly seeds broadcast,
They heavenly harvest bring at last.
We should here like to tell one thing,
That back to memory now doth spring ;
A cold we caught both hard and bad,
For many weeks we serious had.
"Gwyer," said he, "upon our way,
A cough may end in death some day,
Lay up some days and don't go out,
You better not be now about :
Put mustard plaster on the skin,
'Twill drive the cold from chest within ;
Nitre and some medicine too,
Will soon some relief bring to you."
We then restored and well again,
From all our aches and all our pain ;
His free recipe we give to-day,
Cost us but fourpence by the way.
Now Brighton's grace, we've told before,
So of it now we say no more ;
Now Sunday's over, with its rest,
Sure God's day is of all the best,
Strength renewed in body and mind
For active duties do we find.
So up betimes, we clean and oil
Our iron steed for this week's toil ;

We mount aloft and soon espy
The Lewes road on drawing nigh.
To Lewes eight miles now we go;
The sun soon shows with burning glow;
All nature panted for the rain,
But from the sky came not a drain,
But still the ride was very sweet,
The Sussex hilly air we greet,
O give to us the country fair,
With varied landscape everywhere;
The humble living of the swain,
So oft removed from fret and pain.
Now Lewes soon we saw ahead,
Our friendly steed so quickly sped;
Now up the hill we climbed that day:
"What block of building's that?" we say.
"The Sussex Hotel," one then said,
"Of it dear Sir, you must have read."
Some thoughts came quickly to our mind,
Its noted Lewes Jail we find;
Whate'er they lack, there's one thing there,
Its well supplied with fresh pure air.
On Lewes hill it stands well up;
The inmates here on water sup.
If this through life their drink had been,
They'd likely not those dark cells seen.
Their appetites were drawn and wet
In fiery Bacchus Demon's net,
The drink fiends glaring red lights show,
In all the cells that roof below.
But as we've cast the drink away
Of this no more we speak to-day.
Of ancient date Old Lewes is,
We did it search and through it quiz,
We stayed within it for a night,
In morning woke by sun so bright;
The previous day some business done
E'er came the setting of the sun;
From Lewes up to Eastbourne we
With pleasure ride in cheerful glee.
Some fifteen miles or there about,
We place the journey on our route;

Our tricycle did serve us well.
Through all the things that us befell.
Now half way on the road we name,
A curious incident that came ;
A haggler with his pony passed,
Was trolling long the road so fast ;
We followed near behind his cart.
When soon a conversation smart ;
" Take hold, my friend, behind you see,
And take your rest, and talk with me."
In arm chair fashion then we sat
And entered into happy chat ;
We only guided then our steed ;
The haggler walking met our need.
" The country's looking bad," my friend,
" We hope the drought here soon will end ;"
" The farmers," said this man to us
" Are always making grumbling fuss."
" But those who wear the boots that pinch,
Can guage their length just to an inch ;
In all the varied things of life,
We've struggled weary of the strife ;
So kindly we must be to all,
For heavy losses on some fall."
Now we began to tell to him,
Of witty humours terse and trim ;
That which we heard of Lewes Jail,
To him we did repeat the tale
Of what one yesterday had said,
" That's the Sussex Hotel ahead."
The man replied, " Yes, well I know,
Six months last year I there did go ;
I found there not the best of fare,
My stomach oft was empty there."
" Your conduct good," we ask, " or bad ;
That bitter time to spend you had ; "
" Now as you ask the truth you know,
How that I had to prison go :
T'was not for bad I think you'll say,
That I to prison went that day.
You see my aged friend up there,
I rabbits ferreted with care ;

I do allege I there was caught:
The keepers swore with them I fought;
Within those shrubs upon the right,
Was were I ferretted that night;
The sequel this, and thus I went,
And to the Lewes jail was sent."
"Please tell me where you learned this trade,
That for you such sad trouble made,
And life with agony abound
Till you in jail six months were found."
"'Twas Redlynch, Wilts, the county's name.
Where I learnt ferretting's great fame."
"We lived at Redlynch, too, in youth,
And what you say we know is truth."
He further did relate that day,
How he had hoped to leave that way.
"Now shepherd's name was pretty known
By us, for poaching to us shown.
When quite a boy on father's farm,
We used to think it then no harm.
We asked the father for his boy,
To ferret with us then with joy;
Now can you see the drift we ween,
How the commencement thus had been."
We sowed the seed in early youth,
This poor man sad had reaped in truth;
So in the future, every day,
Be only good seed sown alway.
We will not mention here his name,
Or perhaps some day he may us blame.
Suffice to say at Downton School,
We both were taught by the same rule.
Where Mr. Read, a master kind,
Taught both the Bible rules to mind;
Now we this erring brother sought,
By kind entreaties as we ought.
In this lone lane we preached the Word,
As message coming from the Lord;
"Come now to Christ, dear friend," said we,
"He for us hung upon the Tree,
Through penitence and faith we may
Receive His pardoning love to-day."
Though perhaps we shall not meet again

We hope the word was not in vain.
God grant that he a jewel rare,
May in the Master's crown appear.
To Polegate now at last we come,
Sweet converse with our friend is done;
Now Bentley's sales we do pursue,
And a good stroke of business do.
Some four miles now to Eastbourne we,
Of pretty hilly country see;
And up the Eastbourne hill we climb,
When reached we see a sight sublime;
We stand and gaze as struck with awe;
Such beauteous landscape there we saw.
O, God of nature and of grace,
Thine own wise handiwork we trace.
A gentleman with lady fair,
Viewed the landscape with us there,
We sat upon our iron steed,
And penned a poem you can read;
This inspiration very rare,
Did wile away the morning there.
These hilly summits oft remind
Of Pisgah, Moses left behind,
That Charles Wesley did show in verse,
In sweetest hymn, both rich and terse.
So we on climbing up life's hill,
Like Israel's host, aghast stand still.
In looking back on life's rough road,
We long and pant for Heaven abode.
This Eastbourne hill gave us delight,
We never shall forget the sight;
These foretastes of our heavenly rest,
With natures pictured carpet drest.
From growing grandeur on the hill,
To Eastbourne came with right good will;
Our day's hard work is nearly done,
As easy down the hill we run.
With interest all Eastbourne teems,
It really like to Brighton seems.
On Sundays 'tis a sight to see,
The grand parade in front of sea;
Notable places of each kind,
This noble town's nowhere behind.

Of Leaf Hall comfort we partake,
A home of pleasure here we make,
We recommend its fame to all
Whene'er at Eastbourne they may call;
Its near the sea, and you can sight
The blue expanse of waves so bright,
Along the promenade such views
Of dresses rich of many hues;
For winsome mien, and beauty rare,
No nation can with ours compare
'Tis also lighted up at night,
With very bright electric light.
And as we walk the promenade,
We see how fine the place is made
For here a day or two we stay,
To sell our goods, our simple way.
Some orders get at Eastbourne too,
For Bentley's firm so good and true.
Now in the morn we haste away,
With cooling breeze begin the day;
Our carriage clean, and trim and smart,
And oiled well with all our heart
We speed along the level road,
And fly to reach our own abode,
As long the dusty road we run,
We soon begin to feel the sun.
Pevensey Station we arrive,
To halt awhile, we here contrive;
While bread and cheese, and ginger beer,
Solaced our heart and gave us cheer.
On tradesmen here we call and try,
To sell our goods, but these don't buy,
Pevensey castle here we see
With many centuries memory;
Then speed along the beaten track,
The sun's warm rays upon our back,
Ten miles through meadow land we ride,
The grounds seems scorched on every side.
The cattle, too, looked very thin,
Because for months no rain had been;
A farmer said to us that day,
"We soon should starve upon the way;"

"No; not like that my friend," said we,
"God will supply our needs you'll see;
We will not here the dearth complain,
But will in faith ask Him for rain."
We hope the farmer's thoughts that day,
Were drawn from earth to Heaven away,
Then quick o'er level crossing rail,
The wide expanse of sea we hail.
A dip into the sea we gave,
Which perhaps did from a sunstroke save;
And had a good long bathe that day,
As o'er our back the billows play.
We never shall forget this dip,
It gave us vigour for our trip;
We now arrive at Bexhill Town,
Where many Londoners come down;
We ply again our wonted trade,
And here some customers were made:
Some few miles more we have to go,
Before we Hastings reach you know.
Through St. Leonard a pretty spot
Although the summer is so hot;
The shops well stocked, are large in size,
Which here we can well advertise;
We through it into Hastings run,
And so a fortnight's journey's done.
Please keep this fact always in mind;
The coastguards all round cliffs you find,
All through the weariness of night.
They hail each other with delight.
We merely speak of this to-day,
To thank them for their cheery way;
For much depends on them we know,
Our safety watching as they go.
We could, yes, many pages write
Of Hastings varied beauties sight,
For Hasting's has a charm alway,
In cold and wind, and frosty day:
Here warm from north east winds that blow,
'Tis sheltered by the cliffs you know,
Soon invalids restored are,
That come on here, from near and far.

We homeward wend by rail our way,
And muse upon our easy day,
And as we think of all that's past,
Our rhyming verses long will last.
From home a fortnight we have been,
And many pleasant things have seen;
A few of these in rhyme have given,
And thus to please you all have striven.
We put now on the iron road,
Our wheeler for our Penge abode:
While in the train we hie away,
In June, through Kent, that brighest day,
And think of all that we have done,
From morning dawn to setting sun.
Our rambling verse will suit we hope,
Our varied readers every scope.
Their numerous errors please forgive,
We try a useful life to live.
On Friday afternoon we start,
Some eighty miles so trim and smart;
And now the steam draws us along,
Through England's garden full of song.
The land looks dry and scorched, and bare,
But still the Lord for us doth care;
So sure our hopes shall anchored be,
On His sure promise strong and free.
He said, He will supply our need,
If we will follow Him indeed;
At last at home we did arrive,
To pleasant greetings all alive.

BE PATIENT, MOTHERS.

Be patient, mothers, with children fond;
Although their faults make you despond;
I know you have enough to bear,
Your little ones require such care.

Be not too stern with infants, play,
Like kittens, sportive, quick, and gay;
A tender plant, a fragile stem,
Is oft a figure true of them.

A blighting frost, a sudden chill,
These tender buds will often kill,
And so a cold, a cough, or pain,
Can soon your strong heart break in twain.

You may have anxious hours and long,
To test your mother-love so strong,
When your dear child is laid aside,
And oft the swelling tear you hide.

Your darling's face is wan and white;
The eyes have lost their lustre bright;
The parent's eyes are soaked in tears,
Their voices hushed in solemn fears.

The doctor looks, he shakes his head,
The happy spirit now has fled;
This lamb is housed within the fold,
From worldly chilling winds so cold.

To see those eyes with laughter shine,
You'd give all in the world is thine;
Or hear those feet sound overhead,
The music of their merry tread.

Then prize the trust you have just now,
Wear not a frown upon your brow;
While children play with merry glee;
May mother's faces smiling be.

With cheerful song its often given,
That children point the way to heaven;
Your mother-trust is great while here,
Train up your children in God's fear.

Sow well the seed of truth to-day,
In their young hearts while home they stay;
Let your example always be
A copy that the child can see.

With earnest prayer and watching tend,
And God will bless you in the end;
Then soon the reaping time will come,
When you and yours are gathered home.

Ramsgate, August 8th, 1892.

LIFE'S ROAD.

Life's road at times is rough and lonely,
Although 'tis dark, there's light within,
For Jesu's love brings joy and peace;
His blood has washed away our sin.

With Jesus we are never friendless,
For He will never leave, no, never,
His love's an everlasting love,
The world nor Satan cannot sever.

We're often tired and sometimes weary,
For trials come in many a form;
Our daily strength He doth measure,
And guides us safe through every storm.

In saddened days as dark as night,
His fiery cloud protects from ill;
Then we will sing our song of praise,
For all our sorrows He doth feel.

So helpless weak and very frail,
We lean on Jesu's loving arm;
He strengthens us with all His grace,
And nothing then can do us harm.

We're waiting, watching for our Lord,
In hope with patient faith we rest:
Increase these gifts in us we pray,
Then when Thou comest 'twill be best.

So happy then, resigned and safe,
We leave our future in God's care,
Whate'er He sends will be the best,
For gracious blessings it must bear.

Leighton Buzzard, 13th January, 1893.

A SONNET FOR THE NEW YEAR.

Time flies by moments swift away,
And soon will come the closing day,
Another year has quickly passed,
To thousands it will be the last.

Great God, Thy saving truth impart,
Engrave it deeply on each heart;
May we, each moment, as it flies,
Improve and its true value prize.

With deeds of kindness fraught with love,
With gracious impulse from above;
May those who taste of heavenly joys,
Hold lightly all these earthly toys.

The world is still in darkest night,
Shed forth, O Lord, Thy gracious light;
O may the Gospel win its way,
And shine resplendant—as the day.

Break hearts as hard as flinty stones,
And cause to live the driest bones;
Give life, and grace, and faith to those,
And save them from their direst foes.

What'er in store for future life,
May patience bear us through the strife:
And when our days are ended here,
May then our souls in heaven appear.

A TRICYCLE SKETCH, RIDE THROUGH THE ISLE OF WIGHT, JULY, 1893.

Our verse on Isle of Wight received
More praises than we had believed:
When once before we penned our views,
For our kind readers to peruse.

When sketching it a little bit,
We knew but little then of it:
Since then we wandered o'er the isle,
By rail, and road, and coach in style.

Last year we tricycled it too,
And now depict its scenes for you;
We land in Cowes our iron steed,
A hot July it is indeed.

If we could use a painter's brush,
Our scenes on canvas soon would rush,
Some charming ruralistic views,
Of land and sea, and cliff we'd use.

From Cowes to Yarmouth first the ride;
Finding an Inn by the wayside;
Though four miles only had we been,
We beauties all around had seen.

The hostess in a cheerful mode,
Showed us our night's secure abode;
We much enjoyed our home'y tea,
It left a happy memory.

To bed for rest we soon did go,
And peaceful slumbers soon did know,
And woke refreshed at early morn,
To face life's battles, sun or storm.

With eggs and bacon for our fare,
Fresh butter too, a breakfast rare;
Our host and hostess kindly said,
"Of you, dear Sir, we've often read.

Your versatility is great,
You really write, we think first rate;
Perhaps, Sir, you do not know that this
Is just the place, you should not miss.

Wight's Island's highest hill is there,
And if you climb its steeps with care,
A sight you see both great and grand,
Better than any foreign land."

Enamoured of delightful stay.
We climbed its steeps and spent the day,
And sitting on a rural stile,
We thus the time away did wile.

We penned a poem down, so long ;
We call it here our rustic song ;
The sun shone forth with burning ray,
Until the heat chased us away.

Earth's gaping mouths did open wide
With sterile drought on every side ;
We in the beauteous bay did dip,
And land and sea joy both did sip.

Then wandered back through afternoon,
And tea was ready very soon ;
Two ladies staying there did say,
"Will you take tea with us to-day?"

And thus in conversation we :
"Your name is Mr. Gwyer we see,
We've read with interest your verse,
Such pleasant reading nice and terse."

"Your name we see you spell the same,
As did our friend. John Gwyer by name,
He must related be to you."
"He was my father its quite true."

"Well now, dear Sir, we're coming round,
You are the Joseph we'll be bound,
In fifty two to London went ;
We will remember the event."

"If you another person guess,
Myself t'would be still. not be less."
Now forty years of scanning back,
And viewing life's most rugged track.

An object lesson good was sought
From all the mercies God hath wrought,
The tea was ended, then we had
A pleasant ride to make us glad.

We mounted then our iron steed,
And on the road we went ahead :
Life's journeys short we thought at best,
While looking back we all confest.

How short and transient is the span,
Allotted here to mortal man :
It seemed but yesterday we thought,
When first great London town we sought.

So little then it seemed to be,
Such notoriety we should see ;
The scorching sun's hot burning ray,
In cooler eve is fled away.

Through villages we speed along,
As happy as a marriage song :
Some twelve miles now we have to go,
To Yarmouth's pretty harbour know.

We halt awhile, and here we soon
Do sell our goods in best of tune ;
On village grocers here we call,
Get orders ere the darkness fall.

We turn to left, and on the road,
Pass cheerful homes of sweet abode ;
In hedges, honeysuckle grows,
And to our nostrils fragrance blows.

For sickle soon will ready be,
The golden yellow corn we see ;
The horses prancing in the mead,
And lowing cows their stomach feed.

The eventide with cooling breeze,
Sweet blowing through umbrageous trees.
And on the way, what do you think,
We at a cottage asked a drink.

Our verse on Tennyson we gave ;
They other rhymes of us did crave ;
The lady said, "Why, it is strange,
Your rhyming verse takes wide range."

Then she brought us stanzas so rare,
Which we soon scanned with earnest care;
Then pleasant talk; then mount our seat,
Thus friends, our ride was quite a treat.

At Yarmouth late we then did halt;
So sweet the day without a fault;
And Morpheus our eyes did steep,
In nature's sweet restorer, sleep.

This host and hostess, too, we praise,
For all their kindness in our lays—
We early rise, resume our toil,
By giving Iron Horse some oil.

Refreshing breezes now we got,
Although the weather was so hot;
Of Bentley's well-known goods so rare,
A stroke of business did with care.

From Yarmouth then, two miles we ride,
And o'er the country far and wide:
Freshwater too, late honored home,
Of Tennyson whose work is done.

In going down Freshwater hill,
We tried our brake with firmest will:
Alas! alas! it would not act,
We must indeed reveal the fact.

We then were travelling with good speed,
And had a shocking time of need;
The hill was long and very steep,
Our steed its quickest pace did keep.

We thought at once what would be best,
It was an ordeal's trying test,
For killed we thought we sure should be,
But guided to the hedge were we.

The wheels were doubled up like tow,
And we were shaken much you know,
Then had repaired our Iron Steed,
And sold the goods the grocers need.

In quickest haste we search again,
And Bentley's orders soon obtain;
These orders like some fragrant spice,
Come flowing in so very nice.

Now hasten quick to Newport we,
Of scenery fourteen miles to see,
Of hilly country very grand
As we ride through this pretty land.

We should like much to halt a bit,
And try our hand at pleasant wit;
And o'er the Island's widest range,
Our rhyme should ring its merry change.

We hurry our journey on with will,
For we must never here stand still,
The sun is sinking in the west;
Cool evening breezes are the best.

To push our iron steed along
Eight miles an hour is no mere song;
The journey here is quite a treat,
The scenery very hard to beat.

Our form is fifteen stone or more,
Dead weight to drag from hill to door:
Now Newport: soon we hail the town,
Run from its hilly summits down.

Our hostess now in kindly speech,
"From Freshwater now you Newport reach;"
We halt awhile and spend some time,
In penning down our flowing rhyme.

A short time spent at Carisbrooke,
And notes upon the castle took;
The prison house of Charles is there,
And his sweet daughter loved and fair,

Who rested on the blessed Word,
In all the troubles that occurred.
Then tea, with butter fresh, and egg,
We hang our hat upon the peg.

And soon forget the toil that's past.
When back to Newport come at last.
In slippers put our weary feet,
Soft rest to tired souls is sweet.

For rest to bed we soon retire.
Used up by energy's bright fire,
At early morn with vigour new.
Our work with ardour we pursue.

Some orders here at Newport get,
As good as we have ever met :
So pleasure is combined this way
With doing business day by day.

In Newport Church there may be seen.
Placed there by our most gracious Queen.
A monument of marble rare,
To Charles the First's sweet daughter fair.

Reclining on the book with ease.
The precious Bible which did please,
And charm this maiden, princess fair
Within her dungeon sad and rear.

Her Saviour took her while she read
His promise sure upon her bed ;
Ne'er let the darkened days of yore,
Come back again as heretofore.

Good Lord, speed on Thy chariot car,
Send gospel tidings near and far.
Our journey now resume we must,
And face the heat, the stones, the dust.

Though tempting baits of history stand,
Alluring us throughout the land ;
To Brading's village next the road,
Leigh Richmond's cottagers' abode.

The ride transporting is we tell,
O'er hilly country down and dell ;
We've here a moralizing fit,
And on the down sit down a bit.

Of heat and dust, and work we tire,
It draws from us our latent fire;
But our three wheeler we must say
Has been a friend to us each day.

It works with will, it wants but oil,
To roam the Island's fertile soil,
And pass the glorious landscape sight,
Where hill and dale give great delight.

The rippling yellow corn alway,
Is getting riper every day,
And soon with joy there will be borne
Into the barns the ripened corn.

The trees have autumn's lovely tint,
The crowded gardens smell of mint;
From Brading once again we hie
And down the hills we soon espy

The Little Cottager's old home,
And to its pretty thatch we come;
Old thoughts press fast and thick just now,
Leigh Richmond's feet trod here we trow.

Oft up those winding stairs has he,
With loving heart gone there to see
The cottager in sickness laid,
And daily visit to her paid.

To pray and read God's blessed word;
The promise of her blessed Lord.
Old Brading looks of ancient date,
Old things charm us, yes, some first rate.

Old churches and old castles too,
Both draw our commendation true,
While down the village on our ride,
We view the mall house on left side.

These landmarks we can never pass,
Though many vanished are, alas!
'Twas here we heard the vicar had,
His parish school to make them glad.

And often here the Word he spake,
And stony hearts the Spirit brake:
This landscape we cannot forget,
The gems of tour which here we met

Our nature is to moralize,
And some for this call us not wise:
We loose our brake and down the hill,
On tour one cannot long stand still.

No further precious time we wile:
See houses built in ancient style:
Then visit next the church with glee,
And chanced a marriage there to see.

While walking in the churchyard ground,
We heard a very happy sound,
And on enquiry then did stay,
To see a wedlock forged that day.

The rustic church, old fashioned aisles,
With basin pulpit, iron rails,
We thought of all the days of yore,
When scanning Richmond's journals o'er.

Here too, the place where first the light,
Dawned in his heart of darkest night;
When God's great candle did display,
Its sure and saving power that day.

Our reader perhaps, may know, how he
Became empowered his sins to see;
His ruined state by nature lost,
And saved by Christ at such a cost.

This heavenly birth and change so new,
As shown to Nicodemus true—
Dear Wilberforce, a christian grand,
We wish you here to understand,

Was instrument to clear the way,
This gem to bring to Christ that day.
Dear reader, here the motive's told,
That made Leigh Richmond very bold,

The gospel which he preached with power,
Was blessed by God in every hour;
The cottager gave good report,
To young and old of every sort.

And drawn by Jesu's wondrous love,
The theme of Him who reigns above;
Th' Dairyman's daughter was saved too,
Another jewel clear and true.

But here we must not longer stay,
But hasten on our joyous way:
The cottager's saved daughter's grave,
Does just our notice quickly crave.

In churchyard here, close by we see
The stone raised to her memory:
Has Richmond's rhyme both good and terse,
As all the vicar's other verse.

The other relic here we name,
In the old porch of ancient fame:
Close by the churchyard here we tell,
The village stocks once used so well.

Poor drunkards there they used to put;
What numbers now it still would suit,
But if you sign the Temperance pledge,
'Twill save disgrace we do alledge.

Here grocers shops, a few there are,
No pleasure must my business bar,
For Bentley's pays the rent alway,
So we on business ride away.

In calling on some grocers three
For Bentley's good rich order see;
And thus while we descant on themes,
Our pocket with their copper teems.

At Brading Village Inn we stay,
Refreshed by rest upon our way:
The Wheatsheaf Inn its called you know,
From the thatched cottage just below.

Some bread and cheese and ginger beer,
Were relished well you need not fear;
We talked of all our journey past,
And thus the evening soon went fast.

The host and hostess both became
So very kind that both we name:
Some farmers there that spent the eve
Were kind to us, you may believe.

Our readers always will in me,
A really staunch Teetotaler see;
Although we much dislike the drink,
They often of us kindly think.

Our speech though strong, they bear in mind,
If in our teaching we are kind;
They talked of all the Island o'er,
This knowledge added to our store.

The faithful dog, the farmer's friend,
Stuck closely to him to the end;
To weary bodies rest is sweet,
We did that night this blessing greet.

We rose betimes at early morn,
For vigorous health just then is born,
The men who rise up early find
A healthy body, vigorous mind.

We scan the garden neatly kept,
All weeds from it so cleanly swept,
While fruit does hang upon the trees,
Rustled by balmy morning breeze.

The grunters too, are in the stye,
They like a scratch, we know not why;
They talk to us, and grunt with ease,
And very much they did us please.

The cackling hens and crowing cock,
Showed by their number a good stock:
Now breakfast we in best of style,
Much relish it and rest awhile.

To village next, two miles we ride;
St. Helens pretty green so wide;
Our Iron Steed we get astride,
And start again our happy ride.

Here houses built in modern date
Look comely cosy and first rate:
We ply while here our wonted work,
For we our business must not shirk.

For our employers are so kind,
The hours too long we never find,
But then we must not ever tell,
Or scolded we shall be right well.

For our dear friend, John Burns does say,
Eight hours enough for any day.
From Helens on to Bembridge go,
About two miles or nearly so.

We pass close by an old friend's home,
And think of all the good he's done:
At St. Helens we pass the night
With a gardener, with great delight.

About twelvemonths before this time,
We recollect this in our rhyme,
We found that such a man was rare,
And as we'd little time to spare

We asked him where to get a bed,
To lay that night our weary head.
He asked his wife, "Could we not take
This gentleman, my dear, and make

Him comfortable just for a night?"
She answered quick with air so bright,
"Yes John, I'll do my best my dear,
To make him happy don't you fear."

So to the cottage on the hill,
We went at once with ready will;
We shall not soon forget this treat,
When with the gardener we did meet.

They read and pondered poems o'er,
And wanted us to send them more;
No easy rocking did we need,
For we were very tired indeed.

We rose refreshed to start again,
For work doth Providence ordain
To bring us to the needful rest,
Which He well knows for us is best.

We quite at home with them did feel,
Quiet did o'er our spirit steal;
God's providence directs, we know,
Our path through life where'r we go.

Now of Ryde Flower Show we heard,
Just dropped in a most casual word,
This gardener gained the first prize there
For Chrysanthemums, rich and rare.

An honour this we felt so great,
A pleasure we could never beat.
What honour next can be in store,
We thought while pondering this fact o'er.

His brother out of berth we heard,
A gardener till some hitch occured,
While breakfasting a letter came
About a berth and to his name.

"Yes," he said to me, "its true.
Read the kind letter quite all through."
We did do so, and thus it said,
"Will you dear Sir," and then it read.

"Kindly give all the winter through,
A lecture monthly, or perhaps two,
On Botany please write and say,
We want to know without delay."

Well, did we think what can this mean,
How such coincidence has been,
How one should come off with first prize,
And one be botanist so wise.

Exhausted not this strange event,
How strangely there we first were sent;
"Perhaps, Sir, you'd like to go with me,
The glass and garden just to see."

It was a treat of choicest kind
We did in all our journey find,
We carried with the greatest care
Some flowers he gave us very rare.

A member of Parliament lives here
If to his house you keep quite near
'Twill bring you down to Lembridge mart;
You'll see the house is very smart.

Adjoining this of much renown,
Is Lady Lowe's house well laid down:
"Please tell me who this member is?
I should perhaps like his name to quiz"

"Some time with me he oft does spend,"
"And would to you an hearing lend:"
"What is his name, please tell me pray,"
"That we may call on him to-day,"

For royal tokens oft we've had,
St. Stephen's members make us glad.
"Frank Coldwell is his family name,
Of Hackney Wick, won honored fame."

How strange was this; in time of yore,
No friend of ours we liked much more;
Why on the Temperance platform we
Were years ago allied you see.

We'll call on him this morn we vow,
And ask him how he is just now.
While at his door we gently knock,
We feel a kind of nervous shock.

We saw him then with smiling mien.
"Mr. Gwyer where have you been?
Yes years ago we worked together:
Late at night, all sorts of weather."

"Both on the Temperance platform we,
Spent happy hours most earnestly;
Life's varied scenes which here below,
Both calm and storm as well do show

How short and fleeting seems our stay,
When looking back upon our way."
Some twenty minutes now or more,
Of recollections old in store,

Of how we fought the battle old,
The drink fiends curse we often told;
We farther could detail at ease,
Other converse which did please.

Alas! alas! this bitter gall,
That's known and drank by nearly all,
He told us then in plaintive tone,
Of Liberator guilt he'd none;

His character we hope is right,
And out of all he'll come so bright.
Well now we must resume again,
And information too obtain:

We must apologise to you,
For this digression from our clue.
Our tour's on Isle of Wight you know,
Our rhyming verse should easy flow,

So now we hasten on our way,
To Bembridge village there to stay.
Bembridge once a seaport large,
Great ships did here their freights discharge.

But small craft only now do come,
And scarcely any work is done.
The Harbour of late years made long,
By sea wall of cement so strong;

Full many acres thus to be,
Is land reclaimed from the sea.
The Hackney member we have seen,
Has Bembridge Harbour Master been.

He now some months had gone away,
And lives in Croydon to this day.
Renowned the Liberator stands,
As buying of these Bembridge lands.

If purchases like these were made,
No wonder all that has been said,
For thus the strongest bank 'twould break,
Such course but rogues or madmen take.

Now some don't like our open speech,
But we such companies would teach,
That they can't play with honest toil,
Or wind within their artful coil,

And devil's mask, the widows poor,
With starving orphans in the door.
We must not stronger language use,
We hope their prestage they may lose.

They take to aid their wicked plant.
The sacred Scriptures used as cant.
They wrong the poor although they pray,
God sees their heart and knows their way.

At Bembridge short time here we halt,
And of this village can't find fault:
Some lines for Bentley's here we took,
For this indeed we always look.

From Bembridge we to Yarbridge ride,
And view the Island far and wide,
Upon the left, on Bembridge hill,
A mansion grand remaineth still.

And as we view the Park Estate,
We think its beauty is first-rate:
Here lives a head which does contain
The precious ore of fertile brain.

His engineering skill does tell,
In ships like towns he's built so well.
We leave this merchant prince and pray
That we may meet in Heaven some day.

Now down to Yarbridge soon we ride,
And through our minds sweet memory's glide ;
To Shanklin and to Sandown we,
Did there some trade which gave us glee.

Shanklin and Sandown both are known,
With Ventnor, each a beauteous town,
The prettiest places in the Isle,
Which our affections do beguile.

We now returned upon our way,
Again at Brading we did stay,
Through Elmfield, a village sweet,
Where we the folk did kindly greet.

Elmfield to St. John's we come ;
Now into Ryde our journey's done,
We halt awhile, and view the place,
And now of it with give a trace.

The town capacious is, and grand,
As many found in England's land ;
The residents a homelike sort,
And here the fashions all are taught.

And there good business quick we did,
And to the Isle good-bye we bid ;
At Chaplin's store we left our steed,
It was to us a friend indeed.

Our Tricycle at Penge we found,
Conveyed there safe, and trim and sound,
About three shillings was their charge,
We think it not so very large.

Our sketch of Island hill and dale ;
We hope in interest will not fail ;
Some pleasant memories on their way,
We hope they will indeed convey.

Although our hives a little funny.
Leave out the sting and eat the honey,
And when to Isle of Wight you go,
May rich enjoyment to you flow.

How soon a danger might befal
The weary travellers, one and all,
How we scaped danger you have read,
At Freshwater as we have said.

But now another one arose,
Which threatened here to end our woes;
The boat was steaming from the pier,
We thought no danger then was near.

The porter beckoned us in haste,
That we from train may no time waste,
And as we on the gangway stepped,
It fell, and we to jump were left.

We gave a leap, and on the deck
Alighted very near a wreck,
The captain called in language strong,
"What porter did was very wrong."

His deed was kindness meant to me,
It might have been my death you see;
A gentleman in kindly tone,
My danger has to me since shown.

"My friend," said we, "do you not know
How dangers round us ever flow,
How much importance 'tis you see
That we in grace should ever be.

We steamed over with pleasant trip,
Of briny ocean had a sip,
And up to London soon went we,
Safe housed at home as snug could be.

THE ISLE OF WIGHT.

The present governorship of the Island is held by the Queen's son-in-law, H.R.H. Prince Henry of Battenberg, who is also honorary Colonel of the Isle of Wight (Princess Beatrice's) Rifle Volunteers. He is much respected and beloved for his genial urbanity and friendly deportment to all. In 1801 we read that the number of the inhabitants of the Island was only 22,097, but when the census was taken in 1891 it had increased to 78,263. This is owing to the improved state of the Island and to the increased convenience of railway travelling. During the past year was commenced a new branch, running from Merstone through Godshill and Whitwell to St. Lawrence, which will be found a great boon to visitors. When in the Island in the early part of March last, 1895, we heard while riding from Newport to Ventnor, that the previous week the two gangs of workmen had met in the tunnel (St. Lawrence's) and completed it. It is nearly three quarters of a mile long, yet so accurate were the engineers, that when they met they were only some three or four inches out. Certainly this seems remarkable. We hope with the increased railway accommodation the directors will see the desirability of reducing their railway rates, as we are certain that this would prove a benefit, not only to the visitors but to all concerned. Twopence per mile is really an enormous sum nowadays, when the Great Eastern and the Tilbury and Southend Railway Companies only charge about a halfpenny a mile, to say nothing of excursions which are much cheaper. There are, we know, one or two trains run in the Isle on each line for a penny a mile, but they go at inconvenient times.

We wish here to tell the visitors how to cope with this in the cheapest manner. They can get (in summer only) a weekly excursion ticket on either Railways, for 7/6 on the Ryde and Cowes, and 5/- on the Ryde and Ventnor by which they can travel by any train for seven days. Get the ticket directly upon landing at Ryde, Cowes, or any other railway station.

The Island covers an area of 150 square miles, or 95,680 acres, and its circumference is about 60 miles. It is in the County of Hampshire; it is not so small a place after all as some would suppose. The farms and homesteads are numerous. In writing of the Isle of Wight we are reminded of the Americans' complaint as to England, viz:—that he could scarcely turn round without falling into the sea. Such views are held by some we think as to the extent of the Isle of Wight. We heard a laughable, though truthful tale from an old resident of Ryde the other day. He told us that about forty years ago there was a barber in Pier Street, Ryde, named Barnabas Wild, who challenged a London professional walker for a sixty mile walk round the Island. When they had done thirty miles to Freshwater the London walker was dead beat, he could not walk any further. The Isle of Wight puzzled him, as he had only been used to walk on level ground. Wild said to him, "Let us now walk into Ventnor to dinner" (another fifteen miles), but the professional declined saying, he would call the barber in future the champion, at least of the Isle of Wight hills.

Our late tricycle ride revealed to us that it was not such a small place after all, although since then we have had rides in vehicles, and walks in various parts that we did not then even touch, lately forsooth, the ride from Newport to Ventnor, through Godshill, Wroxall, and St. Lawrence was of the most picturesque kind.

To sketch and moralise on all events would take too long, and perhaps become tedious to our readers. Suffice to say, the road from Newport to Ventnor is most ruralistic and enchanting, and the hills and dales of the Island with all its rugged scenery, impart to the thoughtful mind an enjoyable relish for nature in all its pristine beauty and excellence, and feelings of gratitude to the God who paints the lily and the rose, and who will never be unmindful of the needs of His own children.

The new line will give visitors the pleasure of seeing some miles of different parts of the Island. When at Godshill they should pay a visit to Godshill Church, perched right on the top of a high hill; report says it was called by this name in consequence of a curious event. Stones to build this church were carted to the base of the hill where it was intended to erect it. Every morning these stones were found silently taken to the top of the hill during the night by supernatural means, thus this was called Godshill and the church built on the top at any rate. As we were not there to see, we have told the tale as we heard it. If any believe it, they must have a larger gullet than our throat contains to be able to swallow such a theory.

Our tricycle sketch treats only of a small portion of the Isle, as on a ride above narrated from Newport to Ventnor by road we did not trycycle, as also on another very interesting road from Cowes to Newport, which is about six or seven miles. Newport is the capital of the Isle of Wight, the county town where a weekly market is held, and it is the centre of civil and legal authority It is pleasantly situated, and its surroundings, Carisbrooke, &c., are most picturesque and delightful. Most of the wholesale business of the Island is done from Newport, barges and small craft run up to the Town Quay up the Medina river.

Another pleasant walk or ride is from Whippingham Station to East Cowes, about three or four miles. Last August (1894) we quite enjoyed this walk on a beautiful day. We called at

Whippingham Church, and fortunately found the pew opener cleaning the church, who kindly allowed us to look through it. It is a very pretty church and will repay a visit because of its associations.

Here we were shown the chancel, the building of which was paid for by the Queen, and also memorials of the late Prince Albert the Good, and their late son and daughter, Prince Leopold and Princess Alice. We had the pleasure of sitting in the seat in which Her Majesty was accustomed to sit when she attended service here, and of scanning the book used by her.

Here in the house of God all are one, no distinction should be made. All alike must bow before the great King of Kings, and "own Him Lord of all." Leaving the church, I saw the Alms-houses erected and endowed by the Queen, eight in number, which are on the roadside, nearly opposite the church, looking most pleasant and picturesque. When calling at the Almshouses, asking for a glass of water, we were kindly asked in by an old gentleman and his wife, and found the man was pensioned by Her Majesty, having been in her employ for many years in the gardens at Osborne House.

His interesting conversation conveyed to us a high estimate of the character of the late Prince Consort, as the Prince often assisted him with his own hands in the work of planting shrubs and trees on the Osborne Estate. They also spoke in the highest terms of the kindly deportment of the whole Royal Family.

A little way from the Almshouses is the Prince Consort's model farm. The men were busy harvesting, cutting the corn on the estate. A short distance from this is Osborne House and Park, where we enjoyed a pleasant interview with Inspector Frazier, who always accompanies Her Majesty on all her visits everywhere. Coming to East Cowes we ended a most enjoyable ramble, and should advise others to take a walk when there in that neighbourhood.

When writing of the Isle of Wight so many incidents of an interesting character are brought to our remembrance, that were we to indulge and enlarge upon them all they would make a small book in themselves. Riding from Cowes to Newport by rail a short time ago giving away our rhymes, we came across a gentleman who noticed Bentley's name on them, and said to us, "I use Bentley's Relish and like it much." "Yes," we said, "there is a great quantity of it sold in the Island, how long have you used it?"

"About five years," was his reply. "It has not been sold in the Island as long as that." "No," said he, "but I first used it at Brighton for some time and liked it so much, that coming to live at Newport I got my grocer at Newport to stock it, and that I believe was the first introduction of your goods into the Island." Well we know it was sold at Brighton and other places. It was not used at Brighton to any great extent, until we got it into the best houses, about thirty years ago, and sold in one fortnight a very great quantity there and in Hove. This was encouraging and reassuring.

The gentleman still resides at Newport, but we must in courtesy forbear to mention his name. We are reminded by this, of another incident connected with Messrs. Bentley's goods. We had written some verses in memoriam on the death of a Forester brother, connected with (A. O. F.) Court "Alhambra," No. 3146, of Penge, Surrey, which verses can be seen on pages 49 and 50. One of the copies from [illegible] came into the hands of the Secretary of the Newport Lodge, A.O.F., who, we were informed, read it at one of their Lodge meetings, and finding the writer of the lines was a brother A.O.F., and as is known we are very clannish, he, with other members ordered Bentley's goods of their grocer in Newport, who had shops in several towns in the Island and gave me a large order. The foregoing was told me by the son, when paying me for the goods, which was the first I heard of it. We should be pleased to hear of similar occurences elsewhere.

This may seem to be digressing, but it is like the Irishman's pig, found in pages 109 and 110, and all is fish that comes to our net, and fortunately we know how to catch them, as our readers know expenses are incurred in compiling a work of this description, yet we are satisfied if we can but instruct, interest, and amuse our readers and do them good. We are induced to tell another incident of a very singular kind resulting in our buying for a gentleman we know a few months ago a thousand pound house.

This was brought about in consequence of writing as mentioned the verses on our brother Forester. For propriety's sake we must leave out both names here, suffice to say we drew a commision for buying the house, the verses having been my introduction to parties to the business who were relatives of the brother of whom I had written.

We cannot find a better place to mention the fact of our writing verses on a stile, in a meadow at Portsfield, Emsworth,

Shepherd Hill, Northclose, our first halting place for the night on our tricycle ride from Cowes, which verses can be seen on pages 60 and 61.

Seeing a man in the meadow carting, we read them to him. "Very nice," he said, "very pretty verses, I understand your drift." We found he was the dairyman, and rented the farm, and he told us how his young son some years ago had been the means of his own, his mother's, and the whole family's conversion in the village through his inducing them to go to the chapel, and the word was blessed to their conversion. We had a very pleasant and profitable conversation with him and his wife, and partook of bread and cheese and milk at his house. Matt. xi., 25, "Thou hast hid these things from the wise and prudent, and hast revealed them unto babes."

I will tell another incident we heard the other day, in reference to the Local Veto Bill. A temperance speaker at a meeting of the Mizpah Band at the Stratford Conference Hall, told of a little boy who brought home a kitten. His mother at first forbade him to keep it, but on his entreaty relented, but knowing his mischevious tendency told him he could only have part of the kitten, the head must belong to her, the body to his brothers and sisters, and he could have the tail, thinking that thus he would not pull the kitten about. But presently hearing the kitten crying piteously, the mother called, "You naughty boy, what are you doing with the kitten." "Nothing mother, I am only standing on my end, it's your end that's kicking up all the row." So the speaker said, "the Veto Bill is our part of the kitten and we can't help it if the other part makes a noise." If our readers think we digress too much, they must remember we are only standing on our part of the kitten.

While in the Island I met a curate, who informed me that my first verses written on the Island three years ago, had induced him to have the grave of the Dairyman's Daughter repaired and put in good order. We were heartily glad to hear of this.

There is another pretty ride we had from Newport to Sandown through Arreton. Here is the parish church where the grave of the Dairyman's daughter can be seen, and at Hale Common on the right, about three-quarters of a mile away still stands the Dairyman's Daughter's homestead. We saw as we passed the cows grazing in the meadows even as they did in her day, bringing us memories of Leigh Richmond. A little way from this is the village called Lake where two roads meet, on the right to Shanklin and on the left to Sandown.

We will close our sketch of the Isle by advising our readers when at Shanklin by all means to take a walk as we did on one fine summer afternoon in 1892, through Shanklin Chine and the Landslip, one of nature's true phenomenen, through meadows, copse, and wood. As it was towards autumn we picked some nuts, finding at the same work, a family we knew from Upper Norwood.

We soon came out at Bonchurch. The old church will repay a visit. From the hill we saw a fine sight of great grandeur which cannot be surpassed, the hilly Island on one side, and the bright expanse of blue sea on the other.

Thence we came down to sweet Ventnor, nestled in warmth in the winter, protected from the cold north-east winds at the side of the hill. Thus ends the Isle of Wight sketch, which we hope will be read with interest, amusement, and profit.

VERSES ON THE BEAUTIES OF SOUTHAMPTON AND SURROUNDING NEIGHBOURHOOD.

We oft are asked, when penning down.
Our verse on some renowned town :
" How do the thoughts occur to you,
To write such pretty lines so true, ?"

" Ideas from you like heavenly showers
Fall on the dust to raise up flowers :
Your thoughts are like a mine of gold,
A quarry deep, and grand, and old."

Such kind expressions caused that we
Southampton kept in memory ;
Yet yesterday when asked by one,
" The promised lines have you yet done ?"

"No," we replied, with crimson flush,
And then the thoughts began to rush
Into our mind in quickest haste.
We pearls and diamonds must not waste.

Why this renowned old town does yield
A plenteous golden harvest field,
Where sheaves of information lie,
Where Doctor Watts was born to die.

Where the good doctor spent long years,
As in his diary oft appears;
How small events suggested hymn,
Of God's free grace, and man's great sin.

Rich legacy of verse we know
The Church will ever prize below:
No matter what the sect or creed,
They guide and cheer in time of need.

While thousands did the Doctor hear,
With eloquence he preached most clear:
Above Bar Congregational,
Saw many sinners, burdens fall.

One Sunday morn, while here we stayed,
A garland at his feet we laid:
We rose and saw at early morn,
His monumental visage worn.

Our flowing verse must speed along,
And leave the man of Godly song;
Here others climbed the ladder, Fame,
And left on granite their good name.

Lord Palmerston, a burgess too,
Southampton boasts, a man so true:
His manly statue there is placed,
In solid granite nicely faced.

Here preachers, poets, statesmen true,
Have lived and worked for me and you;
And some that's here respected are,
And greatly loved both near and far.

Canon Wilberforce his mark made,
Is loved by all of every grade,
He does the Temperance cause expound,
And strikes the drink fiend to the ground.

He's gone were Canon's oft are heard,
At Westminster, to preach the Word;
Southampton folks do mourn, when here
He tried to dry the widow's tear.

And yet another preacher great,
A Welshman at Above Bar Gate,
Pastor T. Nicholson his name,
This verse we know he's sure to blame

One Sunday staying here was spent,
To Wilberforce's Church we went:
The Gospel thought to hear him preach,
But found he was not there to teach.

The Congregational close by,
We entered accidently:
The pastor Howell touched our case,
We felt attracted to the place.

In language eloquent and true,
He told what daily we should do:
We penned in rhyme his sermon down,
Perchance to scatter through the town.

Last year, one Sunday staying here,
We heard a sermon rich and clear;
Ossian Davies was the preacher,
We thought him a most earnest teacher.

Here the elected Mayor we heard,
Came out in state to hear God's word,
With Councilmen in robes so grand,
A noble sight to grace our land.

The crowd did pack Above Bar Gate;
Such crowds on Doctor Watts did wait,
The preacher's celtic voice so sweet,
Of Gospel matters pure did treat.

Since then when we on Sunday stay,
At Bournemouth fair upon our way;
We wend our steps to his fine church
Which on the steep hillside does perch.

A church, the grandest we have seen,
Lit by electric light serene:
And what a treat is there in store,
True preaching of the Open Door.

Our verse all parsons cannot be,
So now we end this theme you see;
Unless to say that we could write,
Of past and present talents bright.

We are reminded here to halt,
Or we shall find ourselves at fault;
Southampton and not Bournemouth we
Must in our rhyme depicted see.

Its avenues and roads are fine,
With spacious walks and leafy pine;
The prettiest in Old England's land
Southampton environs do stand.

On Sabbath eves some thousands walk,
Young ladies fair, with sweethearts talk,
And homely wives with their dear mate,
And loving children on them wait.

While jubilant song of feathered bird,
On these fine trees is ever heard;
Dog Carlo wagging cosy tail,
His master's word and glance doth hail.

With finest parks, Southampton Town
Is richly blest to its renown:
The shrubs and flowers like garland show,
And trees with beauteous foliage grow.

Fine churches too, of every creed,
To meet the varied fancied need;
Where your Creator you can praise,
All through your earthly pilgrim days.

So much renowned of ancient date,
Southampton boasts Above Bar Gate,
Their Library free, a treasure great
And Ordnance Survey is first rate.

And houses large with gardens rare,
And fruit and flowers grows everywhere;
The people too, in pleasant mode
Home comforts have in their abode.

We saw the debtor's Prison wall,
Its usage gone beyond recall;
It only tells of darker days
When sad oppression marked our ways.

No need of such compulsion now,
In these enlightened times we trow,
May Education free beget,
A moral honour scorning debt.

And this brings us to ask the Town,
Why did they put Prince Consort down
To back a dark old prison wall?
A man so loved by one and all.

Our gracious Queen cannot have seen
The place of her betrothed we ween;
We will not rest until we hear
His statue is removed from there.

No Royal Prince has ever found
More real lovers all around;
Then place his manly form and mien
Near Palmerston upon the green.

A tribute now we pay to one,
A goodly action she hath done,
A drinking fountain shows her care,
For man and beast she placed it there.

A Jubilee remembrance block,
And to keep time a grand Town Clock;
This gift of Miss Sayers we tell,
And all the people thank her well.

Such gifts so generous as these,
Will always worthy people please :
If others rich thus moved should be,
Blessed will be their memory.

Southampton Docks of largest kind,
With foreign treasures full you'll find,
And welcome greetings often seen,
To those who long abroad have been.

The Royal Pier is there so fine :
Electric light so bright doth shine :
Pavilion, too, where thousands meet,
Hear music fine, the greatest treat.

Southampton has Infirmary,
Of Royal note and memory ;
With one hundred and fifty beds,
Where sick ones safe can lay their heads.

In Fanshawe Street its built so grand,
And highly prized on every hand ;
Send author stamp their cause to aid,
And doubly then you will be paid.

The places near of note we'll name
Rufus stone of New Forest fame ;
Were the Red Prince in death laid low,
By Tyrell's arrow shot from bow,

In summer, three times weekly go,
A splendid coach and four you know ;
Where Page's coachmen drive with care,
For a small charge a ride most rare.

If ever there one is locked up,
To Winchester he goes to sup ;
But constables are very kind
To those who keep the law in mind.

We can but praise the Volunteers,
With swords and helmets, guns and spears ;
Their practise is a pretty sight,
And really gave us great delight.

Their large drill hall was lately raised,
And in St. Mary's Road is praised;
This noble army all our days,
We will praise highly in our lays.

To Isle of Wight fine boats do go,
Yes, very often to and fro;
The Island home with beauty scene,
And favourite rest of our good Queen.

Go then, we wish you in our rhyme,
Take holiday when you have time,
Your better half will say we're right,
When at Southampton you alight.

8th July, 1894.

"TRUST AND PRAY."

In times of trial trust the Lord;
"I will not leave thee" is His word,
In troubles six with thee I'll be,
And in the seventh not leave thee.

When darkness hides His lovely face,
He cheers and keeps us by His grace,
The darkest nights brings morning light,
All that He does we know is right.

All things together work for good,
The calm or storm, the smooth or rude;
To those who trust the Lord alway,
He is the Rock, the Hope, the Stay.

Cheer up, ye saints, let happy glee
Upon thy face let worldlings see
The happiness that Jesus gives,
Who died for Thee, yet for Thee lives.

Who reads these lines, and does not know
The joy that Jesus gives below:
Repent of sin, believe the word,
When pardon soon for you is heard.

September, 1894.

IN MEMORIAM PRINCESS ALICE.

Great God we bow before Thy face,
And humbly seek Thy saving grace,
To take us by the hand, and lead
And help us in the time of need.

Death with its sombre cloak has cast
A gloom o'er all the recent past,
By taking one that's loved so dear
That thousands shed the scalding tear.

Our Princess good, was loved by all,
(No matter where), on whom we call,
Her kindness will be treasured long,
And all her kind deeds spread in song.

She nursed her father with great care,
And helped to ease his pain while here,
She sang to him that wondrous glee,
Oh "Rock of Ages cleft for me."

She nursed when ill her brother dear,
So ill, all thought his end was near;
This touching episode will be,
A tribute to her memory.

Her tender care helped him to raise,
For this she well deserves our praise,
Her skilful patience well we know
Was seen in all she did below.

To sick and wounded she became,
At home or hospital, the same,
Like Florence Nightingale, we've read,
Our Royal Princess nursed and fed.

The soldiers all have lost a friend,
Who stuck to them right to the end,
Her worth is known to rich and poor,
Her memory fragrant evermore.

Midst wives she was a model too,
Which they to copy well would do,
And kinder mother never breathed,
This all most surely do believe.

We would condole with all in grief,
And gladly give them some relief,
We know how hard the stroke has been,
To our beloved gracious Queen.

Her husband left does deeply mourn,
Because his wife from him is torn.
Help each, O Lord, "Thy will" to say,
All through this dark and gloomy day.

The Children dear now left behind,
May they their mother's Saviour find,
O Jesu be to them a friend,
And lead and teach them to the end.

Her loss her royal brothers grieve,
The sisters each, O Lord relieve,
We would with all bereaved condole,
Embrace with sympathy the whole.

We mourn not for her royal birth,
But for her love and real worth,
We greatly grieve the loss of one,
So truly great in good deeds done.

The humblest peasant's prayers ascend,
And with the rich they sweetly blend,
Imploring grace in time of need,
To bind the broken hearts that bleed

May this bereavement prove to all,
A voice from heaven that loud may call,
" Prepare to meet thy God " it says,
For death may soon cut short our days.

December 23rd, 1878.

A FEW EVENTS IN THE LIFE OF HER MAJESTY THE QUEEN, AND THE ROYAL FAMILY; AND THE DEATH OF THE DUKE OF ALBANY.

In childhood days when gathering round
  Our humble hearth, I've often heard
From my dear father's lips the praise,
  And my young heart drank every word.

He oft would tell us of our Queen,
  Prince Albert also, too, the Good,
And as in years I older grew,
  I then more fully understood.

At school, again, I too was taught,
  To love and to revere our Queen,
And often my kind master told
  Of loving deeds he'd read and seen.

About her Majesty beloved,
  Prince Albert too, as well the same,
And all these loving lessons taught,
  Grew strong as I a man became.

" Prince Consort, rightly named the Good "
  He once upon a time did say,
The noble Prince had written high,
  That all who chanced to pass that way.

On the Royal Exchange we see,
  A gracious tribute to his praise,
Which follows, " The earth is the Lord's
  And the fulness thereof " always.

If our good Prince, the master said.
  With all his learning, wealth, and fame,
Could humbly say, that all he had,
  Was only lent through Jesu's name.

Now boys, he said, in future mind,
  In all your anxious thought for wealth,
Remember too these gracious words,
  The Lord can give you peace and health.

At early age I came to town.
  Scarce seventeen years, not any more;
It soon began to see the sights,
  As London town I travelled o'er.

I saw the grand procession pass.
  It through St. James's Park did glide,
When Princess Royal was wedded,
  And her betrothed sat by her side.

The thousands congregated there,
  Near filled the Parks that gladsome day,
The hurrahs loud that rent the air,
  Were heard for many a league away.

There sat the bride in colours gay,
  As they drove with steady pace,
The Queen looked happiness itself,
  A smile lit up Prince Consort's face.

The day was cold, intensely cold,
  But packed were we so close together,
T'was there as warm as summer heat,
  We scarcely felt the wintry weather.

The trees were all bereft of leaves,
  And in their naked branches seen
Were boys and men of every clan,
  Rejoicing with their Prince and Queen.

Before I now reverse the scene,
  I here another part portray,
And while I now in verse rehearse,
  I want some tender words to say.

The close of eighteen-sixty-one,
  Brought to us all the deepest grief,
It took from us one loved so dear
  We prayed great God give them relief.

To her our widowed Queen and house;
  Be thou a husband to her, Lord.
Bind up the broken hearts bereaved,
  Console and cheer them by Thy word.

Our gracious Prince had won esteem,
  In every circle far and near;
His loss was keenly felt we know,
  For he was loved by all so dear.

Our lives are changeful, vexed, and frail
  One day with joy we're filled so great,
The next some trials cross our way,
  And then a sunbeam does await.

The years now passed so slow along,
  Such sad reflections of the past,
In sorrow deep our Queen did mourn,
  But hoped dispelled the gloom at last.

Another nuptial now we note,
  The Prince of Wales his wedding day.
I there became an honoured guest,
  Amongst the crowd in bright array.

His Royal Princess how she's loved,
  Her face—betokens her kind heart,
And while along the route they drove,
  The Princess bore an active part.

And as we slowly drove along
  At night, all London shone with light,
For loyal love ran very high,
  It was a dazzling, splendid sight.

God bless the Prince and Princess too,
  Came shining forth from many a gem;
Long may they live and happy be,
  And bless our Queen as well as them.

Another wedding now I note,
  Princess Louise, though nobly born,
We'll give to her our highest praise,
  For wedding in the house of Lorne.

Her husband's gifts are known to all,
  The Princess too has talents rare,
If 'tis thy will, Lord, give an heir,
  And o'er him watch with loving care.

What changing scenes our lives go through,
Hark! so still, not a sound is heard,
At Sandringham where all was joy,
'Tis hushed and still without a word.

The Royal Prince is sick and weak,
His wife is watching by his bed,
His mother looks so anxious there,
And sister Alice props his head.

Some days and weeks in deepest grief,
They wondered ever how 'twould be,
But God his healing virtues sent,
And soon they did His wonders see.

In answer to his people's prayers,
The Lord did graciously attend;
The Prince was soon restored to health,
And prayers and thanks to God did blend.

The Duke of Edinburgh next wed,
The noble sailor true and brave,
We saw the grand procession pass,
And not a ripple on the wave.

Such numbers, 'twas a glorious sight,
The Duchess and the Queen so gay,
The throng they prest on every side,
And loyal cheerings rent the way.

I once in verse tried here my hand,
And sketched the things that struck my [eyes.
So now will cut this short and sweet,
Or I shall not be very wise.

The next event I call to mind,
Was when the Queen the medals gave,
To gallant soldiers from the East,
Who did so bravely there behave.

At Coomassie, too, the strife was quelled,
Sir Garnet with his men we'll praise,
The honours great given on that day
Shall high resound in these our lays.

We witnessed there in Windsor Park,
  The grandest sight we ever saw,
When our beloved Monarch gave,
  Her touching sympathy to all.

Years now rolled on with steady pace,
  Aud softly blew the southern wind,
The Royal house had health and peace,
  And all arouud was blythe and kind.

But, ah ! death lurking in its lair,
  The bow is bent, the arrow flown
And lodges in the fairest one
  That e'er the glorious sun shone on.

Our Princess Alice smitten down
  Just in her happy brightest day ;
The Queen's great sorrow for her loss
  Seemed dark without a glimmering ray.

But hope inspires us with a song,
  For death is but a conquered foe,
Our Royal Princess sought the Lord,
  And all, through grace, is well we know.

Her life was fraught with kindly acts
  Where'er the place she chose to dwell,
And now she's safely housed above,
  Her household bless, O Lord, as well.

We simply note in grateful praise,
  Though dangers thick have flown around ;
The Queen's dear life has been preserved
  And now in health she's safely found.

The deadly weapon once was aimed,
  But God in mercy great was spared ;
And now a joyful note we'll raise,
  And millions too this song have shared.

Last year we note the death of one,
  Who passed away, with deep regret,
Who in the service of our Queen
  A truer servant never met.

From early youth to ripened age
  John Brown did wait on her with care,
No wonder then when called to part,
  She felt the trial hard to bear.

But death makes no distinction here,
  The rich must part, the lowly go,
The summons sure will call for all,
  For all will have to die we know.

Then let us each great kindness show
  To all whate'er may be their lot.
For high distincition soon will cease,
  Our own experience this has taught.

Before I close these simple lines,
  I note a death with deepest grief;
The news from Cannes give all a pang.
  May those bereaved have sweet relief.

Dear Lord, support them by Thy grace,
  Bind up the bleeding hearts we pray;
Our Queen, beloved, and Duchess too,
  Give consolation every day!

The Duke of Albany we know;
  His life we cannot but admire:
His gifts and talents too were rare,
  We'll praise his memory on our lyre.

The mantle of his honoured sire,
  Seemed fallen on his youthful son;
And this inspired our future hope
  To wish his life might long be run.

The nation mourns with deepest grief,
  And sorrowing drops the falling tears;
Great God, with sympathetic eye.
  Help each to cast on Thee their care.

To all his royal brothers dear,
  And sisters too, give comfort Lord;
And may this sad bereavement help
  To cast themselves upon Thy word.

We ask, if 'tis Thy gracious will,
  Spare long to us our Queen to reign,
And in her last declining years
  Do thou her future steps ordain.

Guide our beloved Queen, O Lord,
In all her future course we pray,
Through all her varied chequered life
May light be here along the way.

And when her crown is laid aside,
And all her earthly honours cease,
O may she hear the welcome word,
Well done! for ever rest in peace.

6th April, 1884.

LINES ON THE MARRIAGE OF H.R.H. PRINCESS BEATRICE, TO H.R.H. PRINCE HENRY OF BATTENBERG,

At Whippingham Church, Isle of Wight, July 23rd, 1885.

I'll try to form my muse in verse,
And some few lines will now rehearse,
To write in praise of her just wed,
Who to the altar has been led.

Princess Beatrice, our love has won,
By all the kindly deeds she's done;
The sick have oft her visits had,
To comfort them when they were sad.

This youngest daughter of our Queen,
Who long has her companion been;
And often cheered her aching heart,
When through bereavements called to part.

With kindly words, the daughter's cheer,
Has helped the Queen her cross to bear,
While arduous duties of the state,
Have taxed her energies so great.

We're pleased to hear, she still lives near
Our Gracious Queen, her mother dear.
Will always thus be close at hand
To cheer her in our native land.

But now the nuptial knot is tied,
May sweet affectionate e'er betide;
The happy royal pair through life,
May love abound and banish strife.

May years be many, sorrows few,
And children num'rous given too;
As olive branches round their board,
All blessings earth can them afford.

With health of body and of mind,
Long may the bride and bridegroom find,
May prosp'rous gales speed on their bark.
And Christ be guide when it is dark.

And all along their future way,
The Bible shine as bright as day;
Its truths alone will guide them right,
And lead them o'er the darkest night.

To England's maids we give our praise,
And worthy mention in our lays;
The presentation which they made
A Book whose truths will never fade.

How many a loving earnest prayer
Ascends on high to bless the pair;
From many an English hearth and home,
To keep them safe where'er they roam.

God bless, we pray, the mother dear,
Preserving her when danger's near;
And all her children, too, we pray,
Be brought to Christ, the Living Way.

And when their earthly honours gone,
And all their work below is done,
O may they hear the Master's cheer.
"Come up to heaven and enter here."

To meet the loved ones gone before,
Whose trials here have long been o'er;
Our Queen beloved at eventide,
Protect her Lord on every side.

ugust 3rd, 1885.

IN MEMORIAM OF THE EMPEROR OF GERMANY.

A child of Royal birth,
A man of sterling worth,
Has passed away from earth,
The Emperor of Germany.

He patiently did bear
His sickness long while here,
And we have shed a tear
For the Emperor of Germany.

He's gone to meet above
The ones he used to love ;
And on the shining shore,
With Jesus evermore,
The Emperor of Germany.

VERSES IN SYMPATHY FOR THE BEREAVED EMPRESS OF GERMANY.

The Empress bless, O Lord we pray,
On this her dark bereaving day.
May Gilead's balm soon heal the smart
Of her sad, stricken, broken heart.

May all her orphan children, Lord,
Find true the promise of Thy Word,
Kind Jesus, be to them the way
That leads them to eternal day.

And when their earthly honours o'er,
And they safed housed on yonder shore,
He'll greet them, whom He loved while here,
In Canaan's land, when they appear.

THE JUBILEE OF THE REIGN OF HER IMPERIAL MAJESTY VICTORIA,

Queen of Great Britain and Ireland, and Empress of India.

Again we strike a joyous chord,
Its loyal theme well suits a bard,
In jubilant notes of highest praise,
We'll sound it forth in these our lays.

For fifty years has reigned our Queen,
And many changes has she seen,
Her long and peaceful reign still sheds
Rich blessings on her subjects' heads.

The year of Jubilee is here,
There'll be rejoicing far and near,
Spare longer, if Thy will it may,
Our Queen beloved, O Lord, we pray.

We cannot glance at all the good,
(Since on her brow the crown has stood),
Which lustrous statesmen have achieved,
What aching hearts have been relieved.

The slave has lost his clanking chain,
In her benign and gracious reign:
Though Wilberforce and Pitt have gone,
They heard their Master's word, "well done."

What noble statesmen has she had
To make her country's heart more glad;
Such names as Lawson, Gladstone, Bright,
Would cheer the gloom of darkest night.

But other men have marked their name
Upon the marble scroll of fame,
Who figured high upon the earth
Although they were of humble birth.

Lord Beaconsfield, forsooth, was one,
The nation owned what he had done,
He climbed the ladder from its base,
And did all obstacles efface.

Good Richard Cobden brought a Bill
Before the House, with heart and will;
It took the tax from off our bread,
And starving thousands then were fed.

The tax then in her reign so good,
Removed from papers, that which stood
A barrier great for mind and thought,
Now man is better read and taught.

Yet many more both good and true
Each side of politics we knew,
Whose names would well adorn our verse,
Were we to make a casual search.

We cannot help but mention here,
Lord Shaftesbury to memory dear,
With Morley and Lord Cairns the same
These tell abroad Victoria's fame.

The Queen has played an active part,
(For she has got a tender heart),
Relieving sufferings of the poor,
And helping from her ample store.

Nor can we leave out one great name,
Which o'er the world has spread in fame,
Charles Haddon Spurgeon here we mean
Whose loyalty we all have seen.

The Stockwell Orphanage stands high,
And will preserve his memory,
And as 'twas reared in her sweet reign
Her subjects will its strength maintain.

Our Queen through chequered paths hath trod,
Been chastened well with sorrows' rod;
But still our trials work our good,
Which she, we know, has understood.

One cold and dark December day
When from her heart was torn away,
Albert the Good, her husband dear,
Then on her God she cast her care.

And other trials, sharp and sore,
We wish not here to mention more,
But only say God's grace has been
A help to our beloved Queen.

From many thousand hearts and homes,
Has earnest prayer to heaven been borne,
God save our Queen, we often pray,
In every dark and gloomy day.

At eventide may it be light,
To aid and help her in her fight
As now the shades of night appear,
We pray Thee, Lord, her heart to cheer.

We also pray that God would bless
Her children, too, with righteousness;
For has He not said in His word,
The prayer of faith is always heard.

Then answer, Lord, their father's prayer,
And drive away their mother's fear,
And bless her children with Thy grace,
And bring them all to seek Thy face.

May peace and plenty e'er abound,
Encircling all the world around;
May righteousness exalted be,
In every place of dignity.

And now, in closing this brief rhyme,
We know how quickly flies the time;
And when her earthly troubles cease,
God grant to her a heavenly peace.

1887.

THE MARRIAGE OF H.R.H. THE PRINCESS LOUISE OF WALES WITH THE DUKE OF FIFE,

At Buckingham Palace, Saturday July 27th, 1889.

To-day a Royal Nuptial's tied,
Embracing people far and wide
In kindly sympathy and love,
Which is akin to that above.

Princess Louise and Duke of Fife
Are now united, man and wife :
We pray their future life may be,
In love and health, spent happily.

May life be spared, and wealth abound,
To cheer them through the world around ;
And Olive Branches be in store,
To deck their homes for evermore.

Old England with the thistle too,
Is bound around in union true :
The land of Scot is honoured rare,
With our Princess, beloved, and fair.

May prosperous gales speed on their bark,
And shield them from the tempests dark ;
Great Captain be to them their Guide,
And lead them to Thy heavenly side.

The presents given were rich and rare,
And sent by love, with greatest care,
These tokens of affection may
Be pleasant memories on their way.

The day was bright, and thousands were
In crowds they waited here and there,
And thronged the way along the route,
Which did the smiling ladies suit.

It seems as if 'twas yesterday,
I stood along the Queen's highway ;
For hours I watched the teeming crowd
Then burst hurrahs both long and loud.

This scene described in verse above,
Was seen by thousands, moved by love;
When Prince of Wales and Princess too,
Were both allied in wedlock true.

But years have come and gone since then,
To day the scene's renewed again,
With their sweet daughter, charming bride,
And bridegroom sitting by her side.

We send our greetings on to-day,
To cheer her parents on their way;
They're loved by: all we know 'tis so,
In every clime where e'er they go.

Relatives of the Duke of Fife,
We wish a happy joyful life,
Congratulations rich we send,
On all may heavenly blessings blend.

Nor will we? no, we cant't leave here,
Until her father's mother dear,
Our own beloved and honoured Queen,
Our cordial greeting love has seen.

Our Queen, we pray Thee, Lord, to bless,
And crown her reign with righteousness,
And all her offspring some day meet,
Through grace, in heaven, at Jesu's feet.

IN MEMORIAM LORD SHAFTESBURY.

The noble earl has passed away
To the bright realms of endless day;
His life with fragrant honours crowned,
And many mourning friends are found.

His mem'ry'll long be cherished here,
While thousands shed the falling tear;
But faith has taught us then to know
In heaven he rests from earthly woe.

In early life the Lord he sought,
And well he has the battle fought;
For God has kept him by His grace,
And brought him home to see His face.

His name has been a household word;
For fifty years and more we've heard,
In works benevolent and good
Lord Shaftesbury's name has always stood.

For thirty years we've known him, too,
To be a friend both kind and true;
And often seen his manly form
Presiding meetings large and warm.

The poor have lost in him a friend
Who's kept to them right to the end;
And many mourning children, found
In town and country all around.

At Shortlands station, Dover line,
We saw the noble earl last time;
We shook his hand with hearty cheer,
And said we're pleased to meet you here.

He greeted us with pleasant smile,
And kindly spoke to us awhile;
We told him we had known him long,
His mem'ry's now endeared in song.

'Twas when he opened on the day,
The workmen's talents for display;
The exhibition near the station
Drew ladies dressed in highest fashion.

Two shillings was the ticket price,
We purchased one in quickest trice;
We soon were asked to show our ticket,
We shall not soon forget our visit.

We said, please ask these ladies near
To show their tickets now they're here;
And do not think our coats the test,
A generous heart beats in our breast.

We do not like to think it hard,
Although it happed to be "Penge Bard;"
Our business near was making hay,
Or we had not been there that day.

We shall not soon forget his speech,
It stuck to us just like a leech;
'Twas on the cooking of plain food,
"Said many spoilt it when 'twas good."

"He said few could potatoes cook:"
We put his speech then in our book,
And little thought 'twould serve our rhyme,
Although it comes now in good time.

With other words both good and rare,
"Said art and science too were there:
This does our finest feeling bring
Into the smallest tiniest thing."

We heard friend C. H. Spurgeon pay
A tribute high to him one day:
Lord Shaftesbury's work was nearly done,
His race below was nearly run.

He would arise with heavenly oil,
Anointing one for holy toil:
To fill his place, Lord Aberdeen,
Of all men else is best we've seen.

"Lord Shaftesbury's been a friend indeed,
To me in every time of need:"
This at the orphans' fete we heard,
And can avouch for every word.

Come then lets rally round the man
Assisting orphans all we can:
Now this philanthropist is gone
The children shall not suffer wrong.

Our coster friends will know his loss,
They feel his death a heavy cross;
He's been to them a friend indeed,
And also others in their need.

We shall not soon their gift forget,
For kinder hearts he never met;
The donkey, too, which they gave him,
We hope is still in best of trim.

His death speaks loudly to us all,
And does to highest circles call;
Let those now learn if they would win
The highest fame, they must shun sin,

And consecrate to Christ their life,
'Twill keep them then in every strife
And land them safe on Canaan's shore,
Where all their trials will be o'er.

Shaftesbury's hoary head is crowned,
Because in righteousness 'twas found;
For the bereaved, O Lord, to-day
Bind up their broken hearts, we pray.

A FEW THOUGHTS ON SPRING.

(Written at Elmer's End, Beckenham).

In pensive mood and quiet thought,
From Nature's bounteous stores I sought,
And not in vain: the landscape view
Showed Nature dressed in garments new.

The larks were warbling forth their lays
In songs of sweetest, loudest praise
From out their throats, against the sky
Came grateful praise to God on high.

The cuckoo's plaintive notes were heard,
And songster thrush and sweet blackbird;
If you at night had passed this way
You'd heard the nightingale's sweet lay;

The chaffinch chirp, and cawing rook—
I put their music in my book—
Reminding me the winters' past,
Although so long it seemed to last.

The primrose and the daisy, too,
And other flowers, how well they grew
The tulip sweet and lily fair,
All seemed to say, be banished care.

The springing grass and bursting bud,
And varied trees the landscape stud;
Warm southern breezes fan my cheek,
And Shirley hills my glad eyes greet.

If God, my Father, clothes the field,
With riches plenty makes it yield,
And then adorns the earth with flowers,
And sends us down the April showers,

O! then, my lips, tell forth the praise
Of His great goodness all my days;
For His kind Providence and grace
Through all my journey I shall trace.

I sat upon those stones and mused,
As oft before I there had used;
And now I leave these thoughts with you,
Trusting they'll find an echo true.

A NEW YEAR RHYME.

May the New Year be bright to thee,
Laden with blessings may it be,
Each morn with grateful feelings rise,
To praise thy Maker good and wise;
Throughout each hour and through each day,
As through the year time glides away.
We wish that joy may fill each heart
While choosing Mary's better part.
May health and plenty be around,
And foes be few and friends abound:
Each rolling month as they pass by,
Thy gracious God is ever nigh
To help, to guide, and comfort thee,
For thou shalt His salvation see.

Should trials come across thy road,
And press thee sorely with their load,
Cast then thy burdens on the Lord—
"I'll help thee," is his gracious word.
Should pining sickness be thy lot,
The furnace heated very hot;
In troubles six he'll be with thee,
And thou in seven shall mercy see.
If through the year death's summons call:
Perhaps those we love are marked to fall;
If they're prepared His rod will cheer,
And through death's vale they've naught to fear—
His staff will comfort them the same,
As they by faith plead Jesu's name.
There will be some who read this rhyme,
Who say, "I wish these joys were mine;
My future prospects are not bright;
My soul is sinful, dark as night."
Cheer up, my brother, Christ, the way,
Can turn your darkness into day,
Then cast on Him your every care,
And all your burdens He will bear.
And now you have my wishes best,
Please leave to Providence the rest,
Then all the future of thy life,
If pleasant 'tis, or full of strife,
Thy gracious God will ne'er forsake,
"For bruised reeds He ne'er will break."
May faith be rudder to thy bark,
And Christ the pilot when its dark,
And when your voyage is ended here
May you all in Heaven appear.

THE NEW YEAR, 1886.

We greet the New Year with a song,
And should our days be short or long,
Our grateful thanks to God shall rise,
Whose gracious ways are always wise.
If future dark with clouds we see,

Or bright with sunshine it may be;
If pain or sorrow be our lot,
The promise of our God fails not.
Should there be prosperous days in store,
'Tis only human to want more;
But should adversity be ours,
We can't have sweets without the sours.
These tonics often keep us right,
Or we may stray in dazzling light.
Should some great cross or loss be sent,
May our own wills to God's be bent,
Or should affliction lay us low,
Or sad bereavement to us flow,
May Thy sweet promise be our stay,
"My grace is equal to Thy day."
Then come what may, the rough or smooth,
Life's stormy billows Thou can'st soothe,
And in the tempest's darkest hour,
Can peace proclaim with mighty power.
But should there be as p'raps there may,
Some trembling one to us will say:
"Could I find this heavenly treasure,
To meet life's ills with holy pleasure;
Or know the Saviour died for me,
And gave me pardon full and free."
If this be thy desire dear one,
We point thee to what Christ has done,
He suffered once upon the tree,
To save a sinner just like thee.
And if in penitence and faith,
Thou canst but trust to what He saith
Thou shalt eternal life receive,
Because He died that thou might live.
The year has swiftly passed away,
Some painful thoughts are left to-day
While some we knew and loved below,
Are called away, 'twas such a blow:
Some neighbours too who lived quite near,
Have lost their relatives most dear,
Their hearts we know are sorely grieved,
We wish we could have them relieved.
But human aid is weak and frail,

Yet God's great mercies never fail ;
Then wipe away the fallen tear,
And know thy Saviour God is near ;
If thou canst trust thy Saviour now,
And at His cross wilt humbly bow ;
Then cast on Him thy every care,
For all thy burdens He will bear.
To all our readers, this who read,
We wish a happy year to speed,
And then when life's short journey's past,
A heaven of happiness will last.

A RETROSPECT AND PROSPECT FOR 1888 AND 1889

Suggested through seeing some Children going to a Party.

Our muse shall tell of bygone years,
Before our hearts were filled with cares,
Or e'er the Black Cow trod our toes,
Or we assailed by numerous foes.

We skipped in youth across the mead,
In every game we took the lead,
Our youthful parties had a charm,
Although 'twas lonely on our farm.

God took when young our mother dear,
Before we knew her loving care ;
Dear father mourned her loss in grief,
Found prayer to God his sweet relief.

We used to learn so slow at school,
And oft our palms were crossed with rule,
But still we've plodded on our way,
And have continued to this day.

At the age of sweet seventeen,
Before the world we'd faintly seen,
For London town we left our home,
And in its throngs oft felt alone.

We found its streets were very cold,
Though once we thought them paved with gold ;
Temptations strong, severe, were there,
Oh how we needed God's great care.

In youth His grace touched our young heart,
And bid us choose the better part;
"Give me thy heart," to us He said,
Although in deepest grief it bled.

Believing faith soon brought us joy,
Though oft the world did us annoy,
But resting on the Saviour's breast
We felt a calm—a sacred rest.

Now four-and-thirty years have passed,
But still upon this rock we're cast;
We nothing good, we know can do,
But sovereign grace will help us through.

In all paths of our chequered life,
Amid its trials and its strife,
The Cloudy Pillar be our light,
And Fiery Cloud be guide to right.

And when we land on Canaan's shore,
With all our earthly trials o'er.
Oh may we hear the welcome word,
"Well done"—as spoken by our Lord.

THE COAL CATASTROPHE, MARDY, SOUTH WALES, 1887.

So sad the news that wrings the heart,
And makes us mourn with inward smart
To hear this Christmas time of year,
When most are happy far and near.
The coal catastrophe in Wales
Has thrilled us with its touching tales,
Just at the time when all seemed glee,
Expecting happiness to see.
The shock did rend the village round,
And terror carried with its sound,
At the pit's mouth so quick were seen
Hundreds of faithful hearts we ween.

With pallid face and anxious care
These loving wives were crowding there,
The men in haste, so brave and true,
So quick arranged what they should do,
And soon were ready for the task,
Their lives in danger ne'er did ask.
These brave explorers went below,
And kindest sympathy did show,
And down the shaft they quickly went,
And many prayers were quickly sent—
May God preserve these faithful men
And safely bring them up again.
And as in terror and dismay
They waited patiently that day,
The sad suspense, we know the cost
Expecting those they loved were lost.
How can we write a mother's woe
Or show a father's crushing blow.
The papers tell us what they did
And also words of what was said.
These men of courage soon began
A rescuing their fellow men;
In three short hours of work and thought
Nine hundred men were safely brought
And as each landed on the stage
The touching scenes would fill a page.
A mother's love, it burst the bound
And sent a thrill on all around,
With gushing tears she grasped her boy
Fell on his neck and screamed with joy;
Another mother fainted there,
Was taken home by friends with care,
Two hundred more entombed below
With anxious thought their fate to know,
While friends were waiting in great grief
And there were none to give relief.
A boy of twelve short years was found
His father heard his plaintive sound
Although delirious, sick and weak
Cried, "mother," as if his heart would break.
His father, Davis, heard his cry,
His heart was touched with sympathy,

His faithful, loving dog lay nigh
His side, and cold in death did lie.
"Mine iniquities forgive, O Lord,"
A prayer so fitting there was heard,
He then fell dead upon the floor
And all his sorrows soon were o'er;
Bright angels took his spirit home,
His deacon's work on earth was done.
Dear Jones' prayers are changed to praise
In heaven he'll spend eternal days.
The little boy we mention here
Who said so full of anxious care
"What will poor mother think or say
If she should lose her boy to-day?"
We can't leave out Dan Howell's deed
A friend he was in their deep need;
God bless dear Dan; his sons the same,
May grace write in God's book each name,
No works can purchase Heaven we know,
Yet thanks to them we'll here bestow,
We'd mention others bold and brave
Who tried their comrades there to save
But time forbids and space demands,
Although bound round with loving bands.
As now this simple rhyme we close
We'll ne'er forget the widow's woes;
Be Thou their husband, gracious Lord,
Which Thou hast promised in Thy Word,
To orphan children, too, we pray,
Be Thou their father every day;
Let Thy sweet love and sovereign grace
Wipe tears away from every face;
To all bereaved ones impart
The balm of Gilead in each heart.

IN MEMORIAM OF JOHN BRIGHT,

Who fell asleep, March 27th, 1889.

A noble sire has passed away,
One who has well employed his day;
That mighty voice is hushed and still,
And mind, and memory, with his will.

Yet hark ! I hear beyond the skies
Our friend's not dead—his spirit flies—
And mingling with the blood-bought throng,
His voice to Christ is raised in song.

John Bright's an honoured household word,
Which from our childhood we have heard ;
Our fathers told us his Bright name.
And we have treasured up the same.

He gave his heart to Christ in youth,
And sought and found the God of truth ;
And sovereign grace bedecked his life,
Preserving him amid its strife.

His gifts and oratory we know ;
And generous sympathy did flow
To help the poor wherever found,
In every clime the wide world rouud.

In early life he joined the band,
Not then so numerous, in our land,
The Temperance cause was dear to him,
And many trophies did he win.

His manly speeches oft were heard,
While Temperance truths by him were stirred ;
His maiden speech on it was spoken
In language weak and nearly broken.

We well remember how he fought
With Cobden and the rest : he sought
To give the poor a loaf of bread
That hungry children may be fed.

Free Trade for Corn ! ah, well we know
The Bill was launched 'mid strife and woe,
And by his eloquence and power,
God's richest blessing crowned the hour.

In consort with good Cobden too,
Conferred great blessings not a few;
For soon 'twas passed 'mid shouts of praise,
Which rang amid our youthful days.

How well he fought, and also won,
The franchise Bill; what good its done,
The poor through it a vote receive—
And Ballot Box their fears relieve.

His warning voice was raised on war,
Which thrilled the nations from afar;
The Russian war would ne'er have been
Had statesmen caught his peaceful theme.

And how the Irish Church he sought
To disestablish it; he brought
Both justice, eloquence and wit,
Which proved the key to nicely fit.

Another word in praise we'll say:
His loyalty was seen alway;
Our Queen and Royal House did love
Our world-wide friend, gone home above.

Wreaths which bedecked his coffin lid
Showed loving-kindness deeply hid:
From Queen beloved, down to the poor,
John Bright was loved by all we're sure.

We now will pen another line,
Which will our sympathy combine
To those so dear who mourn his loss,
May Jesus help them bear the Cross.

And now his work on earth is done,
And he has heard the word "Well done;
Come up, thou blessed, and dwell with me
Throughout a long eternity."

IN MEMORIAM—LOUISA SUNSHINE.

I was asked by a relative to write an epitaph on the death of a maiden named Louisa Sunshine, who was a great sufferer for eight years, and who died at the age of sixteen, on the 17th February, 1893. She said before her death, seeing her mother crying by her bedside, "What are you breaking your heart about me so for I know I am going home to be with Jesus, will you dear father and mother and sisters meet me there by and by."

Only a day or two after this she gently passed away at Canning Town, one of the brightest lambs to be for ever in the Saviour's fold. I wrote the following lines, which her relatives printed on her Memorial Card:—

Sweet name, Louisa Sunshine bright,
So radiant now in Heavenly light;
Good-bye, dear girl, our daughter dear,
We cannot stay the scalding tear.

No chilling winds; no aching heart
Will fill again our sorrows smart,
Thou wilt with Jesus ever be,
May we through grace some day meet thee.

ON OUR FIRST VISIT TO BOURNEMOUTH AND NEIGHBOURHOOD.

Down here at Bournemouth we've just spent
A happy week of sweet content,
Of all the seaside towns we've seen,
We reckon this to be the queen.
Its balmy, bracing air doth charm,
In coldish weather seems to warm,
The oily pines with perfume shed
Health's healing virtues on our head.
If wearied out with family care,
And business pressing everywhere,

Take our advice, to Bournemouth go,
And health and vigour you'll soon know.
The promenade and garden fine,
The flowing brook and flowers combine
With warbling birds their music sweet,
To make our happiness complete.
The invalids' fine walk was shown,
By thousands well the place is known:
Protected by the graceful trees,
And seats to rest at cosy ease.
Restore to health, O Lord, we pray,
If this Thy will, without delay,
And may their lives from henceforth prove
The debt they owe, to Thee, of love.
If some, O Lord, are marked to die,
Prepare them for Thy throne on high;
Through Christ may they find pardon here
And then enjoy Thy heaven up there.
Of churches and of chapels too,
In Bournemouth there are not a few;
Most built in Gothic pointed style,
Which makes them look a noble pile
If you would like to have a ride,
See the New Forest far and wide;
The old time coaches, too, are there,
With four-in-hand at moderate fare.
The journey's made almost sublime,
By guide who wiles away the time,
As he depicts the scenes of old,
Which English history doth unfold.
Upon the beach the finest sand
In all old England's happy land,
Where children play with merry glee,
And make sand houses near the sea.
So like those children there, we thought,
We castles in the air have wrought,
Which earthly tides soon swept away
Like Liberator's wicked play.
The boatman, too, yes, one we saw,
He said he was without a flaw,
Of languages said three he knew,

Which made him doubt the Bible true :
We said if thus it is with thee,
A single language best suits me :
For if it makes one doubt God's word,
To learn another is absurd.
These boatmen kind and frank and true,
They'll spin a good yarn out to you ;
Give them a chance to earn a crust,
By rowing you and yours you must.
There's mansions large and hotels rare,
Where you can get most sumptuous fare,
Cafés and restaurants so fine,
Take BENTLEY'S RELISH when you dine,
This lovely sauce has won such fame.
(Please don't forget its well known name),
From Land's End down to John-o-Groat,
In grocer's shops it can be bought.
For us it means our bread and cheese,
So if you'll order, us 'twill please.
The Lemon Squash of Bentley's try,
Their Lime Juice, also, ranks most high.
The tradesmen, too, their shops are grand,
And large as any in the land :
And all your orders they'll discharge,
Esteem them highly, small or large.
So give the local men your trade,
Your name with them will never fade.
You'll find their prices will compare
With Stores in London or elsewhere.
Before you homeward bend your way,
Give pretty Isle of Wight a day ;
The steamers daily ply out there,
A pleasant trip at moderate fare.
If through the Island you should go,
You'll find their charges very low,
But by the rail their charge, O my !
Just walk if able, and them defy.
We must now draw to a quick close,
Though rhyming to us easy flows ;
Our yarn we fear has been too long,
Please reader pardon for the wrong.

IN MEMORIAM—EARL GRANVILLE.

Earl Granville now is gone safe home,
His life's great work was nobly done,
And now is crowned his hoary head,
With grateful thanks as all have read,

We well remember sides he took,
With people whom he ne'er forsook;
A friend was he to all opprest,
In every place his memory's blest.

Some fifty years he guarded well
Great Britain's glorious name we tell;
A statesman good, as true as steel,
And all the world his loss will feel.

We read with pleasure in the *Times*,
Of measures good in all its lines,
Although in pages four contained,
Not one foul blot his life had stained.

In amity he loved to bless,
Mankind of every clime and dress;
In all his measures fraught with good,
Up for the poor he always stood.

With silver speech, yet tongue of fire,
His thoughts were flashed along the wire;
The press took up his every speech,
And did the world his lessons teach.

He aided Cobden pass his Bill,
While many feared this steepest hill,
But Granville saw the good 'twould bring,
And make the hungry folk to sing.

The Exhibition of Fifty-one
Owed much to what he'd kindly done;
His witty sunshine full of glee,
Gives sweetness to his memory.

The cheapened loaf made widows glad,
And children full, who once were sad;
For brothers' weak he made a stand,
And now his praise rings through the land.

For every useful measure wrought,
His powerful influence he brought,
And all knew well which side he'd take,
Good laws our statute book to make.

The Grand Old Man is left behind,
His bosom friend so good and kind;
Granville was loved, we do believe
By every foe, and each colleague.

The humble honored funeral here
Was marked by many a falling tear;
The rich and poor alike have said,
They tribute pay to noble dead.

THE LOSS OF THE ELBE,

With 350 lives, on the 30th Janaury, 1895. A disaster in the North Sea.

The winter night was cold we know,
With frost, high wind, and sleet and snow:
The ocean Liner cut its way
Through rolling billows, ice and spray.

Alas! the Crathie did it reach,
And in its side made deadly breach;
In poured the current of the sea,
And sunk like lead she ceased to be.

Meanwhile the Captain's voice was heard,
For mad excitement all had stirred:
"Launch the lifeboats with all speed,
Women and children take the lead."

In anxious haste the crew obey,
The Elbe fast sinking neath the spray;
Then in the starboard boats did he
Order women and children to be.

Sad and awful the mournful tale,
Those lifeboats were of no avail;
They sank at once beneath the wave,
And none a single soul could save.

Miss Bœcker tells in language plain,
How she, miraculous does remain,
For though her boat was launched with care,
It sunk because no plug was there.

With oar she reached another boat
Which from the ship was safe afloat;
With nineteen men, a night of fear,
Those twenty only saved we hear.

We must within our page enshrine
This herione, with special line;
For she with valour calm and rare
Cheered seaman on to do and dare.

And though immersed in waters cold,
She murmured not, but proved quite bold,
An orphan she, may all her way
Be still as brave; in God her stay.

Karl Hofmann saved with broken heart,
Forced from his wife and child to part;
His story told with patience mild
Of broken heart mid scenes so wild.

And poor Verara's niece was lost,
And nearly his own life it cost;
He saved in a mysterious way
Shares in our sympathy to-day.

Herr Schlegel lost his sister bright,
With hundred others on that night,
Give Lord consoling grace to him,
With all who scaped that awful swim.

Now stalwart men of kindly heart,
In this our verse must share a part:
Their gallant deed both kind and brave,
Saved twenty from a watery grave.

They were the "Wild Flower" fishermen,
Their noble nature shone out then;
With kindly and heroic deed,
To sufferers in their direst need.

Quick from the Palace news was sought,
Condoling messages were brought,
Empress and Emperor both said,
They deeply grieved at that they read.

While too, from our most gracious Queen
The pitying message soon was seen,
Which said her heart was deeply grieved
And sad such news she had received.

Miss Bœcker's since to Osborne been
And paid a visit to the Queen;
From her a portrait grateful took
And wrote her name in Royal book.

Give consolation, Lord, we pray,
To all bereaved by this dark day:
Bind up their riven hearts O Lord,
With the sweet promise of Thy word.

February 4th, 1895.

A SWANAGE LIFEBOAT DISASTER.

Brave William Brown, thy honored name,
If marble stone spread not thy fame,
Yet those heroic deeds of thine
We will in our hearts love enshrine.

Our simple words shall tell the deed,
Of how he helped in time of need;
For many years he sought to save
The seamen from a watery grave.

For fifteen years as coxswain bold,
In Lifeboat service he grew old;
Last Saturday when storm raged high,
He did not think his end was nigh.

But there on duty was he found
While storm and billows raged around,
Full bent on saving lives again,
In spite of winds and bitter rain.

The "Norway Brilliant" was, they found,
Then fast upon the Hook sands bound,
And signals flashing in the air,
Invite the crew to do and dare.

Brown with his crew had braved and been
In fiercest storms that men had seen,
And many a one will shed a tear,
Whom they have saved while death was near.

The Swanage boat met well the wave
When all at once the crew so brave,
Were turned beneath the water cold,
And sudden death faced young and old.

The boat soon righted to again,
And they with horror and with pain
Found two were struggling far away,
And sinking in the twilight grey.

They rescued Smith from out the deep,
But Brown was lost in billows steep
Some hundred yards beyond their reach,
Was drowned, unselfish life to teach.

Yet still, if building on the rock,
Our death comes not with such a shock,
We trust dear Brown, safe from alarm,
In Heaven with Christ is safe from harm.

The crew deserves the best of praise,
And it shall have in these our lays,
To dangers oft exposed they are,
Preserve them Lord, with Thy great care.

Brown's wife and children, seven, O Lord!
Help Thou according to Thy word.
Thou art the helpless widows' stay.
And orphans' guide from day to day.

Success to efforts now put down
By Bournemouth and by Swanage Town,
May many give their money's aid,
To cheer the one a widow made.

21st January, 1895.

A DISTRESSING BOATING FATALITY AT POOLE.

On Monday, 6th May, a distressing boat disaster occured at Poole, by which two young ladies came to an untimely end, namely, Louie Moore and Florrie Burt. Two young men, Arthur Moore (brother of the former), and William Oakley, had hired a boat for a ride to Wareham Chapel. The boat having a small sail they hoisted it and went pleasantly and safely for a time, when a gust of wind caused the boat to shake, and the young ladies being frightened clutching the side of the boat caused it to capsize, and all four were thrown into the water. Florrie Burt sank no more to rise, while Arthur Moore, with heroic valor held up his sister for awhile, until at last his strength exhausted he had to let her go, and both young Moore and Oakley swam some distance to the muddy shore.

Monday was one of the most delightful days we have been having this last fortnight, and the placid Bay of Poole seemed without a ripple, while the sun shone with brilliance. Such were the settings and surroundings of this pleasure party.

All were residents of Poole, and the deceased ladies were much respected. Miss Moore was to have been married in a month, and Miss Burt was to have sung on the following evening at a concert at Poole, for some charitable purpose, as she was a very popular singer and always ready to give her services to any good philanthropic work. They also both were Sunday School Teachers connected with the Church of England, and on the previous Sunday had both been present at the Lord's Table. The late Miss Moore leaves a widowed mother with the brother, to mourn her irreparable loss, while the late Miss F. Burt leaves an elder sister whom she had lived with. We are sorry to say up to this date the bodies of neither of the beloved deceased have been found.

That the Lord may graciously support them all in this their dire calamity is our earnest prayer. The following lines have been penned on the above by JOSEPH GWYER, May 10th, 1895 :—

In ninty-five, the sixth of May,
Such gloomy tidings sped the way,
Spread over Poole's old honored town,
Described by verses here put down.
Two gentlemen, two ladies fair,
Went out in pleasure-boat down there ;
A radiant day, the morning bright,
The sun shone forth with brilliant light ;
Their cheerful hearts with happy glee,
Expected happiness to see ;
One lady in the boat who came
Expected soon to change her name,
In only four weeks from this hour,
Anticipated marriage dower ;
While other on the following night,
At concert down to sing so bright,
So sweet and musical, her voice,
Made all who heard it to rejoice.
In works benevolent and good
Deceased were both we've understood ;
Their hearts by faith, united to
Their Saviour whom they loved so true.
Both teachers in the Sunday School,
The church to love was both their rule.
On Sunday, too, the previous day,
We heard down there upon our way,
The sacramental cup they took,
A privilege great scarce e'er forsook.
They little thought when taking it,
In Heaven with Christ so soon to sit ;
How oft doth life its changes bring,
Of many a pleasured earthly thing ;
How true the precious book doth say
Boast not thyself of future day,
"In such an hour as ye think not",

Grim death hath oft our loved ones sought.
The widowed mother, Lord, to-day,
Bind up her riven heart we pray,
With sister, brother, sweetheart, too,
Each one so sad, their love ran true,
Give benediction from above
Strengthen them all with Thy great love,
Though now they're blinded with their tears,
Let Thy sustaining grace be their's.
Within their wounds pour Gilead's balm :
Lord, sooth the tempest into calm ;
May these sad deaths a warning be
Of boats so small which sail on sea,
They never ought to be allowed
To bring about death's darkened cloud.

THE SOLENT DISASTER.

Lines upon the death of Eight brave sailors, who were killed by the bursting of a torpedo shell used in blowing up a wreck at the Brambles, near West Cowes, Isle of Wight, six of whom left widows and many little children to mourn their loss.

Eight valiant sailors, true and brave,
Lately were carried to their grave :
The shocking news had spread around
How suddenly their death they found.

Such scientific warfare's power
Should safely guarded be each hour,
These deadly weapons dang'rous are,
Requiring the most earnest care.

Yet accidents oft meet our way
When least expected their display.
No human forethought can prevent
When death most certain arrows sent.

We stand aghast when life is lost,
No treasured wealth can pay its cost,
Life's fragile plant in weakly form
Is lost alike in calm and storm.

Yet still for future guidance we
Would ever well directed be,
To turn on Caution's safety light,
And thus be always in the right.

We will not chide for well we know
How erring mortals are below,
But still on science this our thought
More cautious methods should be taught.

In deepest sympathy we mourn
For wives with husbands from them torn!
Give comfort, Lord, to them we pray,
In this their dark bereavement day.

The orphans, too, we pray thee bless,
Kind Shepherd these dear lambs caress,
The widow and the orphan, Lord,
Are promised blessing in Thy word.

When with our wealth and gold we part,
In helping others with good heart,
When widowed poor our gifts receive,
In such a test we do believe.

For Christ hath said in His blest word,
By this we show we love the Lord,
If we to orphans give in love
We then resemble Christ above.

At Osborne late a touching scene,
Took place in presence of the Queen,
Who helped and cheered the widow's there,
And of her purse gave them a share.

The purse of our most gracious Queen
Open once more to need is seen,
Her queenly tender mother love
In pitying sympathy does move.

Rich and poor alike have given
With generous gifts they both hath striven
To earn a place within these lays,
And widows tearful thanks always,

August 12th, 1894.

THE STOCKWELL ORPHANAGE.

God bless we pray, the Orphan Home,
And all the children there who come;
For Stockwell Orphanage has won
Our high esteem for what its done.

The orphan has our tend'rest care,
And loving tribute all will bear,
Upon all hearts, in every place,
Especially those renewed by grace.

For Jesus once, though now above,
(His heart was always full of love),
Said "Feed my lambs," and we obey
His royal mandate every way.

In tender years they've lost a friend,
Whose love their wants did e'er attend,
And as they now are orphans here,
We'll tend their wants with greatest care.

The lady, too, whose worth is known,
And highly in our verse we own,
Who left the sum to start to build;
When soon with orphans it was filled.

Has now gone home to meet her Lord,
And hear from Him the gracious Word;
But still her memory's cherished here,
Who helped to dry the widow's tear.

We'll mention one beloved by all,
In every circle where we call,
Whose deeds of love and works abound,
Encircling all the world around.

Mr. Spurgeon has won esteem,
As President we all have seen
Although at times he suffers so,
Our prayers for him to heaven shall go.

That he may be restored to health,
And long may live in love and wealth,
To preach the gospel to the poor,
And all who need its gracious store.

The Master has our warmest thanks,
From rich and poor, from all the ranks,
For Mr. Charlesworth's name is spread
In deeds of kindness o'er their head.

He also teaches them to sing,
And this a large amount doth bring;
Those little books he writes as well,
Such touching narratives they tell.

He also teaches them the way
To shun the evil of the day:
And if their hearts are drawn by grace,
'Twill lead them then to Jesu's face.

Now, Lord be pleased to bless, we pray,
And lead them all in Thy good way:
That they in youth may call on Thee,
And Thy salvation may they see.

Those who subscribe, yea all who give,
May they be blest, and long may live;
And thousand more, in every stage,
We know will help the Orphanage.

May 28th, 1881.

The following is one of many letters received by the Author, who who has collected altogether about £40 for the Orphanage:—

Westwood, Beulah Hill, Upper Norwood,
June 8th, 1881.

Dear Mr. Gwyer,

I thank you heartily, and all your Subscribers also. You are a faithful servant of our blessed Lord, for you turn your talents constantly to the best account.

The cheque received with many thanks.

Yours heartily,
C. H. SPURGEON.

ON THE ILLNESS OF THE REV. C. H. SPURGEON.

Dear Spurgeon now is very ill,
And at the point of death lies still,
That fertile brain, that power of will
Lies postrate now on Beulah Hill.

Kind watchers round the good man's bed,
Oft gently raise his drooping head,
His own dear wife's soft heart has bled,
While him with nourishment she's fed.

Our prayers to God alternate rise,
For He is gracious, good, and wise;
That if His will, our friend arise,
Though now so weak and low he lies.

Our friend so sick, we all love him,
Like her who touched the Saviour's hem;
We plead Christ's merits full to brim,
His healing virtues never dim.

Thou art, good Lord, our Father, Thou
Cast heal, though to Thy will we bow,
Yet wilt Thou not our prayer allow,
For Jesus sake restore him now.

Though doctors medicine and art
With all their skill is kind and smart;
Great healer do Thy skill impart
And keep his faintly beating heart.

Yes all the prayers sent up to Thee,
On golden file Thy Son shall see;
He pleads for His own saints that we
The answer to our prayers may see.

May he again soon preach the word,
Who we in times gone by, have heard
His eloquence no more deterred,
While we again our loins do gird.

May his beloved wife we pray
Have grace sufficient for this day;
His sons be comforted and stay,
Surrounded by Thy love's bright ray.

As Thou wast wont in days gone by
To scatter blessings far and nigh,
So now on Jesus we rely,
And leave all to His wisdom high.

Nor shall we ever ask in vain,
For Thou dost never give us pain,
Unless Thy will should it ordain,
And then a blessing 'twill contain.

July 14th, 1891.

THE LATE REV. C. H. SPURGEON.

Perhaps it would be interesting to some of my readers to hear of a conversation which took place a short time ago between myself and the Rev. John Rodger, Presbyterian Minister, of Bournemouth, which shews the wonderful memory of the late Rev. C. H. Spurgeon. This minister, with one of the church elders accosted me thus one day in Old Christchurch Road, Bournemouth. "Mr. Gwyer, how do you do." I replied, "very well thank you Sir, but I have not the pleasure of remembering you?" "My name is Rodgers," he said. "The Presbyterian Minister" I said. He said, "Yes." "But how do you know me," said I. "I know you by your writings," answered he, "I want to see you at my manse to-night, can you come up?" I said, "if possible I will." I went as promised, and we had a very pleasant talk together for more than an hour. He told me amongst other things of his meeting with Rev. C. H. Spurgeon, at Mentone, some years ago, and how he had induced his doctor to go and hear Mr. Spurgeon preach in a room of the hotel. The doctor was a German, and a very clever man, and author of several medical works, but was sceptical in his views on religion.

With me Mr. Rodgers said, he seemed to turned everything serious into ridicule, but he like all of us fell under the spell of Spurgeon's sermon, which was on the subject of the "One Faith." I saw he was deeply impressed and felt afraid to disturb the serious thought that his countenance gave witness of, yet I asked him when leaving, 'What do you think of the preacher?' He said, 'I thought he ought to have four tongues, to tell his message to the North, East, South and West, so that all may hear the news.' I cannot say positively that this sermon was the means of the doctor's conversion, but I have every reason to believe it was the beginning of better things in him."

Mr. Rodger told me another incident which remarkably illustrates the tenacity of Mr. Spurgeon's memory. He met him with Rev. Vernon Charlesworth on the cliff at Bournemouth, leaning on his arm as he was ill at the time. Mr. Rodger said he went behind Spurgeon and touched his shoulder; he looked round and bethought himself and said, "You canny Scotsman, Mr. Rodger," although he had not seen him for ten years, and that at a mere holiday meeting at Mentone. Mr. Spurgeon went up in the afternoon to his manse and had a pleasant hour with him and his family.

I can hardly leave this subject without a passing reference to Mr. Spurgeon's death, which sad event occured at Mentone on January 31st, 1892, and his burial which took place on February 11th, at Norwood Cemetery, London, although so much has been written for the Christian public about these events.

Never will the scene be erased from the memory of any of us who witnessed this funeral. The large number of carriages, and the great crowds which lined the road from the Metropolitan Tabernacle to the Cemetery at Norwood, and the impressive funeral service conducted by the Revs. Archibald G. Brown, of the East London Tabernacle, and A. T. Pierson, D.D., the Bishop of Rochester (Dr. Randall Davidson), closing with the Benediction.

Last summer I paid a visit to his tomb, which is a splendid one of granite and marble, with a life-like medallion protrait. As there was no one about, I knelt by the side of the tomb and asked the Lord to enable me by His grace to live such a life as he would have had me live. Whoever may read this, I advise, whenever opportunity occurs, at least once to visit this sacred spot where all that is mortal of our late dear friend is interred.

IN MEMORIAM REV. C. H. SPURGEON,

Born June 19th, 1834, at Kelvedon, Essex; Fell asleep in Jesus at Mentone, January 31st, 1892.

Our friend, safe landed on the shore
With storms and tempests never more,
Has heard his Master's word "Well done,"
His crown of glory now is won.

What must it be to hear Him speak,
Who ne'er a bruised reed did break,
To gaze into his Saviour's face
And drink of His unbounded grace.

Acclaiming angel throngs now raise,
Their jubilant notes of holy praise;
In bright array before His Throne
Presenting Jesus' loved one home.

Redeemed souls take up the strain,
And send the echo back again;
Their Hallelujah's loud proclaim
Hosannas to His mighty name.

Jewels, which in his crown appear,
Shining like diamonds bright and clear,
Which he was here the means to win
From Satan's slavery of sin.

The latest words he spake while here,
Were to his friends who waited near;
"The good fight I have fought, and I
Have kept the faith till now I die."

Without a pang of pain, or fear,
He found the banks of Jordan near,
His happy spirit took its flight,
To regions of Immortal light.

To Mrs. Spurgeon here we send
The tender sympathy of a friend,
Her heart with this bereavement sore
Be stayed on God for evermore.

The Lord sends nought to us but good,
Oft bitters make our sweetest food,
Her faith be strong, her hope be bright,
While walking through this darksome night.

Her "Book Fund" started years ago,
Has Pastors often cheered we know,
May friends still aid this cause to-day,
And well support it—this we pray.

Be Thou to her a husband, Lord ;
And to her noble sons afford
Great strength of heart, we humbly pray,
And grace that's equal to their day.

The aged father left to mourn,
The loss of him, his son first-born :
At eventide to him be light,
As heavenly objects charm his sight.

To his brother and sisters left,
And all the dear ones now bereft ;
May consolation come alway,
From Thy rich stores of grace each day.

Now John Ploughman's work is done,
Where shall we find so strong a one,
And yet the cause is God's, and He
His Joshua soon will let us see.

For all his goodly works we pray
May liberal hearts be moved alway ;
The Orphans find God's people still,
Will guard them in this world of ill.

Their leader's gone, each Christian more,
Must toil to fill God's garner store ;
The Church is in great trial Lord
Thy guiding hand to them afford.

And when our race on earth is run,
May we too hear His word "Well Done,"
And then on Canaan's happy shore,
Our friends shall meet to part no more.

February 4th, 1892.

AN OLD HORSE SHOE.

While at Bournemouth for a stay,
In ninety-five, on fourth of May,
The dazzling sun on steel shone bright,
An old horse shoe gave me delight;
Its diamond brightness in my eyes,
Showed me a treasure of surprise,
Truth 'twas only iron and steel
With five old nails that one could feel.
I saw in it good luck and worth,
Of precious ore dug from the earth;
But who conceived this old horse shoe,
Would bring me treasured honors true.
Yet such we oft in life have found,
Rich treasures at our feet abound,
To bring us wealth if tact we had
To gather them and make us glad.
So I to my dear friend R. White
Gave this old shoe with great delight,
And wrote within its curious tread,
The following rhyme which perhaps you've read.
"I've found on road an old horse shoe
And brought the present, White, to you;
Good luck to you I hope 'twill bring,
And make your good wife sweetly sing."
If you the pleasure wish to quiz it,
Pay Shaftesbury Temperance House a visit,
If some there be who do not know it,
The giver's name is the Penge Poet.
So when at Bournemouth for a stay,
Call at the Shaftesbury on your way;
Hung in the dining room the shoe,
A welcome warm to Bournemouth too.
Where I for years have found a home
When oft to Bournemouth I have come.
My gift is very poor I know,
This old horse shoe and rhyme I show;
But let this gift remind us all
To quickly heed affection's call,
That you in kindness ne'er may tire,
Is here the wish of old friend Gwyer.

THE RAILWAY DOG "HELP" *(See Page 209)*.

As magnets draw the steel things near,
An offered gift I give you here,
For every four books sold for me,
An extra one I'll give to thee.

THE RAILWAY DOG "HELP" AT BRIGHTON STATION.

The railway dog named "Help" is dead,
With deepest grief have many read,
This noble canine Help you see,
Collects for railway orphans he.
One thousand pounds collected sure,
And though now dead collecting more;
For nine long years, "Help" spent his time,
On Britain's varied railway line.
This gallant dog died at his post,
And in the service his life lost,
So may we learn to bless and aid,
Like "Help," the widow and orphan made;
This epitaph be ours when gone,
He cheered the orphan sad and lorn;
So may we live like "Help," to bless
The widow and the fatherless.

PLEASANT REMINISCENCES OF THE ISLE OF WIGHT,

While travelling through it in July, 1892.

While through the Isle of Wight we roam
We find a home away from home,
Most kind respect we have from all,
From everyone where'er we call;
In cot or castle, mansion too,
Yes everyone is kind and true.
Its hills and dales—bold, rugged scene—
Have charmed us much wherever seen;
The cows are grazing in the mead,
The sheep are bleating as they feed,
The horses prance with sportive play
In pastures' sunny holiday.

The hen with their large broods we see,
The clucking mother's ectasy.
From speeding train we see the sight:
The quick-gone bunnies' tails are white.
Wild pigeons in the peas we see,
Look happy as can ever be.
The rip'ning corn on vale and hill
All garners soon will richly fill,
Both man and beast our God supplies,
For his rich mercy never dies.
And fruit of every sort we find,
A luxury for all mankind;
Vegetables how well they grow
To satisfy man's wants below.
Potatoes, too, a floury sort,
We much enjoyed as we took part.
Apples and pears they stud the trees,
And flowers are sucked by busy bees,
And birds they warble in the wood,
And larks on high sing God is good.
The landscape with green trees adorn,
And hills smile back the rosy morn,
The beans entwining round the stick,
And children playing pretty tricks.
Shanklin is our favourite spot,
And if a fortune had been our lot,
A house we'd build and make our home,
To end remaining days that come.
Sandown, too, and Ventnor mild
In wintry cold would suit this child.
To Carisbrooke we went one day,
Though short our visit there to stay;
The Castle put reflection's thought,
And lessons useful us it taught.
King Charles was once imprisoned there,
His face was wet by many a tear;
"Uneasy he who wears a crown,"
Could then with truth be written down.
His daughter, too, a child of grace,
Died in a room in this dark place,
A monument most costly, rare,
Of the young Princess, very fair,

Put there by our Most Gracious Queen—
In Newport Church may now be seen;
Her head reclining on the book,
The Bible blest she, ne'er forsook;
Her happy spirit borne above,
While pondering o'er the Saviour's love.
As Elizabeth so let me die,
Resting on Thy Word, feel Thee nigh;
Hear Thy blest Voice in tender word,
"Enter the joy of Thy blest Lord."
And all the tourists take a pride
In lovely, hilly, blooming Ryde;
The breezy, open promenade,
The finest in the Island made;
The air salubrious, bracing, kind,
All those who visit it will find.
A warning now I give to you,
Spend one penny instead of two;
A weekly ticket of seven-and-six
Will stop the Railway's little tricks,
For by the week you'll find you'll pay,
But little more than cost per day.
Then hie away to Curtis true
For ticket and for guidance too.
His famous dog then ask to see,
Enquire his noble history;
And hear a deed that once he did,
That does the acts of men outbid;
He saved a little seven-years' child
From drowning in the waters wild:
The story and each portrait clear
In the *Animals World* appear.
At Arreton, too, we took a glance,
Which made our hearts with joy to dance.
The Dairyman's Daughter there did go,
As all our readers sure must know,
But should you not, buy soon the book,
And in its pages quickly look.
She went to show her frock so grand,
As proud as any in the land,
But God met her in love and grace,
She sought and found the Saviour's face.

Leigh Richmond good the book did write;
T'has brightened homes as dark as night.
When loving couples kiss and sigh
No doubt they like the hedges high,
But when the landscape I would see
I wish they were cut down for me;
And you would find, O farmer bold,
It would increase your store of gold,
For shading hedges spoil the crop,
So, out with hook, and quickly lop.
The hedges, though, are beautiful
With ferns and flowerets sweet and full,
With honeysuckle, hop and tare,
All join to make the Island fair.
One day to Freshwater we went,
Determined we were, fully bent
Tennyson's residence to see,
We so admire his history.
We were informed he was away
At Haslemere for a short stay.
If we could take a glance at him,
He would our admiration win;
We much should like to speak a word
To him we read and much have heard.
O Tennyson with thy great fame
That ever followeth thy name,
Thy eventide be light to thee
And blessings crown thy memory.
Upon thy brow, with hoary hair,
May God watch o'er thee with great care;
And when thy earthly race is won
Be thine to hear Christ's word "well done,"
And when through grace we meet above
We'll talk together of His love.
We scarce could leave the Island home
Where oft our Queen beloved does come,
And, therefore, down to Cowes we went,
For oft upon her track we're bent.
So we took train, went down to see
The Queen land then upon the Quay—
But our opinion of the town
Was not enhanced by rain poured down.

It is proverbial, so it says,
The Queen fine weather has most days.
Her loyal subjects waited long
Without a murmur 'mid the throng,
And though the rain came down in showers
We waiting spent two happy hours.
Her pleasant face looked calm and bright,
The knows God's dealings with her's right.
We pray God bless our Gracious Queen,
Although in deep bereavement been;
Bind up her wounded heart, we pray,
With Thy rich comforts every way.
The Prince of Wales and Princess, Lord,
Give all, we pray, a cheering word,
And though their hearts were riven sad,
Thy grace can heal and make them glad.

LINES PENNED ON VIEWING THE GRAVE OF "OLD HUMPHREY," 5th APRIL, 1895, IN ALL SAINTS CHURCHYARD, OLD TOWN, HASTINGS.

When there a visit will repay.

" Old Humphrey," thy pen is still, thy voice is heard
In all the printed volumes of thy word,
Beneath this stone lies now thy mouldering clay;
But thy happy spirit's in Heaven's eternal day.
Thou didst while here no plea or merit claim,
But sought for mercy only through Jesus' name;
Who pardoned thee in youth, and thy young heart won;
And through grace kept thee, till thy work was done.
So may I live, O Lord, I pray, to cheer the sad,
Warn sinners, comfort saints, and make them glad:
And when like them my chequered life work's past,
Be mine the joy to hear Christ's "well done" at last.

ON FLOWERS.

The following lines were suggested while watching three young Ladies making Wreaths in a Florists Shop, in Broad Street, City.

Flowers are gorgeous, rich and rare,
Their varied perfumes scent the air,
They speak our Father's love, that's sent
In odourous sweetness to us lent.

The fragrant colours of the Rose
Are beautiful where'er it grows:
The Lily tall, and white its flower
Blooms sweetly in the summer hour.
The Honeysuckle and Violet too
So sweet their scent for me and you;
And when along the lane's we've been
Primrose and Buttercups we've seen.
The Daisy peeps its little head:
At early spring it takes the lead,
The Snowdrops too are dressed in white,
Which gives us all such great delight.
Carnations, Dahlias, white their bloom
Though oft are placed beneath the tomb
While Geranium Alexandras tall
Reminds us too of man's great fall.
For soon we bloom and quickly fade
And then we droop into the shade.
Eucharis Asters so white they grow,
Pancretion, their beauteous colour show,
Pelarnonium white stock they
Impart great joy, on life's rough way;
The Lily from Japan's descent,
Like reeds so feeble oft are bent,
Its fragile stem is very weak,
If we relied on it should break;
To man in all his varied moods
Unstable is and oft deludes.
Lilium Candidum blooms so grand,
Sheds forth their beauty o'er the land
While Bouvardias, Tuberoses tower,
And Gardenia blends the sweetest bower.
We've Harrisi Stephenotis now,
With Gladiolus we must bow;
To make fine wreaths, we must have ferns,
Their back edge white to whiter turns.
Now these have all their varied names,
And each our admiration claims;
There's Bracken, Asparagus fine.
The latter eat when oft we dine,
With Andiantum, Carrot Tops,
They ne'er will suit our city fops;

Frenchmen polite we won't leave out,
We see French ferns when we're about,
If this short rhyme we've penned down here,
Should drive from any one dull care;
The Rhymer will get his full reward,
They lose a weight they felt most hard.
Cheer up reader on life's rough way,
May flowers impart a brighter day,
And may God who the Lily paints,
Place you and me among His saints;
And bye and bye through grace have won,
The Master's welcome word "WELL DONE."

11th August, 1891.

LINES WRITTEN WHILST SITTING ON A SEAT, DURING THE ASCENT OF THE CLIFF AT BOURNEMOUTH, MAY, 1895.

Here the infant and the sage,
We both enshrine within our page;
To each a parting word we send,
Life just commenced and that near end.
The child just climbing up the steep
That won't a minute quiet keep,
Will soon be drawn in life's great stream,
And find it not a fancy dream.
The man in trembling green old age,
With tottering limbs near run life's stage,
We hope his looming future bright
Will end in Heaven, where all is light.
What varied kinds of folk we meet,
While resting on the Bournemouth seat.
Here walking up the hilly cliff,
Some find to be a journey stiff,
In wintry garb a young man drest,
A cancer eating at his breast;
Consumption in its saddest form
Shows soon will end life's calm and storm;
Another young man in Bath chair
Was by his sister drawn with care.

We asked, "how does it fare with you,
The nature of his sickness too,"
He gave a smile, and thus said he,
"A cripple from my birth you see;
And other sickness, too, I have,
No medicine can its ravage save,"
"Are you safe anchored on the rock.
That your decease may bring no shock?"
In language firm, he thus replied,
"My hope is fixed on Christ who died.
For nine long years I've known his love
And soon He'll take me home above."
"Your prospect, friend, is clear as light,
Your anchored hope in Heaven is bright.
On Sunday morn, that sacred day,
To Sanatorium we wend our way
To see a friend we know so well;
For sickness had to him befell;
A deacon loved by one and all,
Upon him we were asked to call.
How closely Christian love doth bind,
The Christian brethren of mankind:
Whilst waiting there we gave a word,
And thus the gospel many heard.
These sick ones have the Master's care,
When'er they ask, His help is near;
We told them then of Christ, the friend,
Who will stick to them to the end.
With Mr. Turk, we then did go,
Heard Ossian Davies just below;
His sermon was a seasoned word
To each of us, sent from the Lord.
If it should be God's will we pray,
Give back his health and speed his way,
To cheer his wife and children dear.
We ask Thee, Lord, be very near.

TUNBRIDGE WELLS AND ITS ENVIRONS.

Of lovely Tunbridge Wells we write,
Its scenic beauties give delight,
With hill and vale, and landscapes grand,
As any in our English land,
These trees and shrubs in spring attire,

With vernal joy our hearts inspire:
These varied tinted greens display
True natures charming holiday.
The beech, and may in sweetest flower,
And fruit trees bloom, a garland bower,
Then charmingly from all around,
The feathered songsters notes resound.
The meadows and the fields now say
The glad springtimes with us to-day,
In nature's every pathway trod,
Her realm shows forth the hand of God;
No single thing His power doth lack,
To cheer us on our Heavenward track.
Our Father's artist work we see
In every blade, and flower, and tree.
Some spots are here from scripture named,
"Mount Zion," thus by ancient famed.
In Tunbridge Wells "Mount Ephraim" stands,
And "Calverley's Mount" does grace these lands.
Fine rock and shingle, shrub and fern
Do greet our gaze at every turn,
And mineral water fraught with good,
Cures sick folk too we understood.
You can quaff all you like down there,
Of healing waters rich and rare:
But if your weary head should sink
And need a cool refreshing drink,
Then Bentley's Lemon Squash will suit,
When in a glass of water put:
Their Orange Cordial, too, is rare,
Both can be bought most anywhere,
While Bentley's Relish when you dine,
You'll cherish much, and say its fine.
Now Rusthall Common, here's a treat,
With here and there a cosy seat,
Where you can rest at perfect ease,
Or stroll about just as you please.
Its shingly hills, its fine cliffs too
Command a charming view for you.
Tunbridge Wells "Penge Poet" does say,
Does the most splendid scenes display:
Its wealth of foliage living green,

And rocks magnificent are seen.
Its lovely landscape views are grand,
So rare and beautiful they stand;
Within a rock a house is built,
And not upon the sand or silt;
The open view we do admire,
Much more than closed rock suits Gwyer.
A visit pay to Toad Rock too,
The God of nature's works to view,
Then if the cash you can contrive,
Take walks and pleasant ride or drive:
The country round is charming too,
Its picturesqueness bright and true.
From some a wondrous thought did flash,
That once the rolling sea did dash
Its waves and spray all o'er this place,
They shells and fish in strata trace.
Upon the Pantiles here at night
Most charming music gives delight;
The Ceylon Band through summer play,
In this sweet spot some twice a day,
This band is thought the very best,
Go and hear it, and thus them test.
A personage of Royal face,
This promenade does often grace,
While Bishops, Dukes, and Earls, and Lords,
With homelier folk, and humble bards,
In carriage gay some ride about,
And titled folk make quite a route.
Here shops capacious are, and large,
Their choicest goods at moderate charge.
We hope you'll spend your money there,
You'll get advantage do not fear.
If you an hour or so can spare,
Visit Calverley's grand park fair;
Old trees of ancient date you see,
Beneath whose branches oft had tea,
Our own beloved Queen we heard
As spoken in her mother's word.
At Calverley House they lived, we're told,
A hotel grand, 'tis now so bold.
In Trinity Church, Mount Ephraim near,
The Duchess of Kent had seats we hear,

So when in Tunbridge Wells they've been,
One worshipper was our own Queen.
In Tunbridge Wells are churches grand,
And chapels fine on every hand,
In costly modern style they're built,
Of real worth, and not mere gilt,
The road from Pantiles, half-moon style,
Repays a walk the time to wile,
Broadwater Church is very near,
A pretty walk on day that's clear;
And Eridge Castle you can view,
T'will well reward a stranger too,
'Tis Marquis Avergavenny's seat,
Two miles away, so grand and neat.
To Frant three miles, and little more,
You have a real treat in store.
From highest rocks of nature's make
You may some beauteous photos take.
At Groombridge on the road that way,
The Bell Rock view, while there you stay,
Its history and curious sound,
Make an impression quite profound.
When struck you hear both loud and well
The note as of a deep-toned bell,
So take a carriage trip and pay
A visit glad to Frant one day.
Near Pantiles, too, a quiet place,
The Recreation Park has space,
With cooling water, fish and swan,
And well cut lawns the ground upon.
When jaded dull with summer heat,
You'll find the Cynus Club a treat,
With swiming bath so large and clean,
A distance you can swim within:
A man is there to teach the art,
Of swimming well, and quick, and smart.
One night to the Town Hall we went,
To Temperance Women's meeting bent,
We heard some ladies wiring in
Who did our admiration win.
With eloquence and humorous wit,
These ladies' speeches well did fit;
If members of the "House" had heard
Each lady speaker's burning word,

In Parliament the "Veto Bill"
Would soon have climbed its steepest hill.
One afternoon, we dared, and went
On information always bent,
To see some ladies cooking food,
And hear a lecture on it good;
Now young folk learn this happy art
Of cooking dishes nice and smart,
This should be learned as well as play,
Quadrilles and music any day.
Thus have we spun a yarn to you,
We leave with you the right to do,
We crave your pardon for the time
You've spent perusing our poor rhyme.

27th May, 1895.

CONTENTMENT AND RESIGNATION.

While through this chequere l world we stray,
Teach us, O Lord, in Thy good way
In prayer and faith to walk;
If trials in our pathway rise,
To make us question Thou art wise,
Then of God's love we'll talk.

For oft the joys of earth are found,
Like cords to bind our souls around,
Our heavenly glow to damp:
Sweet ties of sacred greeting show
To aid Thy saints while here below,
This will our kinship stamp.

Some earthly flowers so sweetly bloom,
But they remind us of our tomb;
So soon they fade away.
God loves the paraclete of grace;
Its everlasting bliss shall trace
Through all their heavenly day.

VERSES ON THE SHOCKING BOATING FATALITY,

Three Young Men from Rochester drowned at Yalding, on Whit-Monday, 1895.

On Monday morn, the third of June,
With spirits high in best of tune,
A happy party rode through Kent,

From St. Margaret's Rochester they went.
Miss Wimble and Miss Streatfield had
Their Bible Class to make them glad;
With them arranged a rural treat,
Two brakes with four-in-hand to meet,
From Rochester to Snodland they
Through Malling Town sped on their way.
The hop was climbing up the pole,
And joy o'er their young spirits stole.
The may in flower so sweet was seen,
The shrubs and trees in living green,
The landscape was a picture grand,
Of Kent, Old England's garden land.
The blooming fruit trees did adorn
The scenery, with its fields of corn.
The larks sang sweetest notes on high,
When soaring up, they touched the sky;
While singing birds of humbler lay,
With music charmed them on their way.
From Malling next at Yalding halt,
And none with them could find a fault;
The horses trotted on so well,
And happiness to each befell.
All at Yalding needed then
Refreshments, both for horse and men.
And all as happy as could be
Within the Institute took tea.
These ladies worked with heart and will,
For love to Christ their hearts did fill,
They cherished much their class we know
As all their loving deeds do show.
Nor will we leave the Curates out,
Both Ayres and Lewis on the route,
For through the day all eyes had seen
Their kindly chivalry and mien.
Alas! the sweetly calm is oft,
More treacherous than the storm aloft,
Speeding on its course so clear
The river's waters glided near.
Attracted these young hearts to cleave,
Alas! the verse we scarce can weave
For chokings in our throat appear

And from our eyes the falling tear;
What strange contrasting fate they greet,
Amid their joy three deaths to meet.
These dear young folk two boats got there,
And up the river rowed with care,
When all at once an accident
Capsized one boat, and down they went.
We scarcely could the truth believe,
Three dear young men were drowned that eve
In river without a ripple,
Young men Bennett, Kemp, and Tipple.
Here we enshrine young Buckitt's deed,
Who risked his life in time of need,
To save his comrade Tipple there.
We praise him that he did so dare,
Both curates on the scene too late,
Yet did their best with bravery great,
Within our verse we will give birth,
To praises of their real worth.
In hopes to save them all alive,
Into the river quick they dive;
Alas! this was to them denied,
We write their loving valour wide.
To the bereaved, O Lord, now send,
With grace their broken hearts attend,
Thy healing balm to them apply,
Assuage the groaning tear and sigh,
To all the friends now wrung with grief,
Give Thou a sweet and calm relief.
To those dear ladies kindly give
Consoling grace that they may live,
For we know well the bitter smart
This sad event strikes to their heart.
The curates and the vicar too,
To each Lord give Thy blessing true,
May this event though sad the tale,
To all be warning not to fail.

JAMES TAYLOR, THE GIPSY (*See Page* 223).

JAMES TAYLOR, THE GIPSY.

The subject of this narrative was born at Rushbrook, near Bury St. Edmunds, in a gipsy tent, surrounded by all the evil influences and hardships to which this wandering class are exposed. His father and mother were gipsies, and James Taylor of whom we write, followed for many years their usual course of life. He had a brother and two sisters. His father died of small-pox when James was only a month old, so that his poor mother was left to struggle and provide for her children the best way she could, and they were often greatly pinched by poverty and anxiety. Those were the so-called good old times; good forsooth in what, save ignorance, poverty and vice, especially among the working classes, with all wages much lower than at present, and all kinds of provisions at fabulous prices, bread three times as dear as now, meat much dearer, tea such a luxury that few could indulge in it, six, seven, and eight shillings a pound, while sugar fetched about 6d. per lb., and clothing and everything of that nature was at an equally dear rate.

Thus those in constant work were only just able to keep body and soul together. There was no free education as now. In such a time, amid such circumstances, James grew to take part in the actions of life, in the greatest poverty, and exposed to all the influences of evil to which his race and craft were exposed, with no father to check his downward course. It is but little surprising that the seeds of sin sown in such a hot-bed of vice soon grew to a rampant harvest.

It may be profitable to follow his history through boyhood and youth up to manhood. He heard scarcely a sentence without oaths and curses; the Bible was unknown to him as he can neither read nor write, and, in his own language, if he could he should never have thought that gipsies had any right to its blessed truths and sweet experiences which he has now known upwards of twenty-three years to be his happy lot, through "repentance towards God and faith in our Lord Jesus Christ." Is not this a "brand plucked from the burning." Oh how erroneous are some of our views respecting the recipiants of "the glorious gospel of the blessed God," for does He not say, "I came not to call the righteous, but sinners to repentance; they that are whole need not a physician, but they that are sick, I came to seek and to save that which was lost."

James Taylor grew up in vice and drunkenness, and at an early age was an inmate of a jail, doing several months at different times for breaking the law. Now came the time when this vessel of God's distinguishing grace and mercy was brought to His feet, that love and grace shining resplendant in the conversion of this jewel for the Master's crown.

James was brought to the foot of the Cross in deep penitence and humble faith in Jesus Christ as his only Saviour and friend. We cannot do better than let him tell us in his own words, which his daughter has written down at his dictation for our guidance in this biographical sketch.

We may say that after hearing him speak at open air meetings in Stratford High Street, to large crowds, in connection with the Stratford "Mizpah Band," on Sunday mornings during the last summer, 1894, and previous year, 1893, we were led to have a quiet chat with him and thought that the simple annals of his life would make an interesting pivot to hang a few thoughts upon, which may, by the Holy Spirit's working, be the means of arresting and converting some who are still in the same blindness, ignorance, drunkenness and sin, which for years was the position of James Taylor. His deliverance from the power of sin and Satan came about in the following way :—

Some twenty-three years ago, three brother gipsies, Smith Brothers, who since have been made most useful companions of James, got savingly converted to God and induced him to go and hear that honored servant of God preach the gospel, Mr. Henry Varley. A revival broke out amongst the gipsies at Ilford, in Essex, and James and many others were converted to God, and now he sings with joy—

> "O, happy day, that fixed my choice,
> On Thee my Saviour and my God ;
> Well may this glowing heart rejoice,
> And tell its raptures all abroad."

For twenty-three years he has been made a power for much good, and many will deck his crown of rejoicing in that day when Christ cometh to number up His jewels. He commenced testifying directly after his conversion and has continued doing so ever since.

He soon abandoned the gipsy life, coming to live in Stratford, joining eleven years ago in the work which is now carried on at the Conference Hall, the "Mizpah Band," that hive of zealous workers in the Master's vineyard. They hold several large meetings during the summer months on Sunday mornings and evenings, and on week nights in various places in the open air, and many listen to the gospel and are led by their instrumentality to receive the blessed message of salvation, and many a home has reason to thank God for these services.

Here James Taylor has worked these long years in faith, prayer, and zeal, as well as preaching and testifying in the lodging-houses and Mission Halls. Visiting race-courses and hop gardens of Kent, his voice has often been heard lifting the Standard of the Cross.

He has been many years an engine-driver in a Canning Town factory, and is much respected by his employés, so he is like Paul who worked as a tent maker while he preached the Word of God. We have often seen the crowd shedding tears while listening to the simple but true story of his conversion. His life with such an ungarnished sanctified testimony cannot but be owned of God to the salvation of many sinners.

He is now fifty-five years of age, and it is the earnest prayer of all who know him, that his life may long be spared to still further do the Master's service. We could enlarge the story of his life's work even to a book, but fearing that would not perhaps attain the ends of a small pamphlet we have withholden, but after reading this, let no one despair of God's mercy, who hath said, "I have no pleasure in the death of the wicked."—EZEK. xxxiii., 11: and "Whosoever shall call on the name of the Lord shall be saved."—ACTS ii., 21. "Him that cometh unto Me I will in no wise cast out."—JOHN vi., 37.

Let none who read this narrative think that because they have not gone to the same length in sin as James Taylor, they do not require the same change, and think they are not so bad as he was: but remember we are all judged according to the light we have. Christ's own words were more scathing to the Pharisees than they were to those who were sinners and knew it. Remember all must have the new birth, which Jesus told to Nicodemus; all need Conversion. "Ye must be born again."

We will now close this sketch with Taylor's own words, written by his daughter at his dictation.

"My name is James Taylor, born at Rushbrook in a gipsy tent, near Bury-St.Edmunds, Suffolk. My father's name was William Taylor, and my mother's maiden name was Sarah Robinson. Shortly after my birth my father was taken ill, and it turned out to be smallpox, and when I was a month old my father died and left my mother a widow with four children, two girls and two boys; the eldest boy's name John, the youngest mine, James; the eldest sister Providence, the youngest sister Matilda. My father was buried in Lavenham Churchyard, Suffolk, so my mother had to get a living the best way she could for her four children, so we were brought up in travelling the country from place to place, by selling a few things that we used to make. The same as most gipsies we never had any schooling nor yet knew the teachings of Christ.

Whilst we were young we were under our mother's care, but after time went along we grew up to be men and women, and my two sisters and my brother got married and left me home with mother. I very soon grew up to manhood, I became careless, did not care for myself nor yet for anyone else, so of course I ran into sin and got locked up different times in my life, and used to grieve my poor old mother very much. So at last I got married to a gipsy girl, whose maiden name was Naomi Buckley, and after her conversion, which took place a short time before mine. Since our conversion we have both lived a most happy life. The result have been ten children, five of whom are married. We pray that all of them may through sovereign grace be one day savingly converted to God, and we live very sociable together. The Lord in His infinite mercy worked in the hearts of sinners, and my wife first called on the Lord to save her. Of course He is always ready to hear the cry of any repentant, and a few days afterwards I went to hear a man of God preach, Henry Varley, became convinced of sin and sought and found the Saviour.

In the first year of my marriage I got into trouble and had three months at Norwich Castle. After I came out I was just as bad after a time as ever, and I felt unrest, I wanted to find pleasure but I could not find any, and I came to London thinking of going to Kent for hoppicking, and I fell in at Ilford with three converted gipsy brothers, Smith Brothers, the honored evangelists."

VERSES ON JAMES TAYLOR, BORN IN A GIPSY TENT IN SUFFOLK.

The grace that won the Gipsy's heart,
  Or cords of love that drew,
Is efficacious still to show
  God's love to me and you.

If we, in penitential grief,
  Confess our sins to Him,
And plead for pardon through Christ's blood,
  He cleanses us from sin.

If a poor drunkard dyed in sin,
  Is tempted here to say:
This can't mean me, I've gone too far,
  Come back to Christ we pray.

He said, "I cast none out who come
  In penitence to Me:
Though your sins be as scarlet red,
  I'll cleanse and pardon thee."

Though perhaps not gone like these so far,
  All wander from the fold.
God's sovereign grace is strong to draw,
  The Bible has us told.

Dear Jesus may Thy Spirit bring
  Some hearts to love Thee, through
The reading of this narrative,
  May there be not a few.

James' loving wife we can't leave out,
  Who took the lead to pray:
Although we have not seen her yet;
  The Lord bless her alway.

May all their children, ten, be saved
  Through sovereign grace and love;
And after all their sorrows here,
  All meet in Heaven above.

30th November, 1894.

N.B.—James Taylor, the Gipsy, can be had in Tract form for distribution, as also the Victoria Disaster, and Biographical sketch of Tipple by applying to writer of same (the author of this book.)

IN MEMORIAM.

A BIOGRAPHICAL SKETCH OF THE LATE ROBERT GEORGE TIPPLE,

Of Grays, Essex. Born 21st December, 1874; Passed away 22nd June, 1893, on board H.M.S. *Victoria*. Also a letter he wrote to his Mother, 14 days before the Disaster, in reply to his Mother's letter informing him of his father's death.

The sad disaster causing the loss of many brave officers and sailors on board H.M.S. *Victoria*, has been depicted in so many papers that it is useless to attempt to convey anything fresh to the tragic scenes already told. Suffice it to say the writer's object is to bring before the public some of the brave, self-denying and heroic deeds of one who, in the humbler walks of life, followed his Lord and Master, buckling on the armour with burning zeal, energy, and fresh grip, being determined to do the right at all hazards, overcoming obstacles arising from the most painful circumstances, through a strength Divinely imparted to him from above—so that he was enabled to "glory in tribulation also, knowing that tribulation worketh patience, and patience experience, and experience hope, and hope maketh not ashamed, because the love of God is shed abroad in our hearts by the Holy Ghost which is given unto us."

It is not ours to make a hero of the departed one, but rather to hope that his deeds are only a sample of those of many more noble tars that found a watery grave in this sad disaster, as well as those of thousands more found in our Army and Navy, and elsewhere, at the present time. Especially to those bereaved parents who have lost their dear sons in H.M.S. *Victoria* do we write now, and whose children suffered the same fate with our friend whose memory we are cherishing, and in whose memories beloved mothers and fathers, brothers and sisters, and relatives, cherish the brightest hopes of their home in heaven, for those who, through grace, "have washed their robes and made them white in the blood of the Lamb." We now tenderly sympathise with them in their deep bereavement and pungent grief, and pray that the Great Healer may bind up their wounds, and pour consolation into their riven hearts. For are we not assured that the deep sympathy of Jesus is with us in the loss of our departed ones? else those significant two words, the shortest in the Bible, would not have been penned, which, at Lazarus' grave, tell us "Jesus wept!"

> "For in every pang that rends the heart
> The Man of Sorrows feels a part;
> He knows what sore temptations mean,
> For He has often felt the same."

Regarding the circumstances of the disaster, it is not our intention to censure or criticise. We are all human, and the best men are liable to err. We know while war exists, and, therefore, the teachings of warfare is necessary, similar events (if not so disastrous) must sometimes be the result. We still think with the lady we have read of, who advertised for a coachman—that the one that kept furthest from the danger was the safest to have, and so, whatever might, under peculiar circumstances, be necessary or expedient in the time of war, would be totally unwise to try when the loss of hundreds of precious lives, as well as a million pounds of the nation's taxes, are at stake, in this, the enlightened and Christian 19th century, when peace and tranquillity, we hope, reign supreme in the hearts and consciences of most men. The court-martial has also acquitted others, so that, we suppose, it is not for us land-lubbers to differ, although we may still be allowed to have our own private thoughts respecting it.

To resume our narrative—R. G. Tipple was born of humble, God-fearing parents, in the little town of Grays, Essex. He was a life-abstainer from intoxicating drinks, and both his parents were also abstainers. He attended the Primitive Methodist Sunday School at Grays. His father was a strict Baptist, although he and his mother often attended the ministry of the Primitive Methodists. We heard from a gentleman, who had known him and his family for eleven years, that his character, before going into the Navy, was Christian, praiseworthy, and most exemplary, he being nurtured in the good way. The seed of God's truth, which liveth and abideth for ever, seems to have germinated and grown in very early life, and, like Timothy, from his youth up he had known the Scriptures, which had made him wise unto salvation; and so he furnishes us with another instance of the Good Book's teaching:—"Train up a child in the way he should go, and when he is old he will not depart from it!"

His letter breathes the aroma of a healthy, consecrated mind, unselfish in the extreme; for while deeply mourning the loss of a beloved and affectionate father, he is tenderly solicitous for his beloved mother in all her struggles in life, with a family of nine (besides himself) depending upon her. At the same time his heart goes out in deepest sympathy with Mr. Hill, who lived next door, aged 70 years, and who had been a consistent Christian for half a century, and a Local Preacher among the Primitive Methodists for nearly the same time (and who, by-the-by, speaks in highest terms of the affection and love of the whole of the Tipple family). Mr. Hill had been unwell, as the letter will describe, and Tipple says he will doubtless soon be with his beloved father in glory in the Heavenly Land. (He is since dead).

Such a letter we doubt but few could write, and he must have had a mind of superior talent, as well as Christian integrity and uprightness, to have penned it, as it was evidently the spontaneous outflow of a devoted, affectionate and Christian heart. Little did he think that such a wide area of readers would shed a tear over the perusal of this loving epistle of a heart full of tenderest love to a devoted, affectionate, bereaved mother. It was not the gushing overflow of a stricken heart alone: here was practical help. "About the half-pay, I am told," he says, "you will be sent another paper"—and again, "Here, mother, I want you to take the one pound a month now; it will help you a little bit, if it will only help with the rent for a good time"—and again, "I have hopes of raising it soon to a little more." The letter is full of texts and props to hang a few thoughts upon. Here is a peep of his inner life:—"He looked pretty well when he bid me good-bye at London Bridge. Little did I think I was looking on his dear old face for the last time on earth; but he has now lost all his trouble and pain, and has left us to enjoy the rest of everlasting peace in the Better Land, where I hope to meet him in some future time. I cannot keep back the tears as I write these lines. It is terribly bitter to lose a good father like ours has been to us." Little did he think that in so short a time—fourteen days at the most—he would also "enjoy the rest of everlasting peace," and his "future time" (so-called) was very short. Perhaps some who will read these lines are thinking, like him, on their "future time," but alas, without his hope. Perhaps life with them, or us, may be very short,

'For dangers stand thick through all the ground
To push us to the tomb.
And fierce diseases wait around
To hurry mortals home."

But, oh! may it be with us, as we doubt not it was with him, that through grace we may have "our loins girt about with truth, having on the breast-plate of righteousness, and our feet shod with the preparation of the Gospel of peace, that we may be able to quench all the fiery darts of the wicked one."

If this should not be our experience, how happy should we be that God has still prolonged for us the brittle thread of life! Then, that His invitations run in this wise:—"Come unto Me, all ye that are weary and are heavy laden, and I will give you rest." "Ho, every one that thirsteth, come ye to the waters, and drink." "I came not to call the righteous, but sinners to repentance." "For the Son of Man is come to seek and to save that which is lost." "For God so loved the world that He gave His only-begotten Son, that whosoever believeth on Him should not perish, but have everlasting life." "For God commendeth His love towards us, in that, while we were yet sinners, Christ died for the ungodly." Cheer up, my fellow-mariner over life's tempestuous sea: in all thy sorrows, trials, temptations and griefs, if thou wilt confess thy sin to thy Heavenly Father, and seek for pardon through faith alone in Jesus, thou wilt find that

Faith in Jesu's blood alone
Can for thy guilty soul atone.

Ask God to give thee repentance—

Repentance unto life bestow,
Through faith in Jesu's blood, to know.

Then sudden death, with thee, as with him, will be sudden glory.

The departed was, as you have read, a life abstainer. His parents were also abstainers for many years. With the temptation of strong drink in the Navy and Army, and elsewhere, with glaring gin-traps, canteens, and such-like, drawing out their poisonous liquors, few such youths would ever have thought of apportioning to their beloved mother £1 a month, hoping to be able shortly to make it more! Here is a noble example of self-denial!

"He dared to be a Daniel,
He dared to stand alone."

Our Bands of Hope are doing an excellent work in training our children in sobriety, and, as the twig is being bent young, we hope that, with God's blessing, our children may be permeated with the Gospel's influence.

Being trained to habits of thrift and industry, if our children are early taught, it may become second nature with them, and then they will only laugh at the taunts and jeers that may be heaped upon them, as we heard one say, the other day, "They may laugh us into hell, but they cannot laugh us out." We pray and hope that all our readers may take a lesson here, as it matters but little what age, rank or position of life we may be in, all who touch the deadly draught of this Upas Tree, sooner or later, if they do not find death in the pot, will find it gives them pangs of sorrow, and be the cause of the most pungent grief to them in some of the walks of their future life, or to their friends. "Touch not, taste not," is the danger flag we hoist, and, from Holy Writ, we would give the warning, "Look not upon the wine," for it will doubtless captivate and drag them down, like it has millions before. There is one redeeming quality—it is a common leveller, as it serves the prince the same as the humblest peasant, should they imbibe much of it.

Young Tipple's life soon ended, and in a most distressing manner, and yet not before his life's work was accomplished, for what could be more heroic than by letter and deed to have the disposition to help his beloved mother! Here comes in the promise, which may seem to us to contradict itself, yet we know it is true, for shall not the Judge of all the earth do right? God had a motive in taking our young friend from the evil to come. The passage we mean is :—"Honour thy father and thy mother, that thy days may be long in the land which the Lord thy God giveth thee." This was a command, as well as a promise, and so we think it is fulfilled, even now, for it is a Heavenly land our deceased friend has entered into, and it will be of long duration, for it will never end: and God's word says, "The memory of the just is blessed, but the name of the wicked shall rot." We were told that at an early age he might be seen on his way with his father to the early Sunday morning prayer meeting, and at the Sunday School he was always in time, and longing to listen to the truths of the Gospel, which came welling up from the heart of his devoted and affectionate teachers Our space forbids us writing more, although we could weave the story of his short life (with his grit and backbone, for he was none of your jelly-fish type of young men) into many pages of foolscap and type, but we are continually reminded our long yarns are not interesting enough. So we will forbear; but we think his acts, his deeds, his life, and last, but not least, his letter enclosed, will show our readers that we have paid no fulsome eulogy to the fragrant memory of this devoted, affectionate son, and Her Majesty's gallant and honoured deceased tar.

We pray that his bereaved mother, his brothers, sisters, relations and friends, who knew him in life, may be comforted by the assurance of knowing that he is now enjoying "his Heavenly everlasting peace,"

"Far from a world of pain and sin,
With Christ eternally shut in,"

and that, with his beloved father—whom he has already greeted on the Heavenly Shore—he will enjoy an everlasting rest of happiness and peace, where he will shed no more "bitter tears," which he so tenderly spoke of as running down his cheeks when penning his epistle; for there will be no sorrow, and "God shall wipe all tears from their eyes," whilst on earth "they are put in His bottle." Let this encourage the tried and tempest tossed saint, "For He knoweth our frame, and remembereth we are dust," and "Like as a father pitieth his children, so the Lord pitieth them that fear Him." Our friend is, therefore, with many more, "Not lost, but gone before," and soon, when the wheels of time shall have run their circle, we shall join him; "For our days are like a vapour, which appeareth for a little while, and then vanisheth away," and "like a weaver's shuttle," and we know how soon, yes, very soon, they glide by.

May the perusal of this simple, unadorned narrative be impressive to every reader, and may sovereign grace

"Teach them to live that they may dread
The grave as little as their bed."

If so, we shall not have written in vain (though imperfectly) this simple, unvarnished narrative of one who, in early life, found Jesus as his Saviour and Friend. That many others may seek Him in a like manner, is the earnest, heartfelt prayer of the writer—for Jesus has said, "I love them that love Me, and those that seek Me early shall find Me," and "I go to prepare a place for you, that where I am, there may ye be also." May this be the happy lot of many, for Jesu's sake.

"Lives of great men all remind us
We can make our lives sublime;
And, departing, leave behind us
Footprints on the sands of time."

COPY OF LETTER.

Thursday Afternoon,
June 8th, 1893.
H.M.S. "VICTORIA,"
WARMARICE.

DARLING MOTHER,

I have received your loving letter this morning, with poor Sarah's. I have been longing for one all this week; I expect it is through being at this out-of-the-way place. I am very glad to hear that you are managing all right with the aid of dear Jack—God bless him. He is worth his weight in gold. Tell him I consider he is acting in a very brave manner.

Dear Mother, it cuts me up very much not to be near poor father when he breathed his last. I am so sorry that Sarah and Fanny were away, too. I know how he must have longed to have seen our faces once again, before he left us for ever, but we must take it for the best.

Dear Mother, the Captain received Fanny's letter safe, and he gave it to our Chaplain. He sent for me to his cabin. I went—he showed me the letter, and spoke to me very nicely indeed. He said he could sympathise with me very much, as he lost his own father when he was about my age. He knows Grays very well, and told me whenever he could do anything for me, he would be very pleased.

Sarah has written me a very nice letter, poor girl. I know she must feel it very acutely, she was such a favourite of father's. Give my very best love to Susan, tell her I am often thinking of her, and I am glad she was fortunate enough to see the last of poor father, and to be at home to give you her great help in your great trouble. Also give my very best love to Jack, Annie, Harry, Albert, and kiss darling little Nellie and Florrie. You must take great care of yourself now, for all our sakes, and do not give way too much; for it will almost break my heart to hear you are in ill-health, for it only makes me wish the more that I was at home by your side to help you on.*

About the half-pay, I am told you will be sent another paper, and it will give you instructions how to go on.

Dear Mother, I will do as you say about leaving the service. I think it is best to let things go on as they are for a time, but you

* Nellie and Florrie are now provided for.

must be sure and keep me acquainted as to the state of things at home. Don't keep anything back, and then I shall really know how you are getting on, and be able to give you the best of my advice.

I am very sorry to hear about Mr. Hills being so queer, poor old chap. I am afraid he won't be long behind poor father. Only to think how father must have borne his pain, and yet never murmured, these last few years; but he looked pretty well when he bid me good-bye at London Bridge. Little did I think I was looking on his dear old face for the last time on earth; but he has now lost all his trouble and pain, and has left us to enjoy the rest of everlasting peace of the Better Land, where I hope to meet him in some future time. I cannot keep back the tears as I write these lines—it is terribly bitter to lose a good father, like ours has been to us; but I must comfort myself with the assurance that I have still got a good loving mother left, I hope, for us for many long years to come.*

Send my best love to our relations. I know you must be grateful to Aunt Ruth, Aunt Rose, and Uncle Kebe. They are proving true friends now, in our time of trouble, as is also everyone who knew us. Thank you very much for the Memoriam Card. It is very nice, and I think that favourite verse of father's is very appropriate.

I think I must draw this letter to a close now, as the time is drawing nigh to do some work. It is a very pretty place we are lying at now—it is in Turkey. I would go ashore, only I don't seem to have any heart now for sight-seeing. We are on the cruise now. We have been to two places, Syracuse and Napplia. I think we sail for Acre next Tuesday. I am getting on all right, and am quite well. Very best love.

I remain, Your affectionate, loving Son,

ROBERT G. TIPPLE.

O. Seamen H.M.S. *Victoria*,
No. 26 Mess (not 16, as you put it),
Malta, or elsewhere.

Write soon, and keep a good heart.

P.S.—Dear Mother, you must excuse me writing to you with white paper, but I cannot get any black-edged on board ship.

---

* His mother is also since dead, only surviving her Husband and Son until the following December, 1893. Verses on her death can be read in this book.

IN MEMORIAM OF ROBERT GEORGE TIPPLE,

Of Grays, Essex. Born 21st December, 1874; Passed away 22nd June, 1893, on Board H.M.S. *Victoria.*

(His Father died five weeks before, and his Mother six months after his death).

Beneath the ever-restless sea,
  My loving son is there,
And hundreds more, whose memory
  To parents' hearts is dear.

For a few days had only passed,
  His father's death was heard;
This o'er his young heart sorrow cast,
  He sent his mother word:

"God bless you, mother dear, just now;
  To Heaven dear Father's gone,
That you shall want I'll not allow
  Now father's work is done.

"For God, dear mother, will provide,
  He's never left us yet;
So we will in Him e'er abide—
  His promise don't forget.

"I saw the Chaplain yesterday,
  Your letter then he read;
He kindly then to me did say,
  'I see your father's dead!

"In youth I lost my father, too,
  And therefore for you feel;
I will do what I can for you,
  And soon your grief will heal.

"I asked him then to portion you,
  My loving mother, dear,
A pound a month I thought would do—
  In London get it there."

In this, our humble lay, you see,
  Though he, with hundreds, more,
Lies sixty fathoms 'neath the sea,
  We praise him evermore.

His loving mother, who's bereft,
  And others loved so dear,
Thou, Lord, the widow's Friend, art left
  For comfort, still, and cheer.

And Thou, dear Lord, wilt never leave
  The widows' cause Thou'lt plead;
Help them this promise to believe,
  The orphan's guide and feed.

THE LOSS OF H.M.S. "VICTORIA."

Can it be true, the tale we've read,
Some hundreds precious seamen dead!
Drowned in the sea, on a bright day,
In waters calm, without a spray!

But such it is, we know it's true;
While war exists these things we rue—
Our ships are handled with such skill
A slight mistake may hundreds kill.

Some statesmen smile, and laugh they may
When war is looming on our way;
Yet still we know the Prince of Peace
Shall haste the time when war shall cease.

If righteousness exalt alone,
What then for warfare can atone?
Whose preparations lead to woe,
And deal out death to make a show.

But, still, we will not furthur chide,
Although our guilt we cannot hide,
Admiral Tryon now is dead—
We cast no slur upon his head.

But yet another word we say:
Such power no single man should sway,
And Markham, like a man of steel,
Should have refused to turn the wheel.

We know the name *Victoria* well,
Though sad the fate the ship befell;
Our Queen beloved (God bless, we pray)
Was deeply touched that awful day.

With heartfelt sorrow now we mourn
For those who from their homes are torn,
Their fathers and their mothers dear,
Sisters and brothers, shed the tear.

Bind up bereaved hearts, O Lord,
Consoling grace send through Thy Word;
Give to them each of Gilead's balm,
And may their future life be calm.

A million precious money lost,
Besides the human gems it's cost!
No wonder, then, the nation smarts
With taxes high and broken hearts.

A ROYAL GRACE.

Lines suggested by a conversation with Stephen Saunders, at Alum Bay on July 10th, 1895, whilst ascending the Chine, who was born at Totland Bay, I.W., on August 25th, 1813, and who has made sand baskets filled with shells and cut sand stones for the past twenty years. In the course of which conversation he related to me his being honoured by Royal patronage, on August 9th, 1887, through the Prince of Wales landing his yacht at Alum Bay for a couple of hours.

Eighty-two years their course have run,
Since first my life on earth begun,
In that small hamlet Totland Bay
I first beheld the light of day.

In troublous times I then was born,
Mid fiercest battles tempest storm;
Old Bonaparte then vainly tried
His spear to thrust in Britain's side.

But One did thrust the tyrant foe,
Old England's God from Heaven we know;
No prowess to our arms give we
For conquering praise belongs to Thee.

When I was two, great Waterloo
Was won by Iron Duke so true;
The cruel reign of Bonaparte
Had sent a thrill through every heart.

But God decreed he stopped should be
In his mad reign of devilry;
The battle waxed both strong and hot,
Soon conquest to our arms was brought.

On St. Helena's lonely Isle,
Old Bonaparte his time did wile;
Soon fled away his warlike mien,
And peaceful joy again was seen.

For pinching poverty did fall
Into the lot of nearly all;
Though sovereign mercy rich and rare,
Was seen all through it everywhere.

In early life a sailor I,
When storms and tempests loud ran high;
For nearly forty years my lot,
A sailor on the ocean wrought.

When in a Bombay typhoon blast,
Near thirty years since then have passed;
My legs, entwined in rigging high,
Were broken both, I feared to die.

But God in mercy spared my life,
Amid the tempest and the strife,
Though could not work for four long years,
Which brought from me most bitter tears.

My wife and I such hard times had,
With our eight children often sad,
The Lord restored me yet again,
Although a cripple oft in pain.

For twenty years on Alum Bay,
In summer on this cliff I stay,
I make sand baskets, filled with shell,
And to my kindly patrons sell.

In eighty-seven, on August nine,
A lady customer was mine,
She quite entranced me with her talk,
And stayed till up her friends did walk.

She asked me then my work and age,
Her tongue so sweet did me engage;
Her husband sat there by her side,
A happier pair I ne'er espied.

She asked the price of all my ware,
Her husband laughed as he sat there;
She paid me double for the same,
And asked me if I knew her name.

"No maam," to her I did reply,
"But lady true, I can't deny;"
She then a sovereign gave to me,
"Princess of Wales in me you see."

"My husband sitting on the bank,
The Prince does for your converse thank,"
The Prince of Wales with laughing face,
With his cigar I now can trace.

"Do you smoke, my friend," he said,
"Yes, jolly tars are sure, you've read;"
He gave his pouch then quick to me,
And lit my pipe with his fusee.

Each Christmas since from them we get,
For eight long years have kindness met,
A sovereign to cheer our home,
We thank them for such kindness shown.

God bless, we pray, the happy pair,
Of Royal personages rare;
Lord give them each Thy saving grace,
May all their household seek Thy face.

The Queen beloved, we pray Thee still,
To bless while climbing up the hill ;
At eventide, be Lord her stay,
And cheer and bless her home alway.

When rich and poor in glory greet,
As in the Heavenly land they meet,
We'll praise the Lord for all His love,
Throughout the endless day above.

IN MEMORIAM OF MATTHEW WENHAM
(OF MARGATE),
Who died August 8th, 1893, Aged 18 Years.

Our hearts are stricken sad and sore,
Our first-born son's short journey's o'er,
The Lord knows well our bitter grief,
And He alone can give relief.

His presence always charms our home,
The cat she purred to see him come,
He made the young ones always glad,
And cheered our hearts when they were sad.

His sickness short and great his pain,
We ne'er shall see his like again,
This rose was cut before 'twas blown,
The Master took him for His own.

Though Jesus wept at Lazarus' grave,
He's mighty still to bless and save,
For He can bind up broken hearts,
His balm can heal their inward smarts.

May His consoling grace be given,
To every heart bereaved and riven,
Speak Thou the word of comfort, Lord,
Send promises of Thy blest word.

Once Jesus touched at Nain the bier,
The great Physician always near,
And though the tears now blind our eyes,
His purposes are kind and wise.

Go with us, Lord, on this dark day,
When to the grave we wend our way,
The Way, the Life, the Truth art Thou,
Give all sufficient grace just now.

And though we leave the form of one
We dearly loved whose race is run,
O Lord, dry up our tears we pray,
In Heaven we'll greet our son some day.

We sisters and his brothers mourn,
Now Matthew from our home is torn.
But we shall meet him on the shore,
In Heaven some day to part no more.

Cheer up, dear friends, he is not dead,
He only sleeps so Jesus said,
This sheep "I'll gather to my fold"
And safe secure from frosts and cold.

August 11th, 1893.

THE FOUR SEASONS.

The spring with all its promised buds,
  And future hope of cheer,
Is come again our souls to bless,
  Soon plenty will be here.

God sends the glowing summer months
  To yield a rich repast;
In beauty and in verdure too,
  Though short they seem to last.

The autumn's waving fields of corn,
  And luxious fruit He sends,
Providing food for man and beast,
  For all our wants attends.

The winter comes with shortened days,
  With cold, and frost, and snow,
With hanging icicles above,
  All show God's good we know.

So may the seasons as they pass,
Speak to our hearts and say,
Improve with persevering grace,
Each minute of each day.

And when life's eventide shall come,
Our work on earth shall cease :
May we enjoy a Home of rest,
With Christ in perfect peace.

ALARMING COLLISION IN THE CHANNEL.

THE STEAMER "SEAFORD" SUNK.

Escape of 300 Passengers and Crew.

The fog did "Lyon" steamer hide,
Which struck the "Seaford" on port side ;
They slackened speed in darkness dense,
The fog in Channel was intense.

Had passengers have known, forsooth,
The time so short, the real truth,
In half an hour t'would sink below,
A panic would have been we know.

But God in mercy oft doth hide
From us great trials near our side,
And often mercy shows us here
The safeguard of His Guardian care.

We will brave Captain Sharp enshrine
In this our simple verse and rhyme ;
His name in future memory
Will long remain and cherished be.

With coolness, yet with quick survey
Heroic deeds were done that day ;
Well he and crew their powers did use,
Without a minutes' time to lose.

Such gallant bravery its true
Have won our praise for chief and crew,
To all their varied posts to haste
A moment's time they did not waste.

In quickest word he gave command :
" All boats be lowered ; on duty stand,
Three hundred souls help me to save
From sinking in a watery grave."

So Captain Sharp's most kindly word
In plaintive tones was plainly heard,
The Captain of the " Lyon," too,
With generous heart was kind and true.

With his good crew did all they could
To aid and help we understood ;
He slackened " Lyons " speed with care
To " Seaford's " port drew then quite near.

In coolness and with valorous speed,
Both Captains then their crews did lead,
All passengers assured to save
Obeying orders that they gave.

If this you do, the Captain said,
All safe to port you'll soon be led ;
No panics or distressing cries
Were heard but most were very wise.

Attended to the orders given,
And terror stricken none were driven,
But truthful still this sketch must be,
A sight of some the crew did see.

They nearly lost their lives 'tis true,
Trying to save their baggage too.
For dear life spared our thanks we give
To Thee, O Lord, while here we live.

Just time to save there lives, indeed,
Thy kindest Providence decreed ;
To this collision sad one came,
Mistress Pearslow was her name.

Into the water she did fall
Just rescued at the seaman's call,
By Moore, the mate, so bold who dived,
With her on deck again arrived.

With broken ankle most severe,
Thank God her life is spared still here;
With broken legs two ladies found,
Command all sympathy around.

One gentleman with broken arm;
These saddened cases gave alarm:
Restore them, Lord, to health again
And quickly heal their aches and pain.

At Newhaven the crowd was great,
With bated breath and fear did wait;
Here we could touching scenes portray;
Congratulations great that day.

From grateful hearts in tender tone,
'Twould melt a heart as hard as stone:
We pray Thee, Lord, receive the praise,
Their humble vows within our lays.

The contrite prayer from hearts that bled,
Be truth of all their future said,
From lips that scarce could speak a word,
Though God alone their vows had heard.

A PLEASANT WALK THROUGH PART OF THE NEW FOREST.

New Forest has great charms for me
When heather and sweet fern I see.
Beech, Chestnut, and the royal oak
Of good old times hath often spoke.
If these could tell their truthful tale
They would so many things reveal.
The pines' rich odour doth us greet,
The scented turpentine smelt sweet:
The blackberries bestrewed my way
Throughout the Forest glade that day,
With luscious ripened fruit that morn,
While fitting background to adorn,
Autumnal tints of varied sheen
Made pictures beauteous to be seen.

A solemn sermon was the sight
Of falling leaf with colours bright;
For we all fade just like a leaf,
Our life at longest is but brief.
Then help us, Lord, our time to spend
In deeds of kindness to the end.
Christmas berries and hoggaes rare
Bespeak a winter grim and bare;
By rich Autumnal colours shown
The artist's handiwork is known.
The birds sang sweet with gleeful song
True music as I walked along,
While rugged scenery did adorn
The forest glade on that blest morn.
The ponies wild with their fine foals
Gave pleasure through my forest strolls,
The milking cows, too, roam at large
And gracious gifts for us discharge:
While pigs and sheep and calves fed there
On grass and acorns, best of fare.
While memory holds her seat I'm sure
It will retain this morning's tour,
I saw New Forest all alive
In October, eighteen ninety-five.
Now to an orchard rich I went,
On apple buying I was bent,
A treasure this I sought to seize
Which hung profuse upon the trees.
Some miles from here I thought, of where,
I bought five hundred bushels there;
My birthplace, Redlynch, was the name,
Where apple-buying won my fame.
There apples were both large and nicé,
But we did differ as to price.
Three miles from Lyndhurst Road I'd walked
And with sweet nature well had talked,
Then Lyndhurst Church spire came in view,
A picture grand 'twould make for you.
Upon the road I'll not forget,
Old Thomas Taylor then I met,
His smiling face gave me delight,
And shovel on his back so bright.

I shook his hand and asked his name.
His avocation, age and fame :
" Daily working this road I ween,
For thirty-five years I have been.
At Lyndhurst Church, I too, was wed,
And born eight miles from here," he said ;
" Lyndhurst Old Church, dear Sir, I mean,
Before the grand new one was seen.
My age is only seventy-four,
And work's a pleasure as of yore.
At Christmas next our wedding day
Quite fifty years have passed away."
" You should not now be left behind.
Keep golden wedding, bear in mind.
And is your wife agreed with you
To pass life's journey loving through ? "
" My wife, her name is Hannah, good,
To me a good wife always stood ;
At birthday next she's seventy-one,
She's won my love for all she's done."
" Then flitch of bacon you have earned
If in each heart love's always burned."
" I've always one," he said, " dear friend,
Which to our wants doth e'er attend."
" Why this is grand," I said, with glee,
" Good bacon on the rack to see,
I much should like a rasher rare :"
" Were you at home 'twould be your fare."
" Now what's the price you get per week ?"
" Twelve shillings is the price I seek."
This noble man does live so high
And with his thrifty wife does try
To garner up their little store,
And plenty had their whole life o'er.
I asked him then, " How do you fare ?
Have you found Christ a Saviour here ?
Are you upon the heavenly road
To our dear Father's blest abode ?
Are you in ' Rock of Ages cleft ?'
Then in the storm you'll not be left.
To all His sheep eternal life
He giveth them, despite the strife."

From me, a stranger, kindly heard,
The old man then had God's own word;
I told him then the Gospel plan
How God could save rebellious man,
Through Christ, the Life, the Truth, the Way
Has open door for us to-day.
If we in penitence and faith
Believe the message Jesus saith:
"Come unto Me ye weary one,
Of all who come I cast out none."

5th October, 1895.

MY SIXTIETH BIRTHDAY.

November seventeenth, ninety-five,
Thank God in health I'm still alive,
For sixty years have passed away
Since first I saw the light of day.
What changing scenes I too have seen,
The rolling years so short hath been,
Our time seems only like a tale,
God's word says this, which cannot fail.
It seems but yesterday to me
I skipt in hopeful youth and glee
O'er heath, and moor, and village green,
The months and years so short hath been.
But still old time to me hath brought
Rich treasures by its lessons taught;
The loving-kindness of my God
I've seen in all his chastening rod.
I will not murmur nor complain
For what is best He doth ordain,
From this my joyful natal day
Give daily grace throughout my way.
My Wiltshire birth-place, Redlynch home,
Is dear to me, though years have flown,
Since Mother lavished on me there
Her rich maternal loving care.
At sweet seventeen from home I start
To London Town, so gay and smart;
I heard its streets were paved with gold,
Not truth I found that thus was told.

Deluded thus and sad misled
Have thousands been, I've heard it said.
God's grace at nineteen years found me
A wanderer from the fold to be,
Christ's love drew my young heart to Him
And conquered then my love for sin.
Sweet pardon at the cross received,
When I a penitent believed,
"My chains fell off, my soul went free,"
I did of God's gift taste and see.
Since then I've told to sinners round,
"What a dear Saviour I have found."
To boast I cannot for I'm weak,
But bruised reeds "He will not break;"
God's grace alone can keep my heart
From Satan's wiles and fiery dart.
Be Thou my guide, Oh Saviour, friend,
Help me to battle till the end
That when draws nigh the day of life,
"Well done," from Christ may end the strife.

Written at Bealing's Temperance Hotel, Northam Road, Southampton.

LIFE-BOAT COLLECTING INCIDENTS.

I was not a little amused at being accosted by a young man as I was collecting for the Life Boat Institution in the Isle of Wight a few weeks ago. This collection, which amounted in seven days to £7, I handed over to the respected honorary secretary, Mr. Shephard, of Newport. Altogether I have collected for the Life Boat Institution, Surf Boat Margate and Dover Home upwards of £24. The young man said, "I should like a job like you have got I suppose you get well paid for it?" I replied "Yes I do or I should not do it." "Just so," said he, "I thought so." "Well, why don't you apply for it," I said "but what sort of a character have you?" "Oh that I think will bear inspection" he said. "But," I said, "Have you nothing to do then?" "No," he said. "But if you were equal to it, could you afford to sacrifice your time; have you any private means?" "No," he said, "but you get paid?" "Yes, well," I said, "but perhaps my pay would not suit you." "How much do you get in the £?" he said. "Nothing," I said, "in that way." He reminded me then of the young man who went to the Saviour. He could not stand this cruisical test. I told him further I had the privilege of putting an advertisement in my book for them free of cost.

But I might have said this is not the only pay we get. I was at Ryde asked by a tradesman "Why do you come boring by your collecting?" and I was told by another whom I styled a crabby stick, "You have the appearance of a company promoter." He had suffered through companies, so I pardoned him.

But another gentleman accosted me on Ryde Pier in a way which well repaid me for all the previous insults. "Will you, Sir, allow me to put a trifle into your Life Boat?" I said, "If you like to." "Yes," he said, as the tears came into his eyes, "myself and six others about five years ago were beating about in a small boat from a wrecked vessel in the Atlantic. A high sea was rolling over us, and we were giving up in despair, when we saw a life boat bearing down upon us, which saved us all. Since then, Sir, I have never seen these little collecting boats without putting a trifle in if I have any."

At Sandown another interesting incident occured. I was passing with my Life Boat an elderly lady with her husband and another gentleman when I heard the lady say, "Now I should like to be able to put something in that boat my dear." I like in all my collections to leave everything to the spontaneous outflow of the people's feelings, and therefore make no remarks whatever unless accosted by suspicious, critical people, but I thought to myself I should like to know how it is you can't afford to give a trifle so I sat myself down on the seat and said, "What a delightful place this is." "Yes," the lady said, "I suppose it is, but every place to me has seemed to lose its charm." "What is the matter?" I enquired. "I had saved £1000, by my thrift from my housekeeping money, as my husband sitting here, who is seventy one years old, was for upwards of twenty five of them in the service of the P. and O. Company, in a good situation. I lost £750, in the Liberator, and my son sitting here, aged 35, is an imbecile, though not bad enough to need putting away. Another £250, a lawyer cheated me out of, and now we are partially kept by my own beloved married daughter." "Well," I said "this is sad, do you know the Friend that sticketh closer than a brother?" "Yes, thank God," she replied. "Then you are not poor, for soon you will exchange this poverty for a crown of righteousness that fadeth not away, and that no Liberator smash or roguish lawyer or breaking bank can rob you of."

This is a sample of many cases I come across when going up and down the country.

THE LATE FIREMAN SPRAGUE (*See Page 251*).

THE STRAND EXPLOSION, October 29th, 1895,

THE FIREMAN SPRAGUE'S DEATH AND FUNERAL.

His post, this gallant fireman found,
Called by his duty to the ground,
He braved the dangers of the spot
And awful death was thus his lot.
Sprague's gallantry and noble deed
We will extol whilst our hearts bleed,
We gladly tell within our verse
How flowers were heaped on the car hearse.
His valour won him true renown
And loving tributes do him crown;
Thousands for miles did line the road
As he went to his last abode.
His funeral was a sight to see
Which will remain in memory,
The sun shone out with radiance bright
And seemed to mock their sorrow's night.
The cortege marked Sprague's gallantry
And glory crowns his memory:
These gallant firemen, true and brave,
Shall have our thanks for lives they saved.
Each doth alike the danger share,
God's providence doth many spare.
With tear-dimmed eyes no one spoke loud,
And every heart with grief was bowed.
They stood in patience close array
To see a fireman's funeral day.
The plaintive sound of muffled drum
Broke in upon the low toned hum,
With solemn awe and music slow
The funeral passed mid murmurs low,
And many a father standing there,
And many a mother breathed a prayer
For noble fireman strong and brave
Who might some day their children save.
The crushed and battered helmet graced
The coffin upon which 'twas placed,

For ten long hours Sprague upright stood,
Midst stone and mortar, brick and wood.
How much deceased was loved, we know
The grand display of flowers did show,
The solemn marching firemen true
Symboled the love of not a few.
Lord Carrington did lead the way,
John Burns too did his grief display,
And Captain Simonds, too, did guide,
The weeping widow by his side.
The constables our praise did share
For keeping such good order there.
The Vicar, too, so kind did come
From out his little village home,
To truly praise Sprague's memory
In funeral sermon tenderly.
In kindest sympathy we'll aid
The widow and the orphan made,
May God support them well, we pray,
In this great trial of that day.
Each relative and parent bless
With saving grace, Christ's righteousness,
To all of us this warning be
In midst of life we death do see.
In such a time as we think not
Our end may come, this death hath taught,
Whene'er the summons us may call—
'Twill come, now soon, to one and all—
May we through grace be ready found,
Our lamps well trimmed with oil abound,
To hear the Bridegroom's blessed word,
Enter the joy of our blest Lord.
Beneath the clods at Highgate rest
The fireman's cemetery corner blest,
The precious dust of heroes grand,
Who did like rocks at duty stand.
Their lives at various fires were lost,
With honours quick at such a cost,
Left wives and children and each friend,
Like Sprague did his, to them we'll tend.
And though we know this rhyme is poor,
We wish that we could offer more.

IN MEMORIAM

SIR HENRY PONSONBY.

Died at Osborne Cottage, Isle of Wight, 21st November, 1895.
Buried in Whippingham Churchyard 26th November.

With deepest sorrow we have read
Sir Henry Ponsonby is dead ;
To Lady Ponsonby we send,
Our sympathy do her attend.

The news his children dear received,
Thus by their father's death bereaved,
We know has caused them bitter grief,
We pray that God may give relief.

Help all to say from God's own word
"Thy will be done, not ours, O Lord."
For forty years he's been the guest
And servant of our Queen, the best.

Her Royal Consort too did share
While on this earth his watchful care,
His fertile brain and tender mien
Made him a noble gentleman.

For twenty-five years he has been
Private Secretary to the Queen,
Sir Henry's death to her will be
A sad and chastening memory.

He served with sword as well as pen
And fought in Crimea with brave men,
He muscle gave as well as brain
And noble grenadiers did train.

Tuesday was seen a solemn sight
In Whippingham Churchyard, Isle of Wight
The warrior brave was laid to rest
Mid sweet love tokens of the best.

The friends that went from London there
Revealed their love and tender care :
And wreaths of beauteous flowers we know
From Queen and all their love did show.

For us his memory long will last
Of courteous kindness in the past,
Some forty letters more or less
From him received we now possess.

Last year's summer we should have met,
But we have not been able yet,
And we must wait till that bright day
When earthly shadows flee away.

THE CHILDREN'S HOME & ORPHANAGE.

Founder and Principal—
REV. T. B. STEPHENSON, D.D., LL.D.

General Treasurers—
J. E. VANNER, ESQ.,
T. B. HOLMES, ESQ., J.P.

Secretary—
MR. JOHN PENDLEBURY, M.A.

Chief Office—
Bonner Road, London, N.E.

The Child: What will he become?

THE Mission of **The Children's Home** is to rescue children who, through the death, or vice, or extreme poverty of their parents, are in danger of falling into criminal ways. It is, therefore, at once an **Orhanage** and a **Refuge.**

The Home receives Children of any age, or any sect, without election. It is conducted on the Family system; is a Religious and Industrial Institution; is a **Training School for Christian Workers;** and is dependent on Voluntary Contributions.

Within the last twenty-six years, over **3,700** children have received the benefits of this Institution. About **930** are now in residence, whilst about **600,** in situations in this country or abroad, are under careful supervision. £16 will maintain a child for a year.

Over **2,770** children have now passed through the Home, and there is the greatest cause for thankfulness to God for the present well-being and for the prospects in life, of a large majority of this great number.

In connection with this work the **Gordon Hall Mission** is carried on in the East End of London; an Agency for the **Protection of Girls** is at work, a Refuge being available night and day; a **Servants' Free Registry** is open, and **Lodgings** are provided for respectable young women during the interval between situations; also a **Mission to the poorest Children** of East London is very successfully carried on. The entire work is greatly in need of more liberal support. The smallest contributions will be thankfully received.

The need of such a work is painfully obvious. Our cities and towns are crowded with children exposed to every evil influence, shut out from all good, living a life worse than that of savages, and as they grow up they naturally take their places in the ranks of the pauper and the criminal. Yet they may be saved. Hundreds of cases prove that these little ones—some of them mere infants—are susceptible of every elevating influence, and need only the care of a Christian home to develop all that is good in their characters, and fit them for reputable and useful lives.

Cheques and Money Orders should be crossed City Bank and Orders made payable at General Post Office.

Remittances to be made payable and sent to T. B. STEPHENSON, *Bonner Road,* **London, N.E.**

A. BANGHAM,

THE ORIGINAL MARGATE CYCLE WORKS,

CECIL SQUARE,

(Established 1872). Near General Post Office,

MARGATE, KENT.

Agent for Singer & Co.'s and other Best Makers of Cycles.

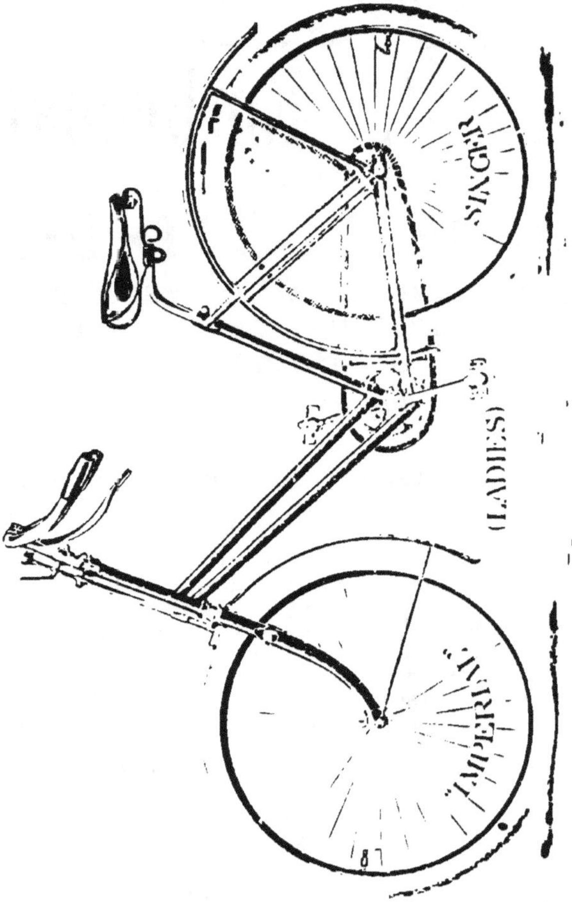

Repairs by Appointment to C.T.C.

Bicycles, Perambulators, Mail Carts & Wicker Bath Chairs for Sale or Hire.

Mangles, Wringers, Gas Stoves, and all kinds of Domestic Machinery.

NOTE THE ADDRESS—

A. BANGHAM, Cycle Works, Cecil Square, Margate.

Sole Manufacturers of the Margate Cycles.

Regular Steam Service between

LONDON, ISLE OF WIGHT, AND POOLE

EVERY THURSDAY. The Fast-Sailing

SCREW STEAMER "DEE"

Will **SAIL EVERY THURSDAY** according to Tide (unless prevented by unforeseen circumstances), from alongside

FREE TRADE WHARF, RATCLIFF, E.

Taking Goods for Cowes, Poole, Bournemouth, and the following adjacent Places:—

BLANDFORD	KINSON	RINGWOOD	WAREHAM
BOSCOMBE	NEWPORT, I.W.	SANDOWN, I.W.	WIMBORNE
DORCHESTER	PARKSTONE	SHANKLIN, I.W.	YARMOUTH, I.W.
FRESHWATER, I.W.	RYDE, I.W.	SPRINGBOURNE	VENTNOR, I.W.

And other Places in the Neighbourhood.

SHIPPERS CAN RELY ON REGULARITY AND DESPATCH.

No claim for Damages will be allowed unless made within 3 days after delivery.

LONDON CARTAGE AGENT:—

CHARLES POULTER, Ltd., 45, Broad Street, Ratcliff, E., or Dowgate Dock, E.C.

and for **LIGHTERAGE:—**

UNION LIGHTERAGE Co., Free Trade Wharf, E., or 60, Fenchurch Street, E.C., or Philpot Lane, E.C.

NOTICE.—The Wharfingers cannot guarantee to ship Goods received after 12 o'clock on the day of Sailing.

Puns, Molasses not Iron-bound are carried only at Owner's risk.

Lucifer Matches, Petroleum and Benzoline will only be carried on Deck, and they can only be received at Wharf on day of Sailing.

FOR FURTHER PARTICULARS APPLY TO—

H. BURDEN, Junr. & Co., West Shore Wharf, Poole.

JAMES GREIG, Wharfinger and Agent for H. Burden, Junr., & Co.,

FREE TRADE WHARF, AND 60, FENCHURCH STREET, LONDON, E.C.

Or to W. T. MAHY, Birmingham Road, Cowes.

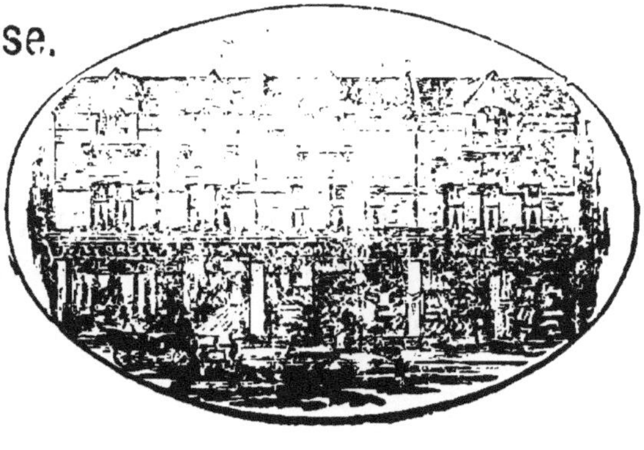

Rev. F. B. Meyer, B.A.

"I have much enjoyed reading 'What the Stones Say.' It brims with the unrivalled power of illustration and genius which we always associate with the name of the late pastor of the Tabernacle: and is a useful addition to his other books of illustrations. It ought to have a wide circulation."

Rev. Geo. C. Lorimee, LL.D. (Tremont Temple, Boston, U.S.A.)

"'The stones speak' indeed in Mr. Spurgeon's lecture, and their varied 'sermons' are full of grace and beauty. What they say ought to be pondered, not only for the value of the lessons taught, but as an illustration of what open eyes and spiritual discernment may gather from the works of God. Nor is the work of Mr. Keys in the volume unworthy of a place by the side of that produced by the master. The information gathered, the facts given, and the arrangement of the whole, are entitled to the highest appreciation."

The Sword and the Trowel.

"Mr. Keys was the privileged possessor of a *verbatim* report of Mr. Spurgeon's notable lecture on 'Sermons in Stones,' and he wisely decided to publish it. In very copious Notes he has inserted extracts from various works, such as he believes the beloved lecturer would have been likely to incorporate into his work if he had been spared to see it printed. All Mr. Spurgeon's friends should purchase this little volume."

The Freeman.

"This volume reveals the great preacher's mastery of the art of illustration; science and art, history and legend, anecdote and simile yielding their lessons at his command. 'Sermons in Stones' were the possibilities of a poet's dream, the book before us is the dream realized. The notes and illustrations by the editor, and a commendatory introduction by Rev. Thomas Spurgeon, enhance the value of the book, the paper, type and binding of which form a worthy setting of a choice mosaic."

London: CHRISTIAN HERALD PUBLISHING CO., Ltd.,
TUDOR STREET, E.C.

May be ordered of any Bookseller, or will be sent, post free, on receipt of the Published Price, J. L. KEYS, 45, Beckenham Road, Penge, S.E.

The following is the Contents of J. Gwyer's Previou[s] Volume, entitled, Life and Poems, Ramble round th[e] Crystal Palace, Glimpses of departed days, &c., &c; 25[0] Page, 8vo, Gilt Edges, 2/-; Published in 1875, 6,00[0] Copies then sold.

As the Author has inserted each of the Religious and Philanthropic Institution advertisments in this book **FREE OF CHARGE** in 2,000 opies, he hopes many readers will be disposed to aid these Noble and odlike Orphanage Homes, and Life Boat Institution, it would be ratifying to know that through this simple means some are induced to ecome annual subscribers and others occasionally sending their smaller gifts.

The Author would also kindly ask, as opportunity serves, all to buy he varied articles specified in these advertisements by the numerous anufacturers and tradesmen mentioned therein. Should any be nticipating removing they would do well to send for an estimate to the urniture removers whose names and addresses they may find advertised erein.

The Author kindly thanks all the advertisers who have kindly given im their advertisements, and by which means has materially helped him o defray the expenses of printing and publishing this work, and he opes this medium may be of great advantage to them all. The Author vill ever feel grateful to his respected employers, T. M. Bentley & Co., y whom, in his travels through the country with their goods he has een able to gather the information and has had time to write many of he sketches inserted herein, which he hopes readers will find interesting nd amusing. Will our readers, both to help them and the Author, indly ask their grocers, chemists, &c., for Bentley's High Class pecialities, which are so liked and largely used, both at home and broad. The trade can have free samples and price lists on application.

Should there be a difficulty of getting this book of booksellers (which here need not be), by sending postal order or stamps 2s. 6d., it shall be orwarded post free by the author,

J. GWYER, Beckenham Road, Penge, Surrey,

see page 63, entitled "An Apt Reply at a Temperance Hotel."

JOHN WALLIS,

RIVERDALE FOOD MILLS,

Lewisham, London,

SOLE MANUFACTURER OF

NUTRITIOUS

GERM FOOD

WARRANTED PURE. ABSOLUTELY PURE.

FOR YOUNG AND OLD.

Supersedes Oatmeal & all other Foods

Young Children may be safely fed on this Food.

None Genuine without the Registered Trade Mark.

The following Letter has been received from a Gentleman :—

"I am **73** years of age, and must say, DOCTOR WALLIS, your GERM FOOD has done me very much good."

———:-o-:———

Sold by all Grocers in the United Kingdom

Price **ONE SHILLING** per Tin.

Study your Health, and take **WALLIS'S GERM FOOD.**

SHEPARD BROS.,

Railway & General Carriers,

Customs' Shipping and Forwarding Agents,

MILITARY CONTRACTORS.

:-o-:

Agents to the LONDON & SOUTH WESTERN, GREAT WESTERN & GREAT NORTHERN RAILWAY COMPANIES

Fast Cargo Boats for Conveyance of General Goods and Merchandise running daily to and from the Mainland.

FURNITURE REMOVED.

PACKED & WAREHOUSED.

Furniture, Pictures, Glass, Pianos, &c., Removed in Large Lock-up Vans by Road, Rail or Sea, without change of Carriage—

ALL TROUBLE & EXPENSE of PACKING AVOIDED.

PERSONAL SUPERVISION. ESTIMATES FREE.

TESTIMONIAL

From the REV. CLEMENT SMITH, Rector of Whippingham, Isle of Wight :—"The removal of the Furniture was carried out in a most satisfactory manner."

Other Testimonials can be seen on Application.

OFFICES--

42, QUAY STREET,
19, SEA STREET, } **NEWPORT** (ISLE OF WIGHT).

And TOWN QUAY, SOUTHAMPTON.

Reviews of the Author's previous writings

We have received a copy of the fourth edition of Joseph Gwyer's Life and Poems (commended by Royalty) published by the author, Ivy Cottage, Penge, and we can only say that Mr. Gwyer's aspirations are most praiseworthy and do him great credit, and that we prefer to refrain from depreciating that which is so well intentioned and so thoroughly indicative of laudable zeal and ambition.—*Lloyds Weekly London Newspaper*, August 26th, 1877.

By kind permission of Messrs. Bradbury, Agnew & Co., Limited, Proprietors of "Punch," the author is enabled to produce the following, which appeared in their edition of July 5th, 1873.

Poem on the Alexandra Palace, Muswell Hill, destroyed by fire, June 9'h, 1873. Composed by Joseph Gwyer, *Potato Salesman, Penge. Half the Profits will be given in aid of Sufferers*:—

We consider this poem no small potatoes. It has its merits, it has its faults, but so has the *Iliad*, and so has *Proverbial Philosophy*. But, as the ancient classic poet, Horace, remarks:—

"Where a thousand potatoes are mealy and white
To rage that a dozen are rotten, were spite."

We remark, *obiter*, that Dryden could not have turned that translation better Mr. Gwyer is what may be called a freehand poet. He has all an Englishman's and potato salesman's scorn and contempt for tryanny, and he refuses to be bound in the rhythmical fetters which, as Mr. Cobbett has told us in *Rejected Addresses*, were invented by the monks to enslave the people. But with a free hand he has a full heart, and we have no doubt that he gives in his business as overflowing measure as he offers in his song. His poetry is much better than most which we have lately been called on to review. If he has not the vigour and subtlety of Browning, at all events Mr. Gwyer never exercises the soul of his reader by compelling him to give a second thought to the meaning of a line. If he lacks the something of the tender grace of Tennyson, Mr. Gwyer successfully resists any temptation which may be presented to him to over-refine his melodies. If he wants the passionate fervour of Swinburne, it is the more creditable to him, for Shakespeare has told that the vegetable in which Mr Gwyer deals has a tendency to soften the heart. And if he is without a good many other things which a good many other people are with, he is himself, an I, an

Ego, and a poet. We shall, therefore, gratify ourselves and our readers by an extract or two from a poem which is sold at four times the price of the original edition of *Orion* :—

" On Muswell Hill there lately stood,
The Alexandra Palace great and good,
Both to our own and foreign land,
It claim from each a prestige grand.

" With works of art it did abound,
Which were wont the ignorant to astound,
The sightly dome for miles was seen,
Surrounded by the pastures green.

" Full many a goodly sir upon the opening day,
Sported with his 'fair one' the time away,
And seem'd to like the stimulating meeting,
For interchange of kindly word and greeting.

" But on the 9th of June the palace caught on fire,
Each moment seemed to send the flames much higher,
Flinging around with consternation spell,
Such sad results as no mortal could foretell.

" The shouts of alarm at this dread afray,
Many were stricken and did prostrate lay,
As if they'd been wounded by some deadly foe,
So painful was the unexpected great blow.

" While some were witnessing this awful view,
Others were anxious as to what they should do,
Some it was seen appeared quite romantic,
While the poor stall girls seemed nearly frantic."

We have then a graceful compliment to the prompt generosity of SIR SYDNEY WATERLOO, the Lord Mayor and to the ready charity of the Directors of the Crystal Palace, who may be said to have heaped coals of fire on the heads of their unfortunate rivals by giving a benefit for the relief of the distressed Alexandrians Then the Bard of Penge boldly reverts to the catastrophe.

" In two short hours it was a blaze,
Which took some years to build and raise,
Grand Alexandra's noble dome,
Alas ! all vanished the Ninth of June.

" I hope when you peruse these lines,
The author's object you'll have in mind,
For ever will his stand point be,
That one great act of charity."

If we hint that we perhaps could, by taking our coats off and thinking our hardest, invent a better—or, at least a more conventional rhyme for "lines" than "mind,"—we say this to show that not even our admiration for a great bard and potato salesman drives us into the unqualified eulogy in which so many of our contemporaries delight. But, as aforesaid, *non paucis maculis*, and there are as few spots upon MR. GWYER'S verses as upon the very best potatoes which he supplies to the fortunate residents at Penge.

See also *The World*, August 19th, 1874, entitled "The New Poet"; *Figaro*, July 16th & August 2nd, 1873, with caricature; *Fun*, July 18th, 1874, *New York Herald; Cincinnati Times; Evening Standard; Scotsman; Amateur World*; and many other London and Provincial Papers.

www.ingramcontent.com/pod-product-compliance
Lightning Source LLC
Chambersburg PA
CBHW021118270326
41929CB00009B/937
* 9 7 8 3 3 3 7 0 9 8 5 5 1 *